Tikal Report No. 23B

MISCELLANEOUS INVESTIGATIONS IN CENTRAL TIKAL: GREAT TEMPLES III, IV, V, and VI

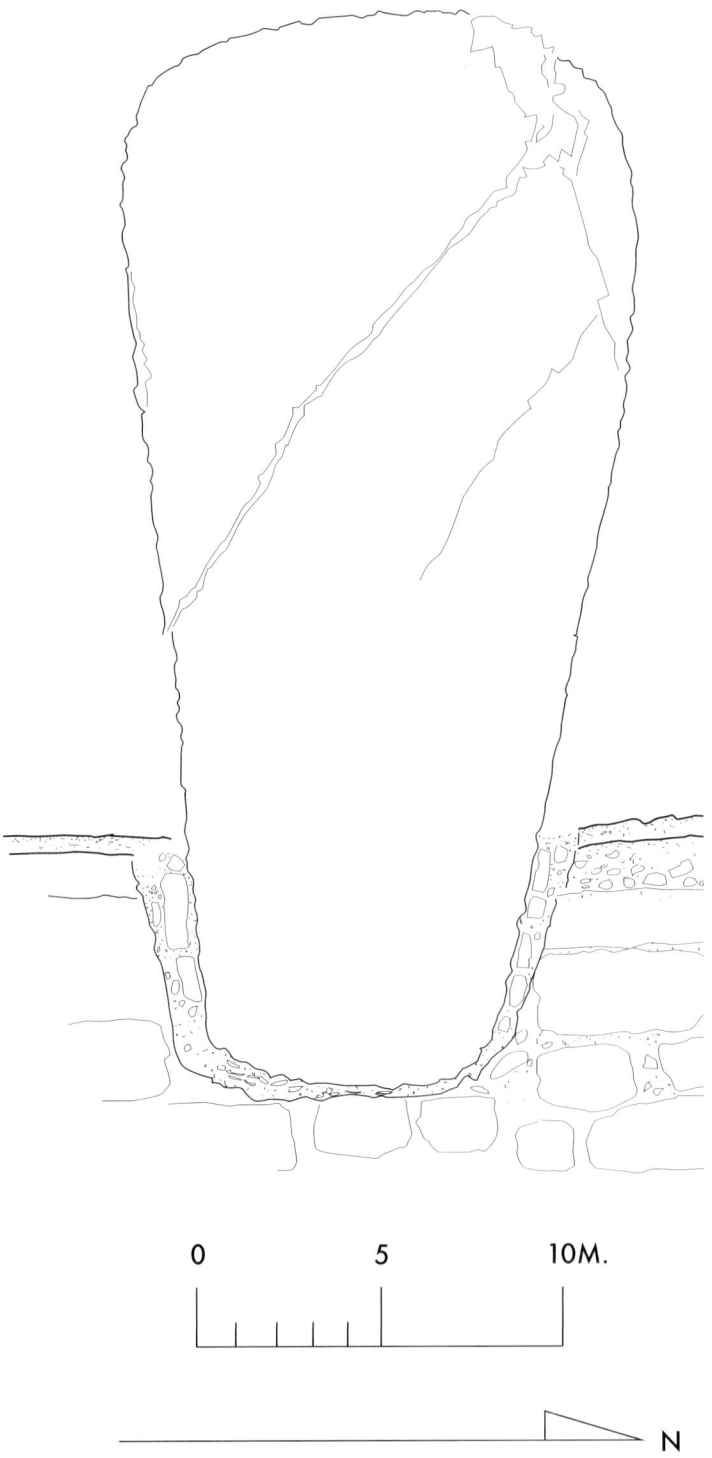

0   5   10M.

N

Frontispiece. Stela P43 after field drawing by Wilber Pearson (scale 1:20).

University Museum Monograph 146

Tikal Report No. 23B

MISCELLANEOUS INVESTIGATIONS IN CENTRAL TIKAL: GREAT TEMPLES III, IV, V, and VI

H. Stanley Loten

Series Editors
William A. Haviland
Simon Martin

Published by

UNIVERSITY OF PENNSYLVANIA MUSEUM
of Archaeology and Anthropology
Philadelphia
2017

CATALOGING-IN-PUBLICATION DATA IS ON FILE WITH THE LIBRARY OF CONGRESS

ISBN 13: 978-1-934536-93-3
ISBN 10: 1-934536-93-8

Distributed for the University of Pennsylvania Museum of Archaeology and Anthropology
by the University of Pennsylvania Press.

Printed in the United States of America on acid-free paper.

Table of Contents

Chronology

Period	Long Count	Date	Ceramics
Early Postclassic			Caban
Terminal Classic		AD 950	Eznab
Late Late Classic		AD 869	Imix
	Temple III AD 801 Temple IV after AD 761 Temple VI between AD 734 & 761		
Late Classic		AD 735	Imix
Early Late Classic		AD 692	Ik
	Temple V AD 650?		
Intermediate Classic		AD 554	Manik
Early Classic		AD 250	Cimi
Terminal Preclassic		AD 150	Cauac
Late Late Preclassic		1 BC	Chuen
Early Late Preclassic		350 BC	Tzec
Late Middle Preclassic		600 BC	Eb
Early Middle Preclassic		800 BC	

Chronology after TR27A: xiv.
Temple dates after Jones 1991:119–20.

Tables

Illustrations

Abbreviations

Alt.: Altar
Bm.: Beam
Ch.: Chultun
Chm.: Chamber
Dr.: Door/Doorway
E: East
Fl.: Floor
Li.: Lintel
N: North
PD.: Problematical Deposit
Rm.: Room
S: South
St.: Stela
Str.: Structure
W: West

Selected Architectural Terms

Note: These are just a few terms that occur in the description of the structures reported here. Some are new and used in this volume, others perhaps just not in general use.

Additions
The most recent additions and/or alterations are designated as "A"-level features; they abut "B"-level, which in turn abuts "C" and so on. The primary structure has a letter designation that depends on the number of demonstrably sequent additions or alterations.

Aggregate
In concrete small stones or gravel are essential as stuff that the cement can stick to. Without aggregate concrete is mere grout with little strength as a mass.

Apron
Substructure and platform faces at Tikal are often profiled with an upper part projecting over a lower part. The whole profile is called an apron but at the same time the upper part is regarded as the apron and the lower part as the subapron. Some apron profiles also have a basal molding.

Architectural Development
Structures erected on top of each other constitute an architectural development. Designation is from the surface feature, 1st, down to those below as 2nd, 3rd, etc.

Arrised Corner
A corner that is sharp rather than rounded.

Ashlar
Facing stones cut and dressed to a regular oblong or square shape are called ashlar. Veneer facings are a type of ashlar, as are block facings. Ashlar has the advantage that relatively little shape adjustment is needed on the job site; stone can be cut to shape at the quarry so that work on the job site goes faster. Nevertheless, we do see a certain amount of notching in some ashlar facings and this must have been done on the job.

Axis
The center-line of a structure, running front to rear is known as the principal axis; some structures also, have a secondary axis running from side to side but the great majority of Maya structures at Tikal have only the principal axis. Symmetry of a facade is worked around an axis, which may or may not be emphasized by a wider doorway opening or a sculptural treatment.

Balustrade
Any raised edge to a stair can be called a balustrade. Strictly speaking a balustrade should consist of balusters like miniature columns supporting a railing. The term is used very loosely in Maya architecture.

Ballast
In floors installed on platforms, a layer of relatively smaller aggregate, ballast, is needed to establish a level substrate for the final surface.

Basal Platform
A platform that sustains a single structure, usually supporting a pyramid, is a basal platform.

Batter
Non-vertical faces are battered. Leaning outward is negative batter, inward is positive.

Beam

A spanning member is a beam. Wood beams are common but stone ones are known, particularly as lintels.

Bed Joint

The more-or-less horizontal mortar layer below stones is the bed joint.

Block Facings

Facing stones proportioned so that their thickness is comparable to their height are known as block facings. Typically they are oblong on the face but less precisely shaped than veneer facings.

Bolster

A raised bench element, also called an upstand, could be called a bolster, though this is a term not generally used.

Building

The part of a structure that contains the accessible rooms is the building. Accessible rooms installed at substructure or roof level generally are not considered as building elements, though upper stories certainly are buildings.

Building Platform

Platforms that directly sustain the walls of buildings are building platforms. Some apparent building platforms are actually fakes, mere moldings at the base of walls, and not the outer faces of actual platforms. Fake building platforms imply existence of platform units sustaining walls when in fact such units had no place in the construction process.

Butt

The parts of beams that bear on their supports are their butts. Some butts are concealed, others exposed.

Capstone

Stones bridging the gap between half-vaults are capstones. Wood members bridging half-vault gaps are known and may be described as wooden capstones.

Cement

The ancient Maya made an adhesive or bonding agent from limestone. The best lime cement was probably made by burning limestone to get lime, which was then mixed with water and fine aggregate or sand to make mortar or plaster.

Cobble

Small stones, about fist sized or slightly bigger and not squared or shaped but just broken to size are cobbles. Walls of Str. 5D-46-C and 46-B1 (second story) employ cobbles as facing stones and also in the hearting.

Concrete

A mixture of cement and aggregate is concrete. As the aggregate gets smaller the cement may be called mortar.

Construction Stage

Major works of architecture at Tikal display a standard set of the following features: basal platform, pyramid, lower substructure platform, supplementary platform, building platform, building, and roof-comb. Building and building platform appear most frequently, and others appear on different structures in various combinations. They are numbered from topmost to basal, but described in reverse order, that is, basal to topmost. Although the terms imply distinct stages of construction, this is not always the case. For example, some building platforms are not stages of construction at all, and many buildings present walls, vaults, and upper zones as distinct constructional modules that perhaps might best be designated as substages, though this has not been formalized.

Corbel

A stone projecting in the manner of a cantilever is a corbel. Some Maya vaults are corbelled, many, particularly "late" vaults, are not corbelled. True corbels do not depend on mortar. Corbels in Tikal architecture are most common as vault springs, medial moldings, and apron springs.

Cord Holder

Interior and occasionally exterior building walls present recessed features with rods or pegs that could be used to secure ties or cords.

Core

The hearting of platforms, walls, and vaults is called

core. In very low platforms—those less than a meter high—hearting may be loose material placed by dumping and may be called fill, retained by masonry at the edges. In higher platforms builders were careful to assemble cores so that they would be internally stable and would not require retention at the edges.

Double-vault Mass

Vaults bearing on spine walls have two soffit faces and constitute double-vault masses. Often there is a more-or-less vertical joint at the center indicating that one half-vault was followed by the other, in order of assembly.

End Joint

In masonry the roughly vertical mortar applications between stones are end joints. Staggering end joints improves stability but most Maya facings were not regarded as load bearing so end joints are often not consistently staggered.

End-vault

Most vaulted rooms at Tikal have four vault facets, two half-vaults, and two end-vaults. The half-vaults do not touch but the end-vaults bond to the half-vaults so as to prevent them from tumbling into the room space.

Epicentral Tikal

This term refers to the parts of the city center that are interconnected by continuous plaster paving. The four structures of this volume are all in the city center, and individual location maps for each one depict part of it. By means of the causeway system the epicenter extends from the Great Plaza to the North Group and to Great Temple VI. Since plaster paving is inherently fragile, maintaining such an extensive paving must have been important and meaningful.

Eyebrow

A roughly horizontal projecting ledge over some feature, usually an inset panel in a facing, may be termed an eyebrow.

Facade Sculpture

Sculptural treatment, usually in relief but sometimes almost full round, in the facade of a building, or anywhere on a structure, can be designated as a facade sculpture and numbered for reference.

Face Surface

The surface of facing stones that remains exposed after setting is the face surface.

Facing Masonry

Outer surfaces of platforms, walls, and vaults, that is, facing masonry, normally have little or no capacity to retain unstable hearting. Facing masonry provides a base for plaster and sets the final form of features such as platforms.

Fake Building Platform

In some "late" work at Tikal we see moldings at the base of exterior walls, usually with shallow projection, that either do not correspond in height to the wall base level, or are not part of any platform installed as a base for wall construction; such features may be called fake building platforms.

Falsework

In preparation for masonry work a system of poles, called a falsework, may be erected to establish angles and heights for the guidance of workers. In vaulting, the practice of leaving a gap between half-vaults may have allowed for projection of falsework members.

Fill

Hearting of low platforms, using loose material such as gravel, and needing retention at the edges, can be called fill.

Floor

A floor may be merely an activity surface flattened by walking, or a distinct constructional element with a thickness, a topping, and a ballast layer.

Floor Pad

A layer of concrete installed to raise the level of a floor may be called a floor pad.

Formwork

Members of a timber falsework intended to actually retain masonry immediately after installation until mortar has reached final set is called a formwork.

Frontality

Tikal structures often have features on the frontal facade that do not appear on the sides or rear. For example, upper zones at the front may have sculptural treatment while those at the rear are plain. On the Great Temples projecting stairs form distinctive frontal features. Emphasis on frontality may have encouraged a sense that the structures, when occupied by non-material forces, could be sentient witnesses to ceremonial performances and sacrifices.

Grading Floor

An application of flooring material that runs part way across some space and feathers out onto a pre-existing floor surface is called a grading floor.

Half-vault

From Intermediate through the Late Classic at Tikal vaults were installed by halves, first on one side of a room and then for completion, on the other side. The two half-vaults do not touch or lean against each other; each is independently stable. Short end-vault units prevent the long half-vaults from rolling into the room space.

Header

A facing stone set with its length projecting into the hearting of the wall or other feature.

Hip Molding

On some upper zones medial and superior moldings are joined at the corners by diagonal hip moldings to create a framed effect.

Inset Corner

Platform terraces at Tikal often have corner elements inset from other face elements. None of these occur in the Central Acropolis.

Jamb

The sides of doorway openings are called jambs.

Lintel

A beam over a doorway, window, or niche is a lintel beam. Most lintels at Tikal employ a number of beams, many seemingly much too small in diameter for the load imposed by the vault mass and they must have been braced until vault mortar had reached full set.

Lintel Bed

Lintels over doorways are normally set some way below wall-top level and support a layer of supra-lintel masonry forming a fair surface on which to install vault spring and medial molding corbels.

Lower Substructure Platform (LSP)

A platform sustaining a building platform is a lower substructure platform unless there is an even lower platform sustaining it, in which case it is a supplementary platform.

Major Substructure Platform (MSP)

This term is introduced as a label for substructure units that cannot be called either pyramids or building platforms.

Masonry

Construction in stone is called masonry whether well-cut and bedded or simply rubble. The core material of substantial platforms at Tikal is masonry, whether bedded or not. (See also Facing Masonry.)

Medial Molding

At wall-top level a corbel course projecting out over the exterior wall surface is known as a medial molding.

Mortar

The adhesive element in concrete is cement, which the ancient Maya made from limestone. When used in masonry as a binder it is called mortar and usually is not as fine grained or pure as plaster. Mortar is usually gray or brown while plaster is white. Ancient Maya builders varied the quality of their mortars using relatively fine mortars for facings and less fine ones for heartings or cores.

Niche

A recess in a wall surface is called a niche. Usually niches are set well up in walls but there are, also, full-height niches that run from floor to vault spring.

Outset

Terraces, walls, and roofcombs, often have elements of surface projected out from other elements. Some may have iconographic significance, particularly rear axial outsets and stair-side outsets. Even side outsets might have carried meanings that would have been known to the people using the structures.

Patch

Deposits intruded into floors are sealed by floor material called patches. This is common in the North Acropolis but rare in the Central Acropolis.

Parging

Finishing a surface with mortar rather than plaster is called parging.

Partition

A non-load-bearing wall dividing a room into two smaller spaces is a partition. Some partitions have upper parts shaped like vaults but are clearly secondary and not load-bearing.

Planing

For application of a thin plaster coat, wall, vault, or terrace facings were often planed smooth after installation by the use of rubbing stones so that the plaster coat could be rendered even while remaining thin.

Plaster

A mixture of lime and finely divided very small aggregate is known as plaster. At Tikal workers hardened the plaster by pounding on it after it had reached initial set. Stress marks can be seen in sections of plaster coats caused by pounding and rubbing. The final finish produced by these processes, where preserved, is usually very smooth, planar, and free of wrinkles. Lime plaster can be burnished and polished to high degrees of luster and even to a mirror finish. Tikal workers certainly burnished plaster surfaces; whether they worked them up to a glossy, reflective state is uncertain.

Platform

An architectural entity built up to provide an essentially horizontal surface is called a platform. Some are free-standing structures, others are parts of structures, and some serve as sustaining surfaces for structures.

Precinct Wall

A wall that encloses an exterior area such as a plaza or patio is here referred to as a precinct wall.

Preplastered

If plaster is applied to a unit of construction before that unit is installed it may be said to be preplastered. So far this is only known to occur at Tikal in capstones of vaults.

Range

Rooms of a building arranged with their length perpendicular to the structure axis constitute a "range." This is the basis of the term "range-type structure." Some range-type structures have more than one range set one in front of the other.

Rear Axial Outset

An outset on the axis at the rear is a rear axial outset. These occur in temples at Tikal and although Str. 5D-66 may be a sort of temple it does not have a rear axial outset. Str. 5D-62, a range-type structure, does have a rear axial outset, though only on the lower substructure platform.

Return Face

This term applies to facets of exterior surface that run perpendicular to the general orientation of facades—for example, end elements of outsets.

Riser

The vertical interval from tread to tread on a stair is a riser.

Rod Row

A series of small holes usually found immediately below a medial molding or a vault spring is known as a rod row. These holes are castes left by dowels only a few centimeters in diameter.

Roof

The layer of hard plaster that provides a seal over the vaulting is the roof of a building.

Roofcomb

A construction standing on a roof surface, usually containing inaccessible interior chambers and exterior sculptural treatment is known as a roofcomb. Str. 5D-63 is the only Central Acropolis structure known to present this feature and it has, or had prior to collapse, no less than sixteen of them.

Roof Structure

A construction standing on a roof surface but not identifiable as a roofcomb may be designated as a roof structure.

Room Floor

A hard plaster application within a room and turning up to the wall plaster is a room floor. In some cases, the plastered top of a building platform serves as a room floor; it passes under the walls rather than turning up to them.

Rope Anchor
A feature similar to a cord holder but very much larger and with a stouter peg is known as a rope anchor.

Run-under
A plastered floor or top surface that extends beneath some other feature is noted as a "run-under."

Scratch Coat
A substrate for plaster prepared using either mortar or a low grade of plaster and deliberately roughened is called a scratch coat.

Sett
Small, roughly squared stones may be called setts. Several Central Acropolis structures, 5D-49, 51 and 55, employ setts as facing stones for the walls of the building.

Side Inset
A recess separating front building parts from rear building parts externally is a side inset; none are known in the Central Acropolis.

Sill
The bottom surface of a doorway, niche, or window is a sill.

Socket
The hole left by a rotted out beam is a socket.

Soffit
The under-surface of a projecting member is its soffit. Vault surfaces over a room are soffit surfaces.

Spall
Small stones that occur in masonry joints and beds are spalls. Some may have been placed so as to provide a correct setting for the blocks, others may have been included in the mortar.

Staggered Joints
Masons often take care not to align the end joints in adjacent courses. Joints are staggered to increase strength. Masons at Tikal did not do this because their facings were seen as skins rather than retentive elements. They took pains to ensure that core masses did not exert outward pressure on facings.

Stair
A flight of steps is known as a stair. A series of aligned stairs could be called a stairway.

Stair-side Outset
Terrace outsets flanking stairs are known as stair-side outsets. They do not occur in the Central Acropolis.

Stair-side Ramp
Some outset stairs present sheer edges, while others have a slightly raised ramp-like edge, also known by the terms "*alfarda*" and balustrade.

Standing Architecture
Tikal ruins include many architectural structures only partially collapsed. Project operations cleared debris away from many of these, but others were left as originally found. These are known as examples of standing architecture and were recorded without removal of collapsed material or vegetation.

Stretcher
A facing stone set with its length running in the plane of the surface.

Subapron
Apron profiles at Tikal are of two main types: two-element aprons and three-element aprons. The two-element type typifies Early Classic work and consists of an upper part projecting over a lower part; the lower part is the subapron. This implies that the upper part is the apron, although the term "apron" is also applied to the whole feature whether two element or three element. In three-element aprons the subapron is the middle part.

Subspring Beam
Beams spanning rooms and set below vault spring height are subspring beams.

Substructure
The parts below the building are known collectively as the substructure.

Subwall
This term was invented for use here to describe a wall-like feature, below floor level, within buildings where they act as footings for walls. Great Temple IV provides the only known example at Tikal.

Superior Molding
A molding at the top of an upper zone is a superior molding.

Supplementary Platform
A platform that intervenes between a building platform and a lower substructure platform is a supplementary platform.

Supra-lintel Masonry
On top of most lintels, there is a layer of masonry filling the gap between the tops of the lintel beams and the wall top.

Surface Dressing
The practice of planing face surfaces of facing stones to provide a fair substrate for plaster is known as face dressing. This is usually done after the facings have been installed.

Tandem Room
A room set in range fashion behind another room is a tandem room. Such rooms are described as set in tandem.

Thick Wall
A wall of a building so thick that its thickness approximates its height is known as a thick wall. None occur in the Central Acropolis.

Thin Wall
Walls of buildings proportioned such that their height is much greater than their thickness are thin walls. All building walls in the Central Acropolis are thin as compared with the thick walls of the Great Temples.

Transverse Room
A room set with its length parallel to the structure axis is a transverse room.

Tread
The horizontal part of a stair between risers is a tread.

Upper Zone
The exterior element corresponding to the vaults and overhanging exterior wall faces is the upper zone.

Upstand
A raised element on a bench is an upstand; alternatively, it can be called a bolster.

Vault
Masonry constructions that span over rooms or chambers are vaults. The vaults at Tikal are unlike arches in that one side does not depend on the other, they do not exert lateral thrusts, and do not require buttresses.

Vault-back
Some vaults have outer surfaces underlying upper zone material; these are known as vault-back surfaces. Some vaults at Tikal do not have vault-backs but most do.

Vault Beam
All known vaults at Tikal contain either wood beams, beam butts, or beam sockets. The beams are known as vault beams and in many cases were installed prior to masonry work as part of falsework and/or formwork. The way that vault soffit stones were cut around beams shows that the beams were in place first.

Veneer Facings
Facing stones proportioned so that their height is distinctly greater than their thickness are known as veneer stones.

Wall
In Tikal Project terminology, a "wall" is an element enclosing a room or dividing rooms. Surfaces of platforms are described as faces not walls.

Wall Top
The top surface of a wall is its wall top. In some cases, these are plastered over, in others, not.

Wing
A part of a building projecting out from the central range of rooms is known as a wing.

I

Introduction & Acknowledgments

During preparation of the topographic site maps for the Tikal Project, a total of 2,120 individual structures were numbered (TR. 11:10). Excavations touched only a fraction of this total and various reports detail their architectural features. The remainder includes many that have fully collapsed—presenting mere mounds of debris—quite a few with features still in place and accessible without excavation. Tikal Report 23A (2002) presents data on some of these "standing" structures, and this volume provides more.

In the nature of things, we have less information for some structures than we have for others; 6F-27 (Temple VI) was partially cleared and a skull burial was excavated; minor excavations, including a short axial tunnel, were done on Temple IV; Temple III had no more clearing than is mentioned below; in Temple V some cuts were made for access to roof-comb chambers. As a matter of policy recording was done with minimal disturbance to the vegetation. In many cases, mortar has degraded so that tree and plant roots are the only things holding these fabrics together. Plant removal would drastically hasten collapse. Measuring had to be done within and around the mantle of vegetation.

A few small cuts were made to locate corners and base lines where it appeared that the data could be obtained with very little disturbance. Some upper parts were measured for plan data along the lines where wall faces emerged from debris. Since many wall faces are not exactly vertical, these measurements include small dimensional errors. In the case of Great Temple IV (Str. 5C-4), restoration was underway at the same time that recording was being done and some features are the restored versions.

Sculptural details, where present, are generally poorly preserved and can be indicated only approximately. One exception to this is the sculptural feature on the upper part of the rear axial outset of Great Temple III. Often vaults have partially collapsed, presenting sectional details that reveal processes of construction otherwise inaccessible.

In TR. 12:37 (1982), TR. 23B was projected to be jointly authored by myself, William R. Coe, and Christopher Jones. Sadly, both Jones and Coe are no longer with us. Jones's material is now to appear in 23C and 23D. As a result, TR. 23B presents data on four of the six Great Temples. Great Temples I and II appear in TR. 14 (1990). The greater level of detail available for these two structures reflects the impact of excavation.

From the start, Tikal was distinguished by a wealth of relatively well-preserved standing architecture. One Tikal Project objective was that of putting on record all accessible details of structures that were not scheduled for more intensive investigation. Since standing architecture was always at risk of collapse due to on-going erosion and tree growth, it was felt as a responsibility that all extant features not concealed by debris should be recorded as soon as possible. This report presents one set of these "standing architecture" examples. Others appear in TR 23A (2002), and TR 23C and 23D (forthcoming).

The four structures presented here, Great Temple III, IV, V, and VI, together with Great Temples I and II, stand as the dominant features of the city center. If tree growth were to be removed, five of these would be immediately obvious as a coherent set of major monuments (Great Temple VI is remotely located but connected with the others by plaster paving). All but Great Temple V represent Late Classic construction and can be associated with known rulers. It is tempting to think of them as funerary monuments, but this is only a supposition. Their relationship with rulers may have been much more complex.

Tikal Project personnel who measured these structures and prepared the drawings that provided the data for this report are noted in the introductory paragraphs for each structure. Manuscript preparation has greatly benefited from the editorial work of Barbara Hayden, Simon Martin, Jim Mathieu, and Page Selinsky. Alessandro Pezzati and Virginia Greene assisted greatly in providing various types of material. Alert outside readers spotted problems and made helpful suggestions. I wrote the reports and must take responsibility for any errors or omissions.

Great Temple IV

Structure 5C-4

As seen from the doorway of Str. 5D-I (Great Temple I), looking W, the superstructure of Str. 5C-4 rises above the forest canopy to the right of Str. 5D-2 (Great Temple II; Fig. 1a,b). Removal of intervening forest would show the two Great Temples (I and IV) as the E and W limits of the plateau occupied by the monumental structures and plazas of epicentral Tikal. Beyond this complex, contours fall away and set the center of the city apart from the less intensive development around it. This effect is heightened by the massiveness of the largest structures. Structure 5C-4, for example, rises approximately 67 m above its sustaining surface, at the junction of the Tozzer and Maudslay Causeways.

Three of the five great temples (II, III, and IV) are located so that from Great Temple I, looking W, all are visible frontally. They are sited so that each stands on a unique axial line. This is true even for Great Temples I and II, located on opposite sides of the Great Plaza. Such obvious separation of axial lines must have been intentional. One possible argument for intentional separation of axes is that each one may have embodied iconographic significance specific to each structure. A consideration such as this may have influenced the site selection of Str. 5C-4 relative to the other great temples. Harrison (1999:fig. 123), noting that 5C-4, 5D-5, and 5D-1 form a right-angle triangle, proposes a different account for the Str. 5C-4 location, not incompatible with the conjecture presented above.

The 5C-4 Pyramid, on top of its basal platform (Fig. 2a,b), measures 88 m across the front (Fig. 3). Height (62 m) appears dominant, despite being less than the width by the ratio of 62:88 or 1:1.42. These proportions give the structure a quality of massiveness and solidity particularly appropriate to its site at the W edge of epicentral Tikal.

When newly built, and while in use, its proximity to the Great Plaza would have been much more apparent than it is now. Intervening forest currently makes 5C-4 seem more remote. A continuous paved surface, the Tozzer Causeway, once extended from the East Plaza through to 5C-4 the size and proportions of which are calculated to match the scale of the causeway, probably not an accident. Indeed, the quality of monumentality is very strongly developed in this structure, both by its own properties and by its position.

The Maudslay Causeway leads from a corner of Str. 5C-4 to the North Group and completes a circuit that returns via the Mendez Causeway to the East Plaza (see TR. 11:Temple IV Sheet). Structure 5C-4 is a major node along this circuit. The wide, plaster-paved, wall-lined avenues seem set up for processional ceremonies. Presumably Str. 5C-4 would have acted as one station-point in ceremonial proceedings staged on the causeways.

A series of quarries is located immediately to the E of Str. 5C-4 and behind it. Stone from these workings might have been part of the fabric of 5C-4; proximity of such a resource surely would not have been ignored. Two groups of small structures adjacent to the quarries (see Haviland, TR. 20A) may have housed the workmen and their families.

Excavations at Str. 5B-6 and 7 (ibid.) reveal Manik and Imix occupation in the area of intensive quarrying. These structures appear to have been continuously occupied from ca. 700 to ca. 869 AD.

Occupants may have worked on Str. 5C-4, but that would not have been their only project.

The basal platform and pyramid of 5C-4 required enormous amounts of material (see the estimates, below). Land previously occupied nearby may have been cleared to bedrock for quarrying. This may explain the paucity of housemounds in the vicinity. Residential trash and demolition debris could have been used in the basal platform. For stability, it seems more likely that quarried stone would have been used for the pyramid.

Not surprisingly, Str. 5C-4 is represented in early investigations at Tikal. Teobert Maler designated the structure as Great Temple IV, cleared it of large trees, and provided photos (Maler 1911:pl. 1, 5) showing vegetation rooted even on the face of the roofcomb, as was still the case years after the inception of the Tikal Project (Fig. 1). This vegetation was removed in 1965 for stabilization (Fig. 4). The foreground in Maler's print shows a tangle of old-growth tree trunks felled to open up vistas for his views of the major structures. These scenes reveal both the extent of forest growth resisted by the architecture over a span of a thousand years and the speed of its subsequent recovery. Although the Peabody Museum did not receive Maler's site map in time for the 1911 publication, Tozzer provided one (1911:fig. 41). It shows a pyramid of nine terraces, probably by analogy with Str. 5D-1. Although higher than 5D-1, which has nine terraces, 5C-4 has only seven.

On-floor debris in the rooms was examined and cleared early in Tikal Project investigations (Op. 5A, 1957). Selective clearing to determine plan lines and terrace profiles was conducted primarily on E and N faces of the pyramid and basal platform terraces (Op. 5B, 1965). An axial tunnel penetrated a short distance into core material at the base of the main stair (Op. 5C, 1965), but did not encounter anything other than construction material.

Wilbur Pearson did the architectural recording in 1965. At that time, the consolidation program had already begun (Fig. 4). For this work, the superstructure was cleared of all debris but the pyramid was left undisturbed except for removal of large trees near the top. Root systems of plants covering basal platform and pyramid terraces have been left intact to maintain stability of masonry facings pending future consolidation.

Construction Stages

The condition of the site prior to construction of Str. 5C-4 is not known. Earlier structures may have been present or the site may have been undeveloped. This latter option seems unlikely given the relatively late date of 5C-4 construction. Hence the kind of work needed to prepare for construction is unknown. The quarrying operation, mentioned above, may have extended over the area covered by the structure.

A hard plaster sustaining surface (see below) on 0.20 m of ballast (small stones) runs under facing masonry at the N corner of the basal platform stair side (Fig. 5a:1). This surface appears to be paving of the Tozzer/Maudslay Causeway. How far W it extends under Str. 5C-4 remains uncertain. The extant surface disintegrates rapidly with distance E from the terrace foot.

PRECINCT WALL

Surface profiles on the site map (TR. 11:Temple IV Sheet) imply that a wall encloses the area containing the basal platform. The term "precinct wall" (Fig. 2a,b) has not previously cropped up in relation to Tikal architecture. It is introduced here and for Str. 6F-27. Although apparently lower and less massive than causeway walls, the precinct wall may define an extension of causeway pavement provided as a sustaining surface for the structure about to be built. Were precinct and causeway walls cleared and rebuilt, Str. 5C-4 would appear to open directly onto the causeways.

Dimensional differences between causeway and precinct wall, as implied by surface contours, suggest that the latter (which was smaller) was seen as part of the structure and, hence, is considered here as a 5C-4 component. Details of height, mass, and position in the sequence of construction operations have not been established. Masonry for the precinct wall is not included in the volume estimates.

BASAL PLATFORM

Surface features indicate the presence of a basal platform (Fig. 2a,b, 5a; TR. 11:Temple IV Sheet). It appears to cover an area of about 150 m N-S by 100 m E-W to a height of about 5 m; this equates to a volume of approximately 102,000 m^3. Surface profiles and minimal excavation indicate a simple rectangular format of two terraces with a stair on the E side debouching directly onto the causeway surface. The 5C-4 pyramid is centered on this platform. It appears to be an integral part of the structure, but this assumption needs to be tested because its plastered top surface runs under the pyramid. Though treated here as a 5C-4 component, the basal platform could belong to an earlier feature (see Basal Platform Sustaining Surface, and Terrace 1, below).

BASAL PLATFORM SUSTAINING SURFACE

At the stair-side excavation, a hard, smooth plaster surface on ca. 0.20 m of ballast runs under basal platform masonry (Fig. 5a:2). This appears to be a resurfacing over an earlier hard plaster surface that was not penetrated. One or both of these floors may relate to causeway construction. These floors raise the possibility that an earlier structure, now hidden by the basal platform, may exist. A drop of 0.10 m in a W to E, 5 m span is indicated along the base of the stair side.

TERRACE 1

The basal platform has two terraces. Plaster run-under (a floor or top surface that continues under a supra-positioned feature) at the top surface of terrace 1 implies that it was built as a distinct construction stage completed and plastered (both face and top surface) prior to commencement of terrace 2. Masonry characteristics, similar in both terraces, suggest they were installed during the same episode of construction (see also evidence for the stair, below).

Profiles, obtained by limited clearing at the junction of stair side and terrace, extend upward ca. 0.90 m with no indication of a basal molding (Fig. 5a). This implies absence of basal moldings and probably also absence of apron moldings, since Late Classic profiles generally do not have one without the other. Preservation did not extend high enough to test this assumption.

An excavation at the NE corner revealed a rounded form with a radius of four meters, greatly contrasting with the sharp corners of the pyramid and upper features. Structure 5C-4 is not unique at Tikal in presenting both rounded and sharp (arrised) corners. This report will bring together the various Tikal structures that possess this property.

BASAL PLATFORM STAIR

Construction of the second terrace coincided with installation of the stair following completion of terrace 1. A run of masonry facings of terrace 1, unplastered, extends 1.5 m behind core masonry of the stair. Terrace 2 facings, on the other hand, stop on the line of stair-side facings. Thus, it appears that the stair was built after terrace 1 had been completed but during construction of terrace 2.

Tread and riser dimensions are projected from the average of in situ observations (Fig. 5b). Extrapolating from limited observations, the stair probably consists of 14 treads, 0.50 m deep, and 15 risers, 0.33 m high, for an estimated total height at the E face of 5 m. Risers are vertical, formed by single masonry units sharply tapered in plan. The stair has no balustrade and the stair side is vertical (little or no batter). Stair-side facing masonry appears to consist exclusively of headers (Fig. 5a,b).

The top of the basal platform is a hard, white plaster surface running under pyramid masonry. A very thin topping, a mere skin coat, overlies this. It disintegrates a few centimeters away from the pyramid foot. The hard surface beneath it hints that an earlier version of 5C-4 may exist within the pyramid.

The basal platform had been resurfaced with a hard, white plaster finish on about 0.06 m of fine topping over about 0.20 m of graded ballast. This floor abuts the foot of the pyramid and precedes installation of St. P43 and Alt. P35. It is unclear whether resurfacing was primary or secondary to plastering of the pyramid terrace. Weathering and erosion have destroyed this floor beyond the zone protected by collapse debris.

PYRAMID

The pyramid (Fig. 2a,b, 6, 7) is distinctly rectangular; 82.2 (N-S) by 64.1 m (E-W mean) at its base as measured at inset corners. These would be the measurements most likely employed by the builders at the start of construction. Setting primary corners is always critical for initial layout. The length-to-depth ratio (length across the front:front to rear, at inset corners) is 1:0.78. That is, the front-to-rear depth is between three-quarters and two-thirds of the side-to-side length across the front. Designers may have arranged this relationship in order to emphasize frontality.

North-to-south lengths, that is rear length and front length at base level to inset corners, are equal as measured by Pearson using tape and transit; east-to-west lengths (N side and S side at base level) vary by 2 cm. In other words, dimensional control appears to have been remarkably precise, at least within the precision of our measuring techniques. The rectangle at the top of the pyramid measures 39.5 by 23 m (at inset corners), a ratio of 1:0.58 (Fig. 6). On axial lines the ratio is 1:0.42. By both measures, the top is distinctly more rectangular than the base. The change reflects the fact that the sides are slightly steeper than the front and the rear is slightly steeper than the sides.

At the pyramid base, that is terrace 1, corner angles measured at inset corners are close to 90° (90° at NE, 88.5° at NW, 91° at SW, and 89° at SW).

The error measured as the differences between lengths of the sides, which would be equal if corners were exactly 90°, is about 2%. The SE to NW diagonal exceeds the NE to SW diagonal by 2.2 m, that is, by 2%.

On the plan (Fig. 6), diagonals drawn to connect the inset corners cross exactly on the central axis at a point precisely midway between front and rear of the building. This is either adventitious or evidence of very careful planning and remarkable dimensional control.

Plan configuration (Fig. 6) is based on numerous small excavations at base level, terrace 2 level, and terrace 6 level. Although presented in broken line in Fig. 6, plan details are reasonably well known (the solid lines provided by excavations are too short to appear at the Fig. 6 scale). There are seven terraces, each with inset corners. North and S sides have side outsets and an extra outset intervening between the inset corner and the side outset. On the rear facade, a comparable arrangement is established by the rear axial outset, extra outsets, and the corner inset. The front stair balances the rear axial outset and stair-side outsets balance the extra side and rear outsets.

North and S rear corners could be regarded as double inset corners. Front corners cannot be seen this way because stair-side outsets are not terrace outsets, and they have different profiles (Fig. 8a,b). This distinction may relate to some sort of significance associated with the stair. This is the only sub-component rising more than one terrace in height, and it extends to full height, base to top. Side and rear outsets are all contained within terrace levels.

A cross pattern, apparent in the plan diagram (Fig. 6), is formed by the stair, side outsets, and rear outset. With the pyramid still obscured by vegetation and not consolidated, this figure is not readily apparent, but ancient Maya users may have been aware of it, and those who designed the structure must have considered it important.

Although all terrace profiles appear similar, setbacks are greater on the front than on the sides and rear. As a result, sides and rear are steeper than the front. The pyramid is symmetrical side-to-side but not front-to-rear. The building component, centered on the pyramid base, is placed slightly forward on the top so that the top terrace is wider behind than in front. There is no effective landing at the top of the great stair. Evidently, this was not a location for staging events.

Plaster surfacing at the top of terrace 1 runs under terrace 2 masonry at the NE corner. This implies completion of facing masonry and plastering of terrace 1 prior to installation of terrace 2 facings (it is not clear how far the top surface runs under terrace 2). The only other exposure of this condition is at terrace 6, where plaster of the terrace 5 top does not run under terrace 6 masonry.

All terrace profiles, except those flanking the main stair, are of the type formed by apron, sub-apron, and basal molding elements (Fig. 8). Apron and basal moldings lie in a common plane. Sub-aprons, which appear as inset horizontal strips, are set at varying heights so that those on outset elements do not coincide with those on different planes. Sub-aprons are set low at inset corners and then alternate in height progressively at outset elements.

In some cases, both apron and basal moldings are cut into masonry after installation. That is, they do not coincide with course levels (see, for example, Fig. 8a:1, 8b:1, 9a:1). At pyramid level, rear axial outsets and the central outsets on S and N sides have no moldings, but at building platform level, aprons are present (Fig. 9a).

Terrace-facing masonry was seen mostly at corners. Away from corners only three stones were actually measured, one stretcher and two headers. They are similar in shape—roughly rectangular blocks—merely set differently and with terrace batter cut into different faces. Representative dimensions for non-specialized facing stones are 0.30 by 0.60 by 0.25 m (the last measurement is the height).

Stretchers and headers appear, more or less, with equal frequency.

Eight corner stones were examined. They are bedded horizontally with batter cut into the surface faces and in three cases with apron outsets or basal outsets cut into the stones after bedding. It seems probable that facing stones were installed with roughly vertical and evenly stepped faces subsequently dressed to conform to the batter of the terrace. No surviving plaster was seen.

Terrace heights vary irregularly, from bottom to top, as follows: 4.90, 4.90, 4.80, 4.55, 4.70, 4.40, and 4.84 m for a total of 33 m. Batter, measured as the angle from the vertical, varies as 20°, 20°, 20.5°, 21.5°, 21.5°, 21°, and 19.5° (bottom to top). Greater batter correlates with lesser height in the middle series of terraces. Reduced batter, that is, more steeply pitched terraces at the bottom of the pyramid, may reflect intent to ensure sufficient area at the top for the planned building. Terrace 7 at the top of the pyramid is the steepest and may reflect the same concern. All observed return faces, between outset facets of the terraces, have zero batter. That is, they are vertical.

In setting terrace batter for such a high pyramid, builders would have been more concerned to avoid excessive batter than overly steep terracing. The former error would have meant inadequate space at the top, whereas the latter would have meant merely a wider space between terrace edge and building—no great problem. Since terrace facings were not designed to retain core masonry, steepness would not risk stability. Hence, they were conservative at the start, more confident in the middle terraces, and finally, conservative again at the top terrace.

On the front facade, the terraces that flank the main stair have superior and basal moldings (Fig. 8). This contrast with regular terrace apron profiles indicates some kind of different identity or perhaps symbolism, possibly associated with the stair rather than the terracing. These are, accordingly, classified as stair-side outsets rather than terrace outsets. Terrace masonry runs under the stair-side masonry. Thus, the stair-side outsets were installed with the stair, not with the terracing.

The volume of construction material required for each terrace decreases with height as follows (bottom to top): 26,038, 20,880, 16,388, 12,129, 9,398, and 6,509 m³. These are, of course, estimates based on reconstructed profiles. They add up to a total of 91,795 m³, including the great stair.

PYRAMID STAIR

The stair has been reconstructed with a total of 110 risers, each 0.30 m tall based on a very meager sample. The three risers measured at the foot of the stair are 0.26, 0.34, and 0.30 m in height. Total stair height is 33 m. There could have been 100 risers at 0.33 m. Stair-side facings are assumed vertical and without balustrades (*alfardas*).

Underlying the first step of the stair is a problematic feature (U. 20) that remains unresolved (Fig. 9b). It presents a single course of block masonry, 0.18 m high, faced with a thick plaster coat turning down onto a hard plaster surface, possibly the top of the basal platform. The plaster facing ends at the top of the blocks in a way consistent with demolition. This feature seems to represent a preexisting construction of some sort, erected on the basal platform and chopped down at the time of pyramid construction. There is no evidence that it extended N-S beyond the area covered by the stair. It could have been a relatively small feature built for some function conducted on top of the completed basal platform. Equally, it may present another hint that the basal platform might be part of an otherwise unknown Str. 5C-4-2nd.

BUILDING WALLS, BUILDING PLATFORM, AND SUPPLEMENTARY PLATFORM

In contrast to the plaster surface of the pyramid top that runs under the supplementary platform, interfaces between the three parts of the next construction stage are merely rough layers of mortar not obviously tamped or hardened (Fig. 11). Such unhardened surfaces do not present clear evidence that each part was completed before the next. Workers could have been engaged on all three at the same time.

The rear axial outset and the front stair extend unbroken through both the supplementary platform and building platform. This reinforces the inference that at least the lower two parts were completed simultaneously. Plastered wall tops enclosing the three rooms of the building provide the evidence for completion of this visually composite part as one construction stage (Fig. 12a,b).

This portion of the work amounts to 3,468 m³ of construction material. The terms "building platform" and "supplementary platform" are retained, but not as construction stages. Here they relate to visually distinct parts of a single construction stage that also includes walls of the building.

At the rear, no plaster run-under was observed between the pyramid and supplementary platform material. If run-under is indeed absent, then the whole of the pyramid top had not been plastered when supplementary platform work began. Still, the pyramid had been substantially completed and at least partially surfaced by this time. Therefore, its classification as a distinct construction stage may be essentially correct.

In 1965–66 workers of the Guatemalan Government Restoration Program, under Tikal Project direction, cleared these upper parts of 5C-4 and consolidated the masonry with new material and mortar. The architectural survey reported here preceded and partly overlapped with this work. As a result, some conjectural broken-line elements in various figures appear as solid masonry in photographs taken later.

The supplementary platform has two levels: a lower front part and a slightly wider, higher rear part, each one-terrace high. These terraces have apron moldings similar to those on the pyramid, that is, apron, subapron, and basal molding. Return faces between the front and rear parts have batter in contrast to the vertical return faces of the pyramid.

A two-terrace arrangement flanks the stair in the normal position of stair-side outsets. Apron moldings without basal moldings, and with apron batter not parallel to subapron batter, distinguish these frontal elements. Return faces are vertical.

The ratio of subapron height to apron height is 1:0.8 (upper terrace) and 1:1 (lower terrace). Apron moldings are infrequent on stair-side outsets at Tikal. This may be a unique instance. They do not resemble Tikal stair-side outsets either in profile or in lateral extent, but because they seem to have been installed with the stair and not with the terracing, they probably should be regarded as such.

The rear axial outset of the combined supplementary and building platform has an apron molding with apron and subapron parallel in straight-line profiles (Fig. 9a). The ratio of subapron height to apron height is 1.9:2.6 (1:1.37). This contrasts strikingly with rear axial outsets of the pyramid, which lack apron moldings. The decision to apply

aprons to these outsets in the construction stage associated with the building must have been deliberate. A guess is that this has something to do with the specific meanings imputed to the different parts of the structure. What such meanings may have been remains obscure.

The stair rising from pyramid top to building floor had deteriorated badly, and had been rebuilt prior to Pearson's architectural survey. The stair illustrated in Fig. 2b and 3 is the rebuilt one.

The building platform is much lower than the supplementary platform but conforms to it in plan, in three levels stepping up from front to rear and with side insets (Fig. 7). Most building platform masonry had eroded down to base level. Apart from stair-side outsets, the consolidation program restored only a small portion on the E (front) facade (Fig. 2b, 3). No plaster survived.

BUILDING WALLS

The walls of the building show three distinct operations that appear somewhat like task-units in the limited exposures that were seen (Fig. 12a). These comprise subwalls, or like footings, with core, facing, and plaster. A small test pit at the N rear corner of Rm. 1 exposed a subwall unit at that location (Fig. 12b:8). It has a roughly plastered top surface. It is suspected that this indicates that it stood exposed for an interval before walls were installed on it. The subwall extended N well beyond the N end of Rm. 1 and not under the end wall. It seems to have been installed to establish the position of the longitudinal wall between Rm. 1 and 2. Probably it was made longer than necessary for expediency. The longitudinal wall between Rm. 1 and 2 also runs N beyond the N end of Rm. 1. Evidently the length of Rm. 1 had not been determined at the time of the subwall and longitudinal wall construction.

Given the relatively indirect relationship between exterior wall faces and the wall elements that actually define rooms (Fig. 12a), a method of locating room walls prior to installation of wall-core material may have been necessary. Subwalls, if they extend beneath both longitudinal walls, would provide this. It may be that interior walls were built to define rooms and then core material was filled in behind them out to the exterior surfacing. If so, then we could expect that room walls have dressed facings only within rooms; the other side of these walls would likely have only rough facings or none at all. Probably a procedure like this would be followed only where rooms are very much smaller than the exterior footprint of the building, as in the case of Str. 5C-4.

The lateral elements of the walls are so thick, extending as solid masses from front to rear, that they do not at all resemble the features normally identified as walls (Fig. 10, 12a). At the N wall of Rm. 1, an excavation probed more than two meters into this zone without encountering any cavity (noted in the field but not drawn). Apparently, these very thick walls are indeed solid and account for 1,343 m³ of material.

This cut provides the only available sample of wall core. It consists of roughly dressed blocks bedded horizontally in conformity with course levels of facing masonry. Hence it would appear that wall construction proceeded course-by-course over the whole extent of the building with core and face units of similar type.

Within the rooms, plastered wall tops are detectable, but the complete surfacing of wall tops remains problematic. Wall-top configuration, as suggested in Fig. 12a, is necessarily speculative. In particular, it is not certain that wall-top plaster extends unbroken over the whole surface. Plaster turns indicate that wall construction began at the rear and proceeded toward the front.

Wall heights vary and there are differences between heights of wall tops in rooms, heights to vault springs, and exterior wall heights to medial moldings (Fig. 12b). Wall-tops, being plastered, are marked by detectable edges where vertical wall plaster turns in, horizontally, over walls. The front wall in Rm. 1 is 3.50 m high to plastered wall top and 4.33 m high to vault spring. In Rm. 2, wall height to wall top is 3.50 m and 4.43 m to vault spring. In Rm. 3, these dimensions are 3.50 and 4.05 m, respectively. The apparent wall height at exterior front from wall base to medial molding is 4.20 m, at side inset 4.20 m, and at rear 4.10 m. The different values result from supra-lintel masonry and floor thicknesses. The rear medial molding is set at vault spring level, but at front and side inset locations medial molding heights do not correspond to either plastered wall tops or vault springs.

Exterior wall faces consist of block masonry set in continuous courses that vary irregularly in height (Fig. 4). A few of the shorter blocks may be headers, but this is not at all clear. Face lengths for a sample

of 100 stones vary from 0.20 to 0.65 m with a variance of 52, a standard deviation of 7.2, and a mean of 0.55 m. Heights range from 0.14 to 0.26 m with a variance of 4.92, a standard deviation of 2.2, and a mean value of 0.20 m. Exterior wall surfaces have moderate batter. Interior faces are vertical. All wall facings were dressed to a smooth surface following installation and prior to plastering.

Scaffolding holes are visible along the base of the walls at the exterior. At the rear (Fig. 13), the holes at wall base are paired with holes about 3 m vertically above. Horizontal intervals between vertical pairs range between 2 and 3 m. Upper-level holes are not visible on front and side facades. Presumably they exist but remain sealed. The scaffolding system probably employed horizontal poles set into wall masonry and lashed to vertical poles at their outer ends. The verticals would reinforce the projecting horizontal poles to ensure support for horizontal working stages.

Lintels: The carved wood lintels of Str. 5C-4 have been extensively reported elsewhere (TR. 6, TR. 33A). Lintels to Dr. 2 and 3 had been removed long prior to Tikal Project operations, leaving plaster impressions that show little or no deflection of superimposed masonry. Evidently, once the mortar had set and dried, the wooden lintels did not actually carry the burden posed by masonry directly above them. This stands as testimony to the high quality of mortar employed in 5C-4 construction. Masonry above these doorways must have acted as a monolithic mass with sufficient resistance to bending stresses to be able to span the openings without deflection.

Lintels 2 and 3 contain extensive hieroglyphic texts that have been the subject of several studies over the years since the Tikal Project. Both lintels record (Fig. 13a,b) the date 9.15.10.0.0 (AD 741, TR 33A:103). Jones (1991:120) cites this as the construction date but, on the assumption that the temple would have been built after death of the ruler interred within it, the construction date would have been much later. Simon Martin has shown that Lintel 3 records a war fought against El Peru in AD 743 while Lintel 2 celebrates Tikal's conquest of Naranjo 191 days later in AD 744 (Martin 1996, 2000:114–22). The last date recorded on the latter falls in AD 747. The precedent of Str. 5D-1 (Great Temple I) calls for construction to follow death of the ruler. Hence a tomb may exist somewhere within the substructure, although Bu. 196, under Str. 5D-73 has been cited as a possible tomb of the Temple IV ruler (TR 33A:103).

In 1977, Christopher Jones deciphered glyphs on Li. 3 (Fig. 13b) as the inaugural date (9.15.3.6.8; 8 December AD 734) of a ruler, known at that time as Ruler B. In TR. 33A, he cites Riese (1979) as the authority confirming the fact that Ruler B was 27th in the dynastic line. Subsequently, his name has been read as Yik'in Chan K'awiil, son of Jasaw Chan K'awiil, in office from 734 to ca. 761 (Martin 1996). It has generally been assumed that Yik'in Chan K'awiil is the enthroned figure depicted on these two lintels. He may have been depicted on the roofcomb as well.

Lintel beams remain in place over the outer doorway. They are roughly squared but not carved. All beams that were either squared or carved are of sapodilla wood (TR. 6:43).

Cord holders with vertical wooden dowels flank the outer doorway on the interior face of the front wall (Fig. 12b:9). Their function demands speculative interpretation. They could have provided anchorage for a fabric or a wooden screen placed across the doorway opening on the inside face of the wall. They might have been used to secure horizontal poles to which a door of sorts could be attached within the doorway opening. Or they might have anchored paired door panels that could swing open inwardly from the cord-holder points. Some alternatives imply interior operation. Others could be opened and closed from the exterior. It may be that some individuals had to spend certain periods of time sequestered in the dark.

ROOM VAULTS

The three vaults over the rooms of the building are all relatively steep (Fig. 11, 12b). Span-to-height ratios as measured from wall surface to edge of the vault cap (i.e., the half-vault span) are 1:5.0 (Rm. 1), 1:10.9 (Rm. 2), and 1:11.2 (Rm. 3). Several vault beams remain in place, set at three levels in each room. Diameters average approximately 0.12 m (see also Table 2.1).

Plaster on soffit surfaces of the three room vaults conceals all masonry details. Soffit surfaces are regular and smoothly finished with straight-line profiles. In the three rooms, the heights from spring to cap

TABLE 2.1
Structure 5C-4: Vault Ratios

Room	Soffit Angle	Wall Height to Vault Height Ratio	Vault Span to Room Width Ratio
Rm. 1	12°	1:0.57	1:0.5
Rm. 2	4°	1:0.57	1:0.25
Rm. 3	5.5°	1:0.63	1:0.24

are very similar: 2.50 m (Rm. 1), 2.50 m (Rm. 2), and 2.57 m (Rm. 3), though spans differ.

At the top of the vault over Rm. 3 application marks show that the upper quarter of the soffit was plastered from above. Workers reached down through the gap between the half-vault units to apply the plaster. They were not able to achieve as smooth a finish as on the lower portions. This provides clear proof that preplastered cap stones were installed after half-vault soffits had been plastered.

As workers placed the first course of vault stones over the rear walls of Rm. 1 and 2, they installed a series of wooden rods or dowels. The holes left by these members are known as a rod row (Fig. 12b:5). They open in the turnout of the vault spring and slant upward into the mortar between vault stones. They span the doorways, but since the rooms—especially Rm. 2—are hardly much larger than the doorways, they effectively extend the length of each room.

Presumably, when initially installed, the rods would have projected out from the wall face. With a diameter of only a couple of centimeters, they could not have projected very far. They could have served as anchors for fabrics or light screens hanging down in front of the rear walls. Such devices would have concealed the two inner rooms and the carved wooden lintels. With the Rm. 2 screen in place and the Rm. 1 screen taken down, Li. 2 would have been visible while Li. 3 remained hidden. With the Rm. 1 screen in place, the front room could have been used without involvement of either lintel. When the screens were up, the lintels might have been regarded as "turned off" and therefore not to be seen.

A plastered vault-back surface is visible off-section on the front facade. Presumably, this plaster extends over all vault-back surfaces, but would likely not be present in double vault cores over interior walls (Fig. 12b).

The rooms and doorways represent a spatial volume of 138 m³. This amounts to 10.3% of wall-masonry volume. In comparison with other Tikal structures, it is one of the highest ratios of wall material to room space, second only to Great Temple V (1.6%).

Clearly Str. 5C-4 designers were not concerned to maximize interior space in relation to gross building volume. Exterior dimensions in this structure are clearly independent of the functional program required for interior space. Side insets imply presence of two rooms rather than the three that are present. From exterior impressions one would expect much larger rooms. Possibly there may have been little or no need for interior space. Settings for the carved lintels may have dictated interior dimensions. Location at the end of the Tozzer Causeway may have required exterior dimensions that would not seem paltry as viewed from Temple I.

UPPER ZONES

Upper zones are in three parts, stepping up from front to rear; total material volume is 1,568 m³ (Fig. 3, 7, 14a,b). The front part and the side inset have medial moldings and superior moldings. Front elements have hip moldings. Sculptural features extend across the front face (Fig. 14a). Preservation is very poor, but extant masonry includes remains of three major mask units. Fragmentary details between the masks may be part of elaborate headdress elements largely lost.

Height of the frontal upper zone is 3.95 m. This compares with frontal wall height (measured as building platform to medial molding) of 3.85 m. The ratio of frontal upper-zone height to frontal wall height is 1:1.03. That is, the frontal upper zone is only very slightly higher than the apparent exterior frontal walls. Frontal batter of 16° appears much greater than other faces, but this may reflect loss of material at the top. Side faces have a batter of 10°.

The middle section of the upper zones, in the side inset, has a medial molding but no other articulations (Fig. 7). Height, including the medial molding, is 4.75 m. Exterior wall height at the side inset is 4.1 m. The ratio is 1:1.16. The upper zone here is distinctly higher than the wall.

At the rear, the upper zone has no moldings or articulations of any sort (Fig. 7, 13). Height is 4.25 m above a wall of 4.15 m. The ratio is 1:1.02.

The rear upper zone is very slightly closer in height to the wall beneath it than is the case at the front. The batter is 8.5°.

ROOFCOMB

The roofcomb is in three stages, representing a total material volume of 1,483 m³ (Fig. 2a, 3, 7, 15). There is considerable articulation of the front face, but due to loss of material no precise delineation is possible. Presumably front surfaces were covered with sculptural detail, almost all of which is now lost or unrecorded. Profile variations suggest there may have been a seated figure at the center base level. Figure 2b illustrates surface articulation schematically.

The lower stage of the roofcomb contains eight vaulted chambers in two levels of four chambers each (Fig. 16a). Masonry of these interior spaces is smoothly dressed and finished with plaster in spite of the absence of any means of access. Vault springs are not outset but rise directly from wall surfaces. In contrast, upper-level chambers (Fig. 16b) have outset vault springs. This seems like a picayune detail, but may indicate some difference in conceptual associations assigned to chambers at this topmost level. In all chambers, workers responsible for interior finish must have crawled out through vault-top openings prior to installation of capstones (slender workers must have been assigned to this task).

The second roofcomb stage also contains four chambers. The total spatial volume represented by all 12 chambers amounts to 92 m³ or 6.9% of roofcomb masonry volume. Chambers at the lower level average 15.6 m³ in volume, at middle level, 5.9 m³, and at upper level, 1.15 m³.

Roofcomb chambers reduce the amount of stone and mortar that had to be carried up to this height, but only to a modest extent. Work entailed by dressing and plastering interior surfaces would seem to overcome any advantage gained by this minor material saving. Other needs must have demanded these inaccessible spaces. Perhaps they were regarded as potential dwellings for supernatural beings.

Two pairs of vertical slots cut through the middle (second) stage from front to rear (Fig. 2a, 3, 13, 15). No obvious function is apparent. At certain times of the year the setting sun shines through them, and certain winds may generate a sound sometimes, though this has not been heard. Above these the upper, third stage is largely fallen. It is reconstructed as a single thick, wall-like element arbitrarily given a height of 2 m.

An axial outset is centered on the rear facade and on this is an inset panel (Fig. 13).

The rear facade of the roofcomb has scaffolding holes along its base level, that is, at rooftop. Here, poles anchored into masonry would not need support, since they would be resting on the roof surface. Their purpose would be that of anchoring vertical supports for an upper level of scaffolding beams. Holes for these members are not visible. They must retain the seals installed after completion of plastering and as the scaffolding system was taken down. Roofcomb construction must have involved a very substantial edifice of timber framing.

Special Deposits

CACHE 203

LOCATION

On the central axis at the foot of the pyramid stair associated with St. P43 and Alt. P35.

CONTENTS

One pottery cache vessel, H. 11.7 cm (Cat. 5B-4/2); 1 partially reconstructed cache-vessel base with a diameter of 12 cm (Cat. 5B-5/2); 9 eccentric flints, Late Classic (illustrated in TR. 27A:fig. 3g; Cat. 5B-6); 9 incised obsidians, Class 6, Late Classic (illustrated in TR. 27A:fig. 45b; Cat. 5B-7).

Sherds and Artifacts

Modest excavations were made around St. P35 and Alt. P43, at the corner of the stair to the basal platform, at various points around the pyramid and in the rooms of the building. Ceramic assessments (from TR 27B:app. III) are Cauac, Late Cauac, and Imix and Ik. The latter, and also the latest, are associated with the altar and stela. Presumably these were placed after construction had been completed and the spread of Imix (ca. AD 700–869) amply covers the expected date of construction (shortly after AD 751). The Cauac ceramics predate construction by several centuries and must represent material secondarily deposited. Artifact collections are scanty and include nothing potentially or obviously diagnostic of function.

Relationship to Adjacent Stratigraphy

A well-made floor surface (Fig. 5a:1) runs under the basal platform. No attempt was made to trace its extent E of 5C-4. A likely connection would be with either the Tozzer or Maudslay Causeway. It could be an extension of the junction of the two.

Absolute Dates

Fifteen samples taken from wooden beams of Str. 5C-4 were submitted for ^{14}C dating (Ralph 1965). Four different laboratories ran tests. The mean for the twelve samples considered "most reliable" centers on AD 746±16 years (the average of the group of dates with their 1-sigma ranges). Jones (1977) presents a construction date of AD 741, very much in line with the above ^{14}C result. Other results fall earlier. Due to post-sample growth, all the results are likely to predate the actual cutting of the timber by an uncertain span of time (post-sample growth is the time lapse between the sample tested and the subsequent tree growth up to the time when the tree was cut if the sample represents inner heartwood). It is also likely that once cut, timbers selected for use as lintel beams would have been stored for some time to dry. Carving might have taken a significant time to complete. These considerations imply a construction date sometime after these "early" date determinations (Ralph 1965), perhaps around the midpoint of the 8th century AD. There are no signs of alterations to the primary fabric (see also Table 2.2, below).

TABLE 2.1a
Lot Groups: Str. 5C-4
Op. 5A

Lot Groups	Lot	Provenience	Ceramic Evaluation
1	1–16	On floor in rooms	Late Cauac

TABLE 2.1b
Str. 5C-4: Distribution of Sherds and Artifacts by Lot Groups
Op. 5A

Study Group	Object	Lot Groups
Pottery	Sherds to Nearest LB	1
Other	Wood chips some carved	15

TABLE 2.1c
Lot Groups: Str. 5C-4
Op. 5B

Lot Groups	Lot	Provenience	Ceramic Evaluation
1	1	Collapse at stela	Cauac
2	Ca. 203	Stela cache	Imix and Ik

TABLE 2.1d
Str. 5C-4: Distribution of Sherds and Artifacts by Lot Groups
Op. 5B

| | | Lot Groups | |
Study Group	Object	1	2
Pottery	Sherds to Nearest LB	2	
Other Pottery	Cache Vessel		2
Chipped Flint	Blade eccentrics	1	*
Chipped Obsidian	Incised eccentrics		*
Ground Stone	Stone sphere	3	
Other	Stela fragments	*	

* indicates quantity not specified

TABLE 2.1e
Lot Groups: Str. 5C-4
Op. 5C

Lot Groups	Lot	Provenience	Ceramic Evaluation
1	1	Collapse at base of basal platform	Cauac
2	2	Axial tunnel at base of stair	E.C. and Cauac

TABLE 2.1f
Str. 5C-4: Distribution of Sherds and Artifacts by Lot Groups
Op. 5C

Study Group	Object	Lot Groups	
		1	2
Pottery	Sherds to Nearest LB	1	1
Chipped Obsidian	Retouched flake-blade	1	1
Ground Stone	Limestone bark-beater	1	
Shell and Bone	*Pomacea flagellata*		1

TABLE 2.2
Structure 5C-4: Time Spans

Time Span	Construction Stage	Other Data
1		Abandonment.
2		Primary use.
3	1–4	St. P43; Alt. P35 Primary construction, 163,205 m³.

III

Great Temple III

Structure 5D-3

Five pyramidal temples rise out of plaster pavement in epicentral Tikal (Fig. 17a); they are the dominant features of the city center and Str. 5D-3 is one of them, perhaps the last. In Maler's 1895 photo (Fig. 17b), looking W from the doorway of Great Temple I, it is the structure on the left (Maler 1911). He reported its height as 54.20 m "adding about three meters for the part fallen down" (1911:38). Our measurement, also at the E facade, is approximately 54 m, with a smaller allowance for fallen material. Prior to our survey, Coe cited Temple III height as 180 feet or 54.90 m (W. Coe 1967:76).

Tozzer presents a plan and section (1911:fig. 41, 42). His plan assumes right angles where we have found acute and obtuse angles (Fig. 18). Since Maler's time, the superstructure has been cleared and consolidated, but upper canopy trees have reestablished themselves on the lower parts. Roofcomb features glimpsed through the forest now seem even loftier as we peer through the treetops. Great Temple III appears to be the steepest, probably because the substructure remains obscured by vegetation. In fact, the proportions of III and I are very similar.

Rudi Larios and Miguel Orrego did the architectural recording in the 1968–69 field seasons, and I converted the inked drawings to a digital format in 2008.

Although the lintel over the outer doorway had fallen by Maler's time (Fig. 19), the inner Li. 2 retains a detailed carving (Fig. 20; TR. 6:17–37, fig. 18). At the foot of the stair (St. 24), there were a number of badly shattered glyph blocks dated to 9.19.0.0.0 in AD 810 (TR. 33A:52–55). Extant readable glyphs on the lintel describe a Tikal ruler called Nuun Ujol K'inich as the father to another whose name is now lost (Martin 2003:33–34). The latter has been identified as "Dark Sun" based on his appearance on pieces of St. 24 and he may be the principal figure depicted on Li. 2. If so, and if construction followed his death, then Str. 5D-3 may have been built well into the 9th century and may be the last major structure erected at Tikal.

Orientation is toward the E, complicated by a series of divergent angles (Fig. 18). The line generated by the exterior front wall of the building component runs 12° E of magnetic N (5°, 59" E of true N as established for the Tikal Base Map; TR. 11:3). North-south lines of the substructure run in parallel with this line. East-west substructure lines run 7° S of E (azimuth 97°). Exterior E-W wall faces of the building component approximately follow this orientation. Interior N-S wall faces follow the 12° E line with E-W faces, approximately perpendicular but not consistent. The pyramid stair aligns with E-W lines of the substructure, 7° S of E magnetic.

By means not well understood, Tikal builders usually kept corner angles close to 90°. By the time of Temple III, they were maximally experienced in this art. It, thus, seems improbable that such pronounced divergence from right angles could have been accidental. With the substructure obscured by vegetation, acute and obtuse angles so glaring in the plan diagram are not discernable. But when initially built, the sharp SE and NW pyramid corners may have been quite evident. If astronomical referents were employed for layout of structures, perhaps multiple targets were involved. If so, unusual plan geometry might have responded to ideological considerations.

The EW lines could have been set by solar positions at sunrise or sunset. The azimuth of EW lines measured at the pyramid base is 111°, not far off winter solstice sunrise for Tikal (N lat. 17°, 33 minutes; W Long. 89°, 35 minutes). The NS lines, azimuth 19°, may have been set by a desire to have the structure face E on an alignment very similar to that of Temples I and II. There is no obvious astronomical target for the NS lines though they are the most consistently oriented at Tikal.

The principal figure on Li. 2 (Fig. 20) looks toward the E as does the structure. This individual may have been a focus of activities conducted in, on, or in front of the structure. At the foot of the stair, Alt. 7 accompanies St. 24. Although badly eroded in places, the altar retains a very clear image of a supernatural head in an offering bowl (Fig. 21a). This image may identify another focus of Str. 5D-3 activities, that is, other than, or together with, the character on Li. 2. These two images may be related in some way to both the EW and NS alignments of the pyramid and the slightly different alignments of the building interior and the stair (see Fig. 18). In other words, the variation in alignments may reflect programmatic considerations.

Construction Stages

There are no less than six distinct construction stages marked by hard, smooth plaster interfaces: pyramid, building walls and building platform, vaults and upper zones, and three roofcomb stages (Fig. 21b). These roofcomb pauses may be only partial construction stages, in that sculptural treatment probably was not completed separately at each stage. Thus, it may be more accurate to count four stages with three roofcomb substages.

LOWER SUBSTRUCTURE PLATFORM

The sustaining surface rises about 1 m from the E facade to the W facade (Fig. 22–24). Workers clearly tried to compensate for the slope. With a few exceptions, heights at the E end of terraces exceed those at the W end. The height adjustment is greatest at the top two terraces so that finally the top surface of the pyramid is exactly level.

Size and proportions of this part of the structure justify referring to it as a "pyramid," as in casual usage. But this term must be understood as broad and metaphorical. The form is so far from pyramidal in the strict geometrical sense that one might consider "pyramidoid," if this were not such an abominable term.

There are nine terraces, each with apron moldings of three-part type: apron, subapron, and basal molding. Profiles are straight-line as far as can be determined from limited clearing and poor preservation. On average, aprons take up 70% of terrace height at the basal terrace and 73% at the top terrace. Subaprons vary similarly from 11 to 9% and basal moldings from 19 to 17%. Subapron heights are most constant, while apron heights vary the most; basal molding heights fall between.

Terrace heights vary as 3.55, 3.15, 3.2, 3.2, 3.25, 3.3, 3.4, 3.65, and 3.75 m (listed bottom-to-top as average values; heights vary slightly within terraces). The first bottom terrace is relatively high; 2nd to 7th terraces are essentially the same in height; 8th and 9th terraces are the highest. The pattern of variation suggests that through middle levels workers were concerned the pyramid might get too high. As they arrived near the top, though, they felt it might be too low. They may have had a specific result in mind. Pyramid height as measured at the center of the E facade is 30.4 m (note: all dimensions cited are derived from 1:50 inked drawings). Discrepancies of more than 5 cm appear in about one-third of instances that provide more than one measure for the same dimension. The maximum disagreement noted was 0.25 m in a dimension of 3.25 m; that is, 8%).

Batter measurements vary markedly (Table 3.1). Some of this probably reflects the difficulty of measuring partially collapsed terracing. Still, there are consistent patterns that seem explicable in terms of construction.

The two ends of each facade, that is, the inset corners, have quite different values for batter in 30 of the 36 cases (four corners, nine terraces). Workers would establish batter initially as a setback laid out at the terrace base level. To control the face angle (batter), they had to transfer the setback up to the level projected for the terrace top. Timber members probably connected to scaffolding could have served this purpose. Diagonal poles lashed to a timber frame might have approximated the batter angle. In such a large structure errors of the magnitude noted in Table 3.1 could easily crop up from one end to the other in each facade.

TABLE 3.1
Structure 5D-3: Terrace Batter at Inset Corners

Terrace Number	Facades							
	North		East		South		West	
	E	W	N	S	E	W	N	S
9	17	13.3	15.3	11.5	12.5	17.5	14.3	17.5
8	14.8	13.2	13.9	10.8	10.5	16.3	14	17
7	15	11.6	11.9	11.6	13.1	12.6	14	13.5
6	16	12.2	12.7	10.6	12	13.6	12.5	16.5
5	15.3	11.4	12.5	11.6	12.2	13.5	13.3	13.8
4	18.9	15.2	16.1	14.8	16.6	18.3	17.3	19
3	18.8	15.1	19.6	10.8	11.9	21.6	11.4	22.8
2	18.8	15.3	19.4	11.6	13.5	17.3	13.7	22.7
1	18.3	15	18.1	13.5	14.6	18.8	14.7	20.1
Average	16.99	13.59	15.50	11.87	12.99	16.61	13.91	18.10
Average	15.29		13.69		14.80		16.00	

Note: Batter is measured in degrees as the angle away from the vertical.

Another consistent pattern is that around the four sides, on average, larger values of batter are found in the lower terraces. Mid-level terraces have the least batter (on average) and the upper two terraces have slightly more. Workers were generous with setbacks at the start, then became cautious in case the top area might be too small, then realized there would be enough room and increased batter again.

Average values of batter are very similar on N and S sides. They differ by only about half a degree (bottom line, Table 3.1). This is an important consideration for symmetry of the E (front) facade. By contrast, E and W average values differ by more than 2°, with the E facade being steeper. This subtle difference probably makes the front (E) facade just a little more imposing, rising slightly more vertically than the rear (W).

Setbacks from pyramid base to top in each facade tell a different story. Average values include 13.80 m for the N facade; 13.80 m for the S facade; 13.70 m for the E facade, and 13.90 m for the W facade. Although N and S setbacks are, on average,

identical, the difference between E and W is 0.20 m. These measurements suggest that workers intended the E and W setbacks to be similar, in spite of applying more batter to W terraces.

A distinctive feature of Temple III pyramid design is the absence of side outsets. In many Tikal structures, side outsets combine with rear axial outsets and front stairs to set up a cross configuration. In ideological terms, this may relate to the importance of the four cardinal directions. Here, however, only two, E and W, are expressed in pyramid form. Whatever the cross associations may have been, they seem to have been suppressed. Perhaps the intent was to let the E-W directional considerations have exclusive presence. This may be another clue that different orientations of E-W lines in the structure were intentional.

The stair, 11.30 m wide, projecting 19 m out from the pyramid base, rises at a slope of 52° (Fig. 25). Based on measurements at the foot, a total of 90 risers is estimated. Treads are horizontal and risers vertical. Nosings are sharp, not rounded. Stair-side ramps or *alfardas* (balustrades) are present. This is a feature found more commonly in much earlier structures at Tikal and usually accompanied by battered risers and rounded nosings. Here it would seem to be a deliberate archaism.

Stair-side outsets flank the stair. They have superior and basal moldings. The return faces have a batter averaging about 2.7°. At pyramid base, stair-side outsets account for 46% of the distance to the inset corner. This increases gradually until the top outset takes up 62% of the distance to the inset corner.

Rear axial outsets have no moldings and each one spans three terraces. They distinguish three levels in the pyramid. This may mean that each set of three terraces has some particular iconographic significance. On the analogy with a natural mountain, the pyramid may be considered as a home for certain supernatural entities. Those of low status might reside in the bottom three terraces, while more prestigious ones occupy upper levels.

Although the corner angles are far from 90° (NW, 84°; SE, 97°), lengths of opposite sides agree fairly well. North and S sides differ in length at base level by only 2% as measured between inset corners. East and W lengths differ by about 2.6%. These diagonals intersect slightly S of the centerline in the building and near the midpoint of the inner doorway. This would not be an intentional relationship, but it shows how well centered the building is on the substructure.

The pyramid represents 56% of the total height of the structure (30 m versus 54 m). The masonry volume needed for its construction, including the stair, amounts to approximately 31,965 m³.

BUILDING PLATFORM AND BUILDING WALLS

The interface between building platform and building walls is accessible at the rear axial outset. Here a rough mortar surface sustains the walls. A hard plaster surface would show that the building platform had been completed and plastered prior to installation of the building walls. In such circumstances, each would be recognized as a distinct construction stage. Absence of such a surface may not be proof to the contrary, but it leaves the option open. The building platform and walls of the building may have been installed in one continuous operation without the clear break indicated by a plaster surface running under the walls. For this reason, these two parts of the structure are classed as substages.

BUILDING PLATFORM

The footprint made on the top of the pyramid by the building platform is even less rectangular than the pyramid base. The NE corner angle is 79° (contained angle) and the SW corner is 80° (Fig. 26). In this much smaller body, departure from the right angle is less likely to be accidental than in the pyramid.

Three parts make up the building platform (Fig. 23). Only one of the three is a genuine three-dimensional body. This is the lower part, a single-level platform with three-part apron moldings, stair, and stair-side outsets. A rough mortar level, similar to that running under the walls, marks its top surface. In many Tikal structures the lower part is frontal only, but here it extends through to the rear.

On this lower member, the apron accounts for 58% of its height, the subapron for 18%, and the basal molding for 23%. As compared with apron members of the pyramid, this height is about one-third less, but height relationships among the three elements of the molding are similar. That is, the apron is greatest and the subapron is least as on pyramid terraces.

The upper-building platform member, at the rear, has the appearance of a platform supporting the rear walls of the building (Fig. 23, 24, 27), but this is a contrived illusion. Figure 28 shows that this apparently three-dimensional body is really no more than a molding at the base of the exterior wall face. It rises higher than the floor level in the rear room, but its base is at the level of the front room. It has no obvious relationship with the rear room, certainly not one of support.

Something similar is true of the apparent member in the side inset of the building walls. This too masquerades as a platform supporting a middle room, though there is no middle room. The side inset aligns with the inner doorway, not with the inner room. Members apparently analogous, hinting at a middle level within the building, non-existent in this case, have a long history at Tikal. Early Classic structures with this member often do have a middle room at a middle floor level.

The rear axial outset rises to the top of the upper building platform member. It is, thus, part of both lower and upper members. In contrast with the rear axial outsets on the pyramid, it has an apron molding. The apron part of the molding takes up 59%

of the height, the subapron takes up 13%, and the basal molding 27%. In other words, the apron proportions are almost identical with those of the lower building platform member; the subapron is less, and the basal molding is relatively higher.

Unlike the pyramid, the stair has no balustrade, but like the pyramid there are stair-side outsets with superior and basal moldings. This may be a unique arrangement at Tikal.

The exterior appearance of the building platform, as for a building of three rooms stepping up from front to rear, may have acquired iconographic significance over the centuries at Tikal. It may have developed a function as a kind of glyph and this aspect may have been allied with its physical function sustaining the building. In Str. 5D-3, as in a number of similar cases at Tikal, only part of the building platform actually sustains the building.

The particular significance of building platforms probably emerged early in the Early Classic period. Their original significance, whatever that was, may well have changed over the years. Yet some issue of ideological content must have remained powerful enough to be incorporated as a surface image into the last known major architectural undertaking at the site, in which a building platform may have been absent, at least in the rear part. Masonry for the building platform, mainly the lower member and the stair, takes up about 560 m^3 in volume.

WALLS OF THE BUILDING

A hard plaster wall-top surface is present at the rear of the building (Fig. 28). This indicates that walls were installed and finished prior to construction of the vaults. Application of plaster across the top surface of the walls marks completion of the construction stage initiated by building platform work.

In plan, walls follow the parallelogram geometry of the building platform with noticeably acute angles at NE and SW corners (Fig. 26). Except for the short elements beside the two doorways and the stretch along the rear of the inner room, one can hardly speak of walls at all. It might be more appropriate to speak of wall "mass" rather than "thickness." Exterior wall faces mostly define a solid volume rather than a series of walls in the conventional sense. The two rooms appear to have been hollowed out of the wall mass rather than enclosed by wall elements.

The ratio of room area to gross building area provides a measure indirectly reflecting wall thickness. In Str. 5D-3, room area, not including doorway area, amounts to 19% of gross building area. The advantage of this measure is that it applies to all structures that have building components with rooms, including those that have several different wall thicknesses and those like 5D-3 in which wall thickness is not a valid measure.

Facets of exterior wall surface describe a conventional formation with side insets and rear axial outset. Front elements project beyond rear elements and this attribute does correspond to interior arrangements; the front room is indeed longer than the rear room. But side inset location is too far forward to fully correspond to the front room. Its position seems rather to have been determined by a desired proportional relationship between front and rear parts of buildings. The rule apparently was that front parts should appear narrower than rear parts when viewed from the side. Tikal Report 34B will set out the variations in this relationship. Its effect in Str. 5D-3 is to place the front edge of the side inset in line with the rear wall of the front room. Thus, N and S elevations (Fig. 27, 23) give the impression of a front room much narrower than it actually is.

Although the step-up from Rm. 1 to Rm. 2 is only 0.28 m, the rear medial molding is 0.78 m above the front medial molding (Fig. 23, 27, 28). The difference is due to rear wall elements being 0.23 m higher than front wall elements. This distinction is accompanied by concomitant variations in the batter of wall faces. The rear exterior face at the rear axial outset has a batter of 4° (Fig. 28). At the front, exterior face batter is 2.3°. On the S facade, exterior wall faces have a consistent batter of 3.6°. The N facade batter is 1.5°. Between these are several wall faces with zero batter (vertical). Similar batter variations are evident on interior wall faces.

Exterior wall-facing stones appear to be entirely headers. A sample of 100 stones varies in face length from 0.21 to 0.33 m, with a mean value of 0.26 m, a variance of 6.9, and a standard deviation of 2.6. Heights in the same sample range from 0.21 to 0.30 m. That is, face proportions are nearly square. Depths appear to exceed face dimensions and for this reason it seems the stones are all headers. Face surfaces have been dressed following installation to a smooth regular finish. The stones remain in good shape with little erosion. No plaster survives on accessible surfaces. Wall volume is 700 m³ of masonry.

VAULTS AND UPPER ZONES

With walls completed, workers installed timber lintels over the two doorways. Maler (1911:37) reports that the outer doorway had a lintel of "six broad and thick *tsapotl* beams" (sapodilla, *Manikara zapota*, *Achras zapota*, chico zapote). He considered that the beams had not merely decayed, but had been removed. Satterthwaite suggests that it was probably not carved since no other outer doorways at Tikal are known to have carved lintels (TR. 6:73). In the current reconstruction, eight beams are estimated (Fig. 28).

The lintel over the inner doorway presents on its underside the carved depiction of a figure wearing a jaguar skin (Fig. 20). This lintel originally had ten beams, one of which has been either removed or completely eaten by carpenter ants (TR. 6). The Proskouriakoff style-date (1950:51) for this lintel is 9.19.0.0.0+/-2 1/2 katuns. That would place it anywhere between AD 760 and 860.

No vault-back surface has been noted, therefore, vaults and upper zones are included together in the same substage. The two vaults differ mainly in dimensional attributes. That over Rm. 1 has its spring level set 0.50 m above the wall top. Its soffit rises at an angle of 74.6°. The Rm. 2 vault is much smaller, narrower, and lower. Its spring is set 0.30 m above wall top and its soffit angle is 85.7° (note: wall top was detected by means of plaster turns at both interior and exterior surfaces). Both vaults have preplastered capstones. The gap between half-vault units is 0.17 m in Rm. 1 and 0.08 m in Rm. 2. There are two levels of vault beams in the outer vault and only one, high up, in the inner vault. One surviving intact beam remains in the inner vault as evidence of timber falsework. Both have straight-line soffit profiles.

The narrow inner vault may have been partly assembled from above. A timber falsework would have been set up for the half-vault unit above the spine wall and for the spring of the outer half-vault. Workers finished and plastered these elements and then dismantled the timber that had been used partly as scaffolding and partly to set the height and soffit angle. Then standing on the masonry over the rear wall they installed the reminder of the outer half-vault, plastering each course in turn from above. The result

is a less smooth surface readily observable from within the room. This relatively rough surface rises from a plaster turn on top of the spring course of the outer half-vault unit. The space between soffits is too narrow for workers to have done the whole installation from within the room.

A vault of these proportions raises a question about vault function. At vault spring level, because of negative wall batter, the room is only 0.40 m wide. A horizontal stone could easily span this distance. The demanding work of vault assembly could have been avoided. Clearly the vault is not there for practical reasons. Its presence probably relates to ideological issues inherent in construction of structures of this type. Ideas of cave and mountain as domains of supernatural beings or ancestors may have been best embodied through vaulting. In most cases this issue is not so obvious because vaulting spans exceed the capabilities of individual stones. The same ideological directives may have been active in much wider rooms, their presence masked by the practical function of accomplishing the span. In the case examined here, the vault may have been carried just high enough to provide the requisite character to the inner space. It occupies just 28% of height from floor to vault cap. In Rm. 1 this ratio is 35%.

Upper zones are on two levels, the rear part set 0.78 m higher than the front part. The rear profile is plain with a batter of 2.8° at the rear axial outset and 7° at the S facade. The E upper zone has medial moldings, superior moldings, and hip moldings. Batter is 7.5° on the E face and 9.6° on the S face. The E face contains three masks (Fig. 22, 29a,b) and the S face has a sculptural feature resembling an inset panel (Fig. 29c).

The E facade masks, badly eroded, represent a partly human, partly grotesque face flanked by rectangular ear panels (Fig. 29a,b). The S and N masks partly survive but the central one disappeared along with the lintel. It is illustrated in dotted line as identical with the two flanking masks, but this is merely a matter of indicating the likely presence of a central mask of some kind. Central mask features usually are more elaborate than flanking ones. Above the two non-axial masks, a masonry block extends upward through the superior molding. These units may indicate vertical extension of headdress elements. Figures 29a and 29b indicate this possibility, but with little solid basis.

Hard, smooth roof plaster running under roof-comb material marks the top surface of the upper zone and defines it as a construction stage. It cannot be denied, however, that upper-zone sculptural work may have been incomplete as roofcomb construction began.

ROOFCOMB

As seen from the E (front), the roofcomb rises in three steps, each narrower than the one below (Fig. 30). Workers assembled it in three construction stages separated by hard plaster surfaces. Ordinarily these would define construction stages, but details show that this would not be correct. The first of these plaster levels comes at the elevation 292.27 m, about 0.25 m below the first step (Fig. 31). Sculptural treatment on the E face shows no horizontal break at this level. Therefore, it seems more likely that the two plaster levels running through roofcomb fabric are just floor surfaces carried right across the masonry. This would serve to seal wall and vault masonry below, but may not mean that lower units were entirely finished before upper units were started. In particular, sculptural treatment of the E facade probably was not done in separate stages. Although three divisions of sculpture are visible, central features extend upward without any breaks at chamber floor levels. The issue, at first, appears similar to that of the upper zones just cited. But the roofcomb sculpture runs continuously through the levels marked by the floor plasters, which is not the case with upper-zone work.

Surviving details convey the intricate character of sculptural treatment even though much has been lost (Fig. 30). In the middle, and at the second level, two circular elements suggest ear ornaments. If that is what they are, then a probably seated human figure could be inferred, partly in the second step area and partly in the first. Such an image would have been visible from ground level but many of the smaller details would not. In particular, the motifs located at the base of the roofcomb could only have been seen by the artisans who put them there.

Four chambers are known to be present within the roofcomb (Fig. 31). It seems likely that two more might exist at basal level. A probe cut downward from the center of the lowest-known chamber (Fig. 28) failed to reach a lower chamber. This means either there are no lower chambers, or there are two lower chambers and the probe descended between them. This latter possibility seems the most likely. The total, then, would be six chambers, alternating pairs and singles at each level.

All known chambers were inaccessible when initially built, but during the many years of abandonment openings have been made by root action and collapse. Some of the chambers now have deep deposits of bat dung. All were finished with plaster, but some applications are quite rough. In part this is the result of finishing having been done from above with workers standing on partly constructed vaults. In some cases, it appears that vault-soffit facing stones were preplastered before installation. In others, workers seem to have been leaning in and applying plaster by the handful. Hand application-marks are clearly visible in upper parts of vault soffits on the N side. The S half-vault units were finished first, from within the chambers, and then upper parts of N half-vaults were completed from outside and above. The procedure is the same as that used for the inner room in the building. All capstones are preplastered.

Interior facing stones within roofcomb chambers are roughly finished and not standardized either for size or shape. Face surfaces were not dressed after installation. If these chambers were intended for occupation by supernatural beings, the roughness of finish seems somewhat inappropriate.

Each chamber has vault beams set at vault spring level. These clearly were put in place prior to installation of vault masonry. It was likely then, when one half-vault and the spring of the other had been set, that they were removed to clear the way for completion as described above.

A rear axial outset extends vertically to the full height of the roofcomb, or at least to the top of surviving material (Fig. 24). Just above mid-height is a sculptural panel (Fig. 29c). A deity head is alluded to by a few key elements: an eye image with square iris, mouth curls, side flares, and a supraorbital plate.

Full height of the roofcomb, with an estimated allowance for material fallen from the top, amounts to 25% of structure height. That is, the roofcomb is about half as high as the pyramid. Masonry volume, with allowances for fallen material and for a fourth level of chambers, comes to approximately 500 m³.

Given the late date of construction, not long before collapse of elite systems, lack of any secondary modification is not surprising (see Table 3.2, below).

Special Deposits

CACHE 123

LOCATION

On central axis at foot of stair, below level of platform floor.

CONTENT AND ARRANGEMENT

Five cache vessels, 9 incised obsidians, 9 eccentric flints, obsidian and flint fragments, human bone fragments, and 1 metate fragment. Ceramic assessment: Imix and Ik (Table 3.1c).

Sherds and Artifacts

Ceramic assessments range from Chicanel to Imix. The latter could be contemporary with construction and also with installation of Ca. 123 associated with St. 24. Sherds found in roofcomb chambers assessed as Imix most likely represent pottery in use by workers during construction and, hence, current at that time. Other samples, assessed as Cauac, Late Cauac, and Early Classic and Cauac, represent much earlier production recycled either accidentally or intentionally as aggregate in mortar.

Artifact samples are sparse in quantity though they include a wide range of different kinds, most arising from St. 24 investigations. Oddly, a giant flint eccentric turned up in a roofcomb chamber.

Absolute Dates

Two samples were tested, P-949 and P-950, from outer surfaces of the vault beams of Rm. 1. The wood is *Achras zapota* (sapodilla or chico zapote). Averaged date results from three and two runs are: AD 607±39 years, and AD 613±45 years ([14]C Dates for Tikal Samples, September 10, 1965, Tikal Project Archives, unpublished [14]C Lab Reports). Since the generally accepted construction date is AD 802 (Jones 1977), these may be re-used beams taken from an earlier, demolished, structure.

TABLE 3.1a
Lot Groups: Str. 5D-3
Op. 8A

Lot Groups	Lot	Provenience	Ceramic Evaluation
1	1–13	n.d.	Late Cauac
2	14	n.d.	n.d.

TABLE 3.1b
Str. 5D-3: Distribution of Sherds and Artifacts by Lot Groups
Op. 8A

Study Group	Object	Lot Groups	
		1	2
Pottery	Sherds to Nearest LB		
Other	Zapote carved lintel fragments	13	1

TABLE 3.1c
Lot Groups: Str. 5D-3
Op. 8B

Lot Groups	Lot	Provenience	Ceramic Evaluation
1	1,2,3,4	above floor	Late Cauac
2	5	in trench, sealed by floors	Tzakol and Chicanel
3	6	in trench not sealed	E.C and Cauac
4	7,8,9,11,13	Collapse debris	Cauac
5	10,12	Stela pit, Ca. 123	Imix and Ik

TABLE 3.1d
Str. 5D-3: Distribution of Sherds and Artifacts by Lot Groups
Op. 8B

Study Group	Object	Lot Groups				
		1	2	3	4	5
Pottery	Sherds to Nearest LB	*	*	*	*	*
Other Pottery	Censer fragments	8				
	Modeled pendant	1				
	Cache vessels 1–5					5
	Figurine fragment					1
Chipped Flint	Flake blade fragment	1				
	Unmodified chips		5	1		2
	Used flake			1	1	
	Unused core				1	
	Modified flake				1	
	Eccentric					7
Chipped Obsidian	Flake blade fragment	1				
	Used blade		5			1
	Blade				1	
	Incised					8
Ground Stone	Mano fragment	2			1	
	Basalt mano fragment	1				
	Limestone mano fragment		1			
	Quartzite metate fragment					1
Shell and Bone	Unidentifiable fragments			2		
	Human bones, teeth					*
Other	Carved stone fragment	2			1	
	MS-149				1	

* indicates quantity not specified

TABLE 3.1e
Lot Groups: Str. 5D-3
Op. 8C

Lot Groups	Lot	Provenience	Ceramic Evaluation
1	1,2	Roofcomb, Ca. 25	Imix/Ik transition

TABLE 3.1f
Str. 5D-3: Distribution of Sherds and Artifacts by Lot Groups
Op. 8C

Study Group	Object	Lot Groups 1
Pottery	Sherds to Nearest LB	
Chipped Flint	Giant eccentric	1
Shell and Bone	Fish bones	

TABLE 3.2
Structure 5D-3: Time Spans

Time Span	Construction Stage	Other Data
1		Abandonment.
2		Primary use. St. 24; Alt. 95.
3	1–4	Primary construction; 31,400m^3, approximately.

IV

Great Temple V

Structure 5D-5

Located immediately E of the South Acropolis, Str. 5D-5 (Great Temple V) is one of the major features along the S edge of the epicentral complex (Fig. 32a). Since no major excavations were planned for this structure, its recording fell to the Tikal Standing Architectural Survey, and Miguel Orrego did the work in 1968. To avoid the need for subsequent consolidation, he had to obtain whatever data he could with no more than minimal clearing. Hence, it is mainly the superstructure that he was able to convey in detail. Despite dense undergrowth and tree coverage, Orrego achieved a remarkably complete record of the structure as a whole. (For subsequent investigations of Str. 5D-5 see Gómez 1998, 1999; Gómez and Vidal Lorenzo 1997, Muñoz 1997.)

Maler (1911:49–50) designated the fabric as Great Temple V. He measured its height as 57.3 m (our measurement is 54 m) and noted excavations in the roofcomb attributed to Modesto Mendez in 1848 (W. Coe 1967:12). Curiously, Mendez dug upward through three levels of roofcomb chambers and out at the top. Gómez (1999) measured the height as 50.5 m.

Maler claimed to have seen masks in the upper zone and "the most elaborate ornamentation imaginable" on the roofcomb (1911:50). In 1968, these features were hardly visible and many could only be recorded with such extensive clearing that a consolidation program would have been needed afterwards. Only a few are illustrated here, and these only in bare outline (Fig. 33). Many more remain in situ, held by matted roots of trees and bushes. Tozzer (1911:fig. 33) provides a plan that reflects Maler's description rather than fresh observation. It shows nine terraces, with inset corners on all but the lowest. Orrego's survey reveals a very different arrangement.

The structure faces N. The line defined by E and W corners of the front wall of the building runs 5.5° S of magnetic E (noted on plan illustrations as 5.5° E of magnetic N). This is not a very reliable datum, however, since there are hardly two parallel lines in the parts of the structure that could be measured. The pyramid plan illustrated in Fig. 34 (in broken line) should be taken as an estimate.

Prior to Orrego's survey, debris had been removed from the foot of the great stair where a stela might have been expected (Op. 86A). This work found no evidence of a stela ever having been present. Also prior to Orrego's survey, debris from the Mendez tunneling had been removed from within the single room (Op. 86B). Consolidation work was done during 1987–92, and in 1997–98 a tunnel was cut unto the pyramid at base level on the NS axis. This latter work suggested a construction date of ca. AD 650 (Gómez 1999).

Construction Stages

The site is a level surface extending E from the South Acropolis. Whether this was established specifically for 5D-5 or for some earlier feature is not known. It is not considered here as a part of 5D-5, but the question remains open.

As far as can be determined without more exca-vation, construction appears to have proceeded in three main stages. The first includes the pyramid, building platform, and walls of the building. No definite pause-lines appeared between these parts of the structure. Plastered wall-top surfaces mark completion of this composite stage. The second stage includes vaults and upper zones, and the third consists of the roofcomb. Both second and third stages contained inaccessible chambers and presented sculptural features.

PYRAMID

Several small probes around the base (Fig. 34) established dimensions and footprint/plan outline with reasonable accuracy. From this level, the pyramid (Fig. 34–36) rises up in seven terraces averaging 4.23 m in height: total height equals roughly 30 m. Because of advanced collapse and vegetative coverage, no probes were attempted above base level. Apron profiles indicated in Fig. 34 are estimates. Only the stair-side outsets were profiled above debris level (Fig. 36). Terrace heights are based on these stair-side outset heights and terrace tops are assumed level (Fig. 35).

The plan is distinctly rectangular. Length (side-to-side) relates to depth (front-to-rear) as 1:0.73 (depth not quite three-quarters of the length). Corners are generously rounded and not inset. Side and rear outsets are set well back from the corners so that they read clearly as outsets (Fig. 34). If they were closer to the corners, these would appear inset. Either the designers did not want inset corners or, perhaps more likely, the idea of inset corners had not yet been applied to pyramid design at Tikal. It may be that inset corners were introduced to embody some aspect of meaning not at issue when 5D-5 was built.

Stair-side outset profiles (Fig. 36) present superior and basal moldings, possibly for the first time at Tikal. Profiles are convex. Batter, measured on lines struck from base to top edge (ignoring convexity) increases through third, fourth, and fifth terraces, then decreases sharply (12.5°, 15°, 16.5°, 11°, and 5°, respectively; the bottom two terraces are under debris). At the same time, terraces 6 and 7 (the top two) are distinctly lower (4.15 and 3.5 m) than average (4.23 m). Builders may have become concerned that open space at the top would be too restricted for the kind of building they had in mind.

The state of preservation does not provide detailed information about terrace profiles. They could be convex like the stair-side outsets, but this is uncertain. Side outsets may lack apron moldings. Rear axial outsets are assumed similar to side outsets, but are even less clear.

The fully outset stair has stair-side ramps or *alfardas* and a generous width of 16 m. Structure 5D-5 may present one of the latest appearances of stair-side ramps at Tikal (but see Great Temple III, above). From dimensions for the bottom two or three risers, the total number is estimated as 91 risers (with a low level of confidence). Masonry volume in the stair is 3,467 m³. This may be the largest stair at Tikal.

The only accessible sample of pyramid masonry is that of in situ facing stones on the W stair side (Fig. 35). These are consistently coursed, horizontally bedded headers and stretchers, rounded, and cushion-shaped on face surfaces. Mean stretcher length is 0.59 m (n=100) with a minimum of 0.40 m and a maximum of 0.68 m, a variance of 23, and a standard deviation of 4.8. That is to say, dimensions are not rigorously standardized although face shapes appear consistent. No plaster has survived, but no doubt all facing masonry was originally plastered over.

The total volume of masonry for the pyramid, including the stair, is 36,753 m³.

BUILDING PLATFORM

The building platform is in two bodies, a wider front part and a narrower, higher rear part (Fig. 33, 35). Base levels slope sharply up from front to rear. The sustaining surface is unclear. No pyramid top was encountered and so it remains unclear whether this also sloped upward to the S. There is no clear evidence for a break in construction between the pyramid and the building platform.

The building platform is largely a feature of surface articulation. Rear parts in particular do not correspond to any core body other than wall material. Except at the front, there is no relation between the exterior form and interior arrangements. The front part does relate to core material sustaining the room. Rear parts are nothing more than basal moldings, elements of exterior wall faces. Corners are rounded and profiles are plain (with no aprons).

The only masonry that can be assigned exclusively to the building platform is that under the room, and involves 73 m³ of material.

BUILDING WALLS

The term "walls" hardly applies unless undetected chambers exist within the core mass (Fig. 37). Exteriors imply a wider front part and a narrower rear part, but there is only a single room much smaller than the outer wall dimensions. Similarly, walls appear to be set at two levels, lower in the front and higher in the rear (Fig. 33, 35), but since there is no known rear room or chamber, the exterior impression is illusory. Accordingly, rear-wall masonry is assumed to extend down to pyramid-top level. This could be erroneous if there is a concealed building platform under the rear walls.

A plaster surface defines the wall top (Fig. 38) and this is the first pause-line detected in the survey. Mean length of exterior stretchers is 0.58 m (n=65; minimum is 0.51 m, maximum is 0.61 m, variance is 9.7, and standard deviation is 3.1). These facing stones are similar in shape and size to those illustrated (Fig. 36) in the W stair side but much more standardized dimensionally. Exterior wall surfaces have a batter of 1.5° at the front, 0.5° at the rear, and 2° at the W side.

The room represents 1.6% of gross building area. This will probably prove to be the lowest ratio of room area to gross building area (to be discussed in TR. 34B).

Four cord holders with vertical pins flank the doorway on the inside wall surface (Fig. 39). These could have served to secure some kind of device for closing the doorway. Using them from the outside would have been awkward if not impossible. Whoever used them from within would have been shut up inside the room. Participants in ritual activities requiring prior periods of seclusion and fasting for purification might have used the room for this purpose, but hopefully not too many at any one time.

Karl Taube has proposed that in temple structures "a curtain-covered doorway probably indicated that the god was asleep in his resting place" (1998:429). If the doorway curtain had to be secured from the inside, the god was not sleeping alone.

Nineteen holes are visible at the base of exterior wall elements (Fig. 33, 35, 37). Their spacing varies from 1 to 6 m with a modal interval of about 2 m. The wider spaces probably contain holes not visible either due to debris cover or intact seals. They penetrate between 0.50 and 1 m into wall-core material. Most likely these are scaffolding holes. Normally a

second set of holes appears above those at wall base. If they exist in the walls of 5D-5, they may have been well sealed when the scaffolding was dismantled.

Two subspring beams span the width of the room at each end, close to the end walls and at the height of the lintels. Hammocks could have been slung from them. Alternatively, beams spanning the length of the room, resting on these lateral members, might have provided for overhead storage.

The volume of masonry in walls amounts to 696 m³.

VAULTS AND UPPER ZONES

These parts represent a definite construction stage defined by plaster surfaces at wall top and roof levels. Work would have begun with wood lintels over the doorway set on plastered lintel beds installed integrally with the wall tops. They support about 0.40 m of supra-lintel masonry building up to vault-spring level. The vault is much steeper than strictly necessary for structural efficiency (the soffit angle is 8°). In part this may reflect the modest room width (0.80 m). Designers may have been concerned with a height relationship between the vault and the walls. Here the ratio is 1:0.69; that is, vault height is about two-thirds of wall height. Soffit profiles are straight-line. Preplastering of capstones remains unclear. The set of vault beams (Fig. 41), including many surviving stubs, appears excessive for such a small vault. This may be the most closely packed set of vault beams recorded by the Tikal Project (to be addressed in TR 34B).

Presence of a vault-back surface remains indeterminate. Upper zones are in two parts, the front part lower and the rear part higher, following the lead of the building platform and bearing no relationship to the room system. The front part has two levels (Fig. 35), stepped back across the front. The rear upper zone is a single level approximately as high as the combined front levels with plain profile set at 2.5° of batter. This is a unique design of upper zones at Tikal (as will be shown in TR 34B).

Front upper-zone elements appear to be elaborated sculpturally. Rough masonry outlines imply three large sculptural features across the front, but no similar treatment on E and W faces (Fig. 42a). Intention to display these large sculptural images across the upper zone may account for the apparent disjunction between exterior form and interior arrangement. Designers may have wanted a wide building for exterior effect. Interior space may have been a significant functional requirement, but one that could be met by a small room. If the iconography had anything to do with mountains and caves, a constrained, cave-like space might have been entirely appropriate.

The core mass between upper zone and vaults contains at least six inaccessible chambers (Fig. 38, 39, 41). They are crudely built and low, with no distinction between wall and vault, have very uneven surfaces, and capstones of light timbers. An additional three chambers could be present to the rear of the known ones (Fig. 41). Despite their informal character, they may have been plastered like similarly rough chambers in the roofcomb.

Ignoring the possibility of additional chambers, the volume of masonry in vaults and upper zones totals approximately 836 m³.

ROOFCOMB

Externally, the roofcomb rises in four stepped levels (Fig. 32b,c, 35, 37, 38, 40, 41, 43–45). These divisions apply only to the exterior. Internally, chambers are arrayed in three levels that do not align with the exterior steps. This circumstance may represent additional evidence that designers considered exterior features and interior arrangements separately and somewhat independently.

All together there are twelve chambers, four at each of the three levels. In the top level (Fig. 42b), the central two chambers are interconnected. None of the chambers were accessible prior to partial collapse and the 19th-century excavations.

Debris on the floor of Chm. 2 (Fig. 45) was sampled in three places. Bat guano had accumulated to an average depth of 0.10 m on the floor. An average of 0.20 m of dust and plaster debris overlies the bat droppings. Clearly bats had been able to access the chamber for a long time prior to plaster disintegration. This chamber retains some in situ plaster. Others accessed during the survey presented bare masonry. Chambers 5 and 8 have on-floor debris that could consist of fallen plaster. Chamber 6 has no evident plaster and no debris layer. Therefore, it seems, some chambers were plastered and others not.

Roofcomb chambers in the lower two levels have masonry capstones. Vaults rise from spring levels set flush with wall facings (not outset). In the upper level, where chambers are much lower, there is no consistent distinction between wall and vault elements.

Beam sockets are present in all accessed chambers, both at wall and vault level. They probably served to support scaffolding and falsework for masonry installation.

Interior facing stones for wall and vault elements appear identical in the accessed chambers (Fig. 45). They are cushion-shaped, inconsistently coursed or bedded, similar to masonry elsewhere in the structure but smaller and less carefully installed. Some stones are set on-end, some in sloping beds. Dimensions vary greatly but not in any pattern that might suggest headers and stretchers. Surfaces are uneven. For a sample of 51 stones drawn from Chm. 6, average face length is 19.3 cm with a standard deviation of 5.8. This value for standard deviation equates with a low level of standardization, but more than what was seen in substructure and building facings. Exterior facings were not sampled.

The roofcomb consumed 53% of pyramid height. Total volume is approximately 960 m³ of masonry; this is a smaller value than might be expected from exterior impressions. The numerous chambers clearly reduced the amount of masonry needed, limiting the load on the walls and lessening the amount of material that had to be carried up to roofcomb level. As it is, the whole superstructure represents 80% of pyramid height.

Special Deposits

BURIAL 172

LOCATION

On central axis at foot of stair in shallow earth above platform floor.

GRAVE

No grave preparation such as walls, edges, or cover.

INDIVIDUAL AND ASSOCIATED MATERIAL

Intact, articulated individual associated with obsidian flakes, worked shell, pottery candeleros, and a large, weathered jar fragment (Table 4.1b). Above the burial, a concentration of censer fragments (PD. 123, Table 4.1b) may be a related deposit. The assessment from TR 27B Appendix C, is Terminal Imix.

DISCUSSION

Appears to be an ordinary burial made without ceremony—other than PD. 123, above—in an extraordinary location. According to the ceramic assessment, above, the burial was made long after construction of Temple V at a time when earth had accumulated above the platform floor.

PROBLEMATIC DEPOSIT 123

A scatter of 104 censer fragments in the dark earth above Bu. 172, more or less concentrated above the burial.

Sherds and Artifacts

Sherds collected during investigations of Temple V (Table 4.1a,b,c,d) range from Cauac to Terminal Imix, the latter associated with Bu. 172. The spread of artifacts is unremarkable except for the concen-

tration of censer fragments (PD. 123). Imix sherds might have been current at the time of the burial.

Absolute Dates

Two samples were tested, P-947 and P-948 (*Piscidia piscipula*, Jamaican Dogwood also known as Florida Fish Poison Tree and Fish Fuddle Tree), from the outer surfaces of vault beams of the single room vault. Averaged dates from two runs each are: AD 698±43 years, and AD 647±51 years ([14]C Dates for Tikal Samples, September 10, 1965, Tikal Project Archives, [14]C Lab Reports). These ^{14}C results accord well with date estimates based on architectural attributes (outlined above) and ceramic assessments (Gómez 1999).

My guess is that Str. 5D-5 was built during Intermediate Classic times, a style date really based on wall facing attributes, face surfaces not smoothly finished, rounded terrace corners, and balustraded stair. There is no evidence of any alterations or additions (Table 4.2).

TABLE 4.1a
Lot Groups: Str. 5D-5
Op. 86A

Lot Groups	Lot	Provenience	Ceramic Evaluation
1	1,4,5,7	PD.123 in collapse at base of stair	E.C. and Imix
2	2,8	Bu. 172, in collapse at base of stair	Terminal Imix
3	3	Surface in general area	Cauac
4	6	W stair corner	n.d.

TABLE 4.1b
Str. 5D-5: Distribution of Sherds and Artifacts by Lot Groups
Op. 86A

Study Group	Object	Lot Groups			
		1	2	3	4
Pottery	Sherds to Nearest LB	8	4	8	12
Other Pottery	Censer fragments	104		2	
	Miniature vessel	1			
	Modeled sherd	2			
	Figurine fragment			1	
	Weather jar fragment	1			
Chipped Flint	Core fragment	2			
	Biface	1			
	Blade fragment	1		2	
	Flake blade	2			
	Unused chip	2			
Chipped Obsidian	Flake blade fragment	1	4	8	
	Green flake blade fragment	1	1	2	
Ground Stone	Basalt metate fragment			1	
	Whetstone			1	
Shell and Bone	Poss. human bone fragment	1			
	Worked shell tinker		1		
	Unworked human bone		13		
	Animal tooth		1		
	Intact skeleton (Bu. 172)		1		
Other	Monument fragment	1			
	Modeled plaster fragments	2			

TABLE 4.1c
Lot Groups: Str. 5D-5
Op. 86B

Lot Groups	Lot	Provenience	Ceramic Evaluation
1	1,4,5,7	PD.123 in collapse at base of stair	E.C. and Imix
2	2,8	Bu. 172, in collapse at base of stair	Terminal Imix
3	3	Surface in general area	Cauac
4	6	W stair corner	n.d.

TABLE 4.1d
Str. 5D-5: Distribution of Sherds and Artifacts by Lot Groups
Op. 86B

Study Group	Object	Lot Groups 1
Pottery	Sherds to Nearest LB	1
Other Pottery	Worked shell Perforated eccentric sherd	1 1
Chipped Flint	Used flake Unused flake	2 1
Chipped Obsidian	Used flake blade fragment	3
Shell and Bone	Unworked animal bone	3
Other	Chalcedony lump	1

TABLE 4.2
Structure 5D-5: Time Spans

Time Span	Other Data
1	Period of abandonment and partial collapse.
2	Period of use as initially built.
3	Period of construction; approximately 36,430m^3 of masonry.

V

Great Temple VI

Structure 6F-27-1st

Antonio Ortiz, a local Petenero, reported the existence of Str. 6F-27-1st in 1951 (Berlin 1951; W. Coe 1967:87). Both Maler and Tozzer missed it (Tozzer 1911). Hence, Berlin's detailed description of architectural features is the first account of this structure. The text for which the structure is named—The Temple of the Inscriptions–has been discussed in several publications since (Jones 1977:53; Stuart 2007; Martin 2015). Intriguingly, the text refers to very ancient times and deals with the mythology of the Tikal kingdom by reference to a ruler-deity we call "White Owl Jaguar" (Stuart 2007). Dates mentioned include 1143 BC, 456 BC, and 157 BC. By the time of the last date, monumental architecture had been installed at the North Acropolis and Str. 5C-54 (in the Lost World Plaza). But the earliest date may possibly precede settlement and development at Tikal.

As shown in Fig. 46a, 6F-27-1st occupies a SE location approximately 1 km away from the Great Plaza. This explains why it was not discovered until so very recently. A paved causeway runs uphill from the site to the central complex. This avenue connects 6F-27-1st to the series of epicentral structures that are all linked together by paved plaster surfaces. Ancient Maya officials could circulate through this zone without ever stepping off plaster onto mere turf. In effect, then, 6F-27-1st must have been considered an integral part of the central zone despite its remoteness. After all, it is only slightly farther from the Great Plaza than the North Group, which is also connected by causeways.

Surrounding 6F-27-1st is a precinct wall enclosing an area roughly twice the size of the Great Plaza (Fig. 46a, 47a:1). Precinct wall construction appears to coincide with the construction of 6F-27-1st. Surface contours (TR. 11:Temple of the Inscriptions Map Sheet) show two levels within the precinct, a higher level sustaining the structure and a lower one to the W. The higher level appears to have been paved, although the surface has weathered away (Fig. 46b).

It seems likely that 6F-27-1st was erected over an earlier structure, 6F-27-2nd, which was, perhaps, partially dismantled. The precinct was either smaller or less well defined prior to construction of 6F-27-1st. Entry points through the precinct wall other than the causeway are evident at the E and S edges. Altogether this setting must have been very impressive, monumental, and able to accommodate large numbers of people.

Andras Nagy (1965 season), Gordon Echols (1965 season), Rudy Larios (1969 season), and Miguel Orrego (1969 season) did the architectural recording. Karen Mohr (1965 season) and Susanna Ekholm (1966 season) excavated and recorded problematical deposits. Glyph panels were recorded by Linton Satterthwaite and Christopher Jones (1965), and inked by William R. Coe (Jones 1977:53). Using both field sheets and large-scale drawings produced by these investigators, I wrote the report, and constructed the figures in 2008. Occasionally, inconsistent data had to be reconciled. Otherwise, the figures faithfully present the investigators' findings.

Orientation is toward the W. The line generated by the rear exterior wall-face runs 4.7° E of magnetic N (approximately 2° E of true N as determined for the Tikal Project base maps; TR. 11).

Construction Stages

Construction stages, when most clearly evident, are separated by plastered surfaces. Such surfaces indicate completion of a stage, including plastering, prior to initiation of the next. This is a practice not always followed at Tikal. Architectural forms apparently reflecting staged construction may mislead in this respect, especially in later work. One morphologically distinct part, such as a substructure platform of several terraces, may have been started prior to completion of an apparently previous part, such as a basal platform. In some cases evidence for staging of construction is unclear or inconsistent. For these reasons stages and substages are based on both superficial morphology and interfaces between apparently distinct parts.

BASAL PLATFORM, MAJOR SUBSTRUCTURE PLATFORM, BUILDING PLATFORM, AND BUILDING

There is no evident break between any of these major parts of the structure and hence they must be regarded as substages. They superficially present distinct elements of architectural form, but the construction process may not have proceeded from one to the next sequentially. Details recorded by three different investigators failed to detect any major pauses from the base level to the roof of the Building. Evidence does not clearly indicate that any part below the roofcomb was completely finished and plastered prior to initiation of the next. Mortar levels may be present within core material but, lacking plaster, such pause-lines are not diagnostic of completed construction stages.

BASAL PLATFORM

Figure 47a shows a thin, rough floor (Fl. 7) running under the basal platform. This is one of several features that hint at an earlier structure contained within 6F-27-1st. Its roughness may reflect weathering. The bedrock surface immediately beneath Fl. 7 has been leveled. Floor 6 (Fig. 47a) turns up to basal platform masonry installed prior to basal plat-

form plastering. Plaster application may have been delayed until completion of the major substructure platform (MSP). Apparent absence of a plastered interface between the basal platform and the MSP implies a more or less continuous construction sequence lacking major breaks.

The basal platform is roughly 1 m high and extends well beyond the MSP to the W (Fig. 49, 50). It is nearly square in contrast to the rectangular proportions it appears to sustain. In similar contrast, its corners are generously rounded. There is an outset of sorts on the central axis at the W face flanked by twin stairs. The basal platform upper surface to the W of the MSP is not level but slopes down to the W (Fig. 52). The central, frontal outset, supporting St. 21 (see below), has vertical faces partly cut in bedrock. Other basal platform surfaces have a batter of roughly 15° at the E face. South face batter is close to 19°. There are no surface articulations such as apron moldings. At the W edge, the line of the basal platform facing has been cut into bedrock (Fig. 50).

Volume of material needed for the building platform is problematic because bedrock rises toward the center W and an earlier feature appears present. Maximum volume is 1,300 m³. A rough estimate might be about two-thirds of this, or 900 m³ required for the building platform.

MAJOR SUBSTRUCTURE PLATFORM

In the absence of an established term for a substructure with 6F-27-1st properties, MSP is employed as a working label. The term "supplementary platform" does not seem appropriate here. It applies to a substructure platform intervening between a pyramid and a building platform. Here, absence of a pyramid calls for a different term. "Pyramid" needs to be reserved for components much higher than this substructure.

The 6F-27-1st substructure platform has three terraces with front, side, and rear outsets and a broad frontal stair (Fig. 49–54a). Terraces other than those flanking the stair have apron moldings of three-element type (apron, subapron, and basal molding). Terrace heights vary: 2.9, 2.6, and 3.3 m for terraces 1, 2, and 3, respectively. Apron corbel levels are set at 38%, 34%, and 24% of terrace heights in the outset elements. Terrace faces between the outsets, at the four corners, have apron levels set about 0.10 m lower.

Upper parts of terraces have fallen, but surviving fragments suggest aprons have straight-line profiles (Fig. 54a). Batter is roughly 15° on the E facade and 19° of the S facade.

The elements that flank the stair have superior and basal moldings (Fig. 54b). This type of profile is common at Tikal on stair-side outsets, though usually such outsets have return faces with little or no batter (near vertical). In 6F-27, the return faces are sloped at an angle similar to terrace faces (Fig. 52). For this reason, they are referred to here as stair-side terraces rather than stair-side outsets.

Figure 47b shows that Fl. 5 runs under the stair, while Fl. 4 turns up to the bottom riser. Excavations did not expose the comparable condition at the E facade. If Fl. 5 relates to an earlier structure, its E face may lie somewhere within the MSP. It is not clear, however, that Fl. 5 runs under the MSP.

The possible existence of an earlier structure raises problems for estimation of MSP volume. Floor 2 (which only showed up at the north end of Rm. 1 and was not evident elsewhere) and Fl. 3 lie only slightly below the building level (Fig. 55) and appear to be elements of 6F-27-2nd. They are higher than the 6F-27-1st MSP but might be surfaces of a 6F-27-2nd building platform. One possibility is that the 6F-27-1st MSP may be little more than a resurfacing on the earlier construction. On the other hand, the earlier feature might be much smaller in lateral extent. In either case, the MSP makes up 31% of the height of 6F-27-1st.

Building Platform

Figure 52 shows a building platform of two levels. The lower front part extends laterally beyond the higher rear part. The effect is that of two separate platforms that overlap. Surface profile is straight-line with no apron molding. Batter is about 12°. Probable existence of an earlier structure prevents accurate calculation of the volume of material needed to build it.

A stair of three risers is shown (Fig. 49, 50, 52, 53) in front of the central doorway. This stair was not seen, and a limited excavation in front of the N lateral doorway found no stair. Since the building platform is 0.70 m high at the front, a stair seems necessary. The stair shown, providing access to the central doorway only, is entirely conjectural. Unlikely as it may seem, there may be no stair at all.

Building

Key building attributes include two rooms in tandem, three doorways, a rear axial outset, a front part wider than the rear part, and a rear axial outset but no side inset (Fig. 56). Gross building area is 140 m^2. Total room area, excluding doorways, is 45 m^2 (32% of gross area).

The floor in Rm. 2 runs under the rear wall (Fig. 55). In Rm. 1, both Fl. 1 and Fl. 2 turn up to the N end wall (Fig. 57). These seemingly contradictory observations may mean that wall construction began at the front and proceeded toward the rear, so that by the time rear wall construction began, room floors had already been installed. Since there is no evidence of a plastered building-platform top at the rear exterior, it may be that the floor surface only runs a short distance under the Rm. 2 E wall.

The surface of Fl. 1, where exposed along the central axis, shows many signs of burning. No plastered wall tops were noted despite the presence of a plastered lintel bed at the W axial doorway. Walls of the building employed a total of 230 m^3 of masonry, including both core and facing stones.

A total of about 2,000 masonry units were cut for wall facings. They are veneer type (which is exceptional – see Chapter 6), rectangular, with sharp corners, with an average face length of 0.50 m (n=100), a minimum of 0.40 m, a maximum of 0.58 m, and a variance of 14. A standard deviation for stretcher lengths of 3.7 indicates a relatively high degree of dimensional standardization. After wall-masonry installation, face surfaces were dressed to a smooth, even finish by a process of shaving and rubbing. The finish of other surfaces was not determined. The survey did not distinguish between headers and stretchers. A single thin coat of white plaster covers interior wall surfaces.

The rear room, originally 15 m long, has been reduced to 4.2 m by secondary installation of masonry that fills the two ends. The effect of this modification is to reduce the rear room (Rm. 2a) to only 10% of the front room in area.

This change might have been motivated by structural considerations. Dwarf walls in the roof-comb chamber above Rm. 2 (Fig. 58a) are located directly above the two ends of the room blocks. The purpose of the dwarf walls is not clear, but their presence may have caused some anxiety for users of 6F-27-1st.

Floor 3, below Fl. 1 (Fig. 55), appears to be an element of Str. 6F-27-2nd. Floor 3 steps up 0.38 m to a higher level beneath Rm. 2. It may be the top surface of a building platform that had been plastered on completion (unlike the 6F-27-1st building platform).

Immediately in front of the step-up (W) is PD. 168, intruded into Fl. 3 (Fig. 55, 59a). The chop in Fl. 3 for installation of the deposit removed part of a set of lines incised in the floor, possibly constituting a *patolli* game. The opening was sealed with a roughly circular stone and then buried within the 6F-27-1st building platform. Items in the deposit include human bone and skull fragments distributed vertically from top to bottom (see PD. 168, below).

Floor 8, installed on Fl. 3, is absent directly above PD. 168. The cut for the deposit went through this floor as well as Fl. 3. If this assumption is correct, Fl. 3 must be a 6F-27-2nd resurfacing. Problematical Deposit 168, on the other hand, must have been installed at the time of 6F-27-2nd termination.

Vaulting: At the W wall of Rm. 1, two supra-lintel masonry courses appear beneath the vault spring. These drop to only one course at the spine wall. The Rm. 1 vault has four soffit courses topped by a leveling course (Fig. 59b). Soffit profiles are essentially straight-line with slight convexity. Capstones are preplastered. The soffit angle is 35° in Rm. 1, and 23° in Rm. 2.

Vault beams are in two levels, staggered so that upper and lower beams are not vertically aligned (Fig. 57). Lower-level beams rest at vault spring level and upper-level beams are set at the third-course level. This raises the possibility that vaulting may have dispensed with prior installation of a timber falsework. Preplastered capstones indicate that soffit surfaces were plastered prior to capstone installation. Normally, at Tikal, this practice is associated with a falsework of poles used to establish soffit angles and vault-top level. Scaffolding for soffit plastering would have been needed.

Proof for a timber falsework usually depends on vault-beam sockets falling between masonry course levels. In these cases it is often evident that soffit stones had been cut to fit around the beams, thereby showing that the beams had been installed prior to the masonry and, therefore, set up within a timber falsework. When the beams fall at course levels, as here, the timber falsework is not so certain. Tikal

Report 34B will test the frequency with which preplastered capstones occur together with vault beams not at course levels. It may emerge that preplastered capstones themselves provide evidence for timber falseworks.

Room floors and upper-zone levels step up from front to rear, but vault springs do not. Hence interior walls in Rm. 2 are 0.35 m lower than in Rm. 1. Although vault springs are at the same level, capstones in Rm. 2 are 0.38 m higher than in Rm. 1.

Vault-height to room-height ratios are 1:2 in Rm. 1 and 1:1.5 in Rm. 2. Vault-height to span ratios are 1:1.5 in Rm. 1 and 1:0.9 in Rm. 2.

Upper Zones: Profiles are plain across the rear part of the building and near vertical. The front part has uncertain profiles, probably including sculptural features that have either fallen completely or are too badly preserved to suggest original form. Front upper zones are approximately 0.40 m higher than rear elements. The ratio of upper-zone height to wall height at the rear (E) is almost exactly 1:1.

North, S, and E facades carry panels of glyphs on both upper zones and roofcomb surfaces (Fig. 60–62), discussed in detail by Jones (1977). Martin and Grube (2000:50) note that the texts identify 6F-27-1st as a "wayib'il," literally, 'sleeping house' (a symbolic dormitory for a god, or, perhaps, the place in which its effigy was kept in seclusion)" (see also Stuart 1998:399–401). From the ancient Maya point of view, the notion of a sleeping house for a god might not be merely symbolic (Freidel, Schele, and Parker 1993:188). If supernatural forces were held to be real and to inhabit features in the landscape, then a structure such as 6F-27-1st might be regarded as one such place (Haviland and Haviland 1995:306; Taube 1998:429).

Vault and upper-zone portions of the structure required approximately 400 m³ of construction materials.

ROOFCOMB

This feature is perhaps the most impressive part of 6F-27-1st because of the hieroglyphic text that runs most of the way up the E facade on the rear axial outset and continues on the N and S sides (Fig. 60). A dedication statement in AD 766 (9.16.14.17.17) is linked to the period ending 9.16.15.0.0, which took place just 3 days later. The name of the ruler in office at this time is hard to make out in this eroded inscription, but since he comes between the 27th and 29th in succession he presumably occupied 28th place in Tikal's count of kings (TR 33A:129). Nonetheless, there are strong signs in the text that this was a second dedication of the structure, indicating an earlier construction date (see Discussion below).

A mask survives at the base of the roofcomb on the W side (Fig. 53, 63a,b), possibly flanked by sculptural detail that has been lost. The mask has a skeletal lower jaw and fleshed upper parts with tendrils emerging from the eyes. Earplug danglers flank the image. It is some kind of supernatural reference, possibly a form of Kawak monster, a personification of mountains and the forces within them. The ancient Maya may have seen Str. 6F-27-1st in similar terms.

Two major spaces, or "chambers" occur within the roofcomb (Fig. 58a,b). The lower and larger space (Fig. 58a) contains two dwarf walls that divide its lower part into three compartments. These may have been meant to stiffen the outer walls of the roofcomb. Without such bracing-members, these would be the largest runs of high walling at Tikal not supported by lateral bracing of some kind. Some runs of walling at Tikal may be longer, but none are so high.

Chamber surfaces are irregular, probably because facing stones were not smoothed after installation. The finish is a thick undulating coat (0.05–0.13 m) of soft plaster, similar in appearance to mortar or grout. Facing stones are much smaller than those used in other parts of the structure. Average unit heights are in the 0.10 m range.

At the top level, there is a longitudinal space that apparently runs almost the full width of the roofcomb (Fig. 55). Seventeen square openings visible in both E and W facades (Fig. 53, 60) penetrate this otherwise inaccessible space.

Workers employed on roofcomb construction used roughly 680 m³ of stone and mortar. Roofcomb chambers total approximately 170 m³ of void. They reduced the volume of masonry required by about 25%.

Associated Monuments

Stela 21 and Alt. 9 stand on the basal platform near its W (front) edge. Altar 9 rests on a plaster floor. No higher floor is evident at this locus. Unless Fl. 4—seen at the foot of the stair (Fig. 47b)—feath-

ers out onto Fl. 5 farther W, the surface under Alt. 9 must be Fl. 4. If this is the case, Alt. 9 was set in place after construction of the basal platform, perhaps following completion of the structure. Presumably St. 21 is contemporary with Alt. 9 and bears the same relationship to Str. 6F-27. Stela 21 refers to the Long Count 9.15.3.6.8 3 Lamat 6 Pax, which is the inaugural date of Tikal Ruler B in AD 734. The monument itself was dedicated at the period ending 9.15.5.0.0 in AD 736 (TR 33A:48). Ruler B, Yik'in Chan K'awiil (Jones 1977:34–35; Martin and Grube 2000:48) was the father of the 28th ruler.

Out in front (W), on a paved surface that abuts the bedrock base of the basal platform, there are two other stela/altar pairs (Fig. 49) and a third pair (not illustrated) W of them.

DISCUSSION

Satterthwaite excavated St. P74 in 1956 (Fig. 48b). David Stuart (2007, 2012; also see Martin 2015) has made numerous observations concerning the roofcomb text, several in support of the suspected earlier structure mentioned above. He also cites Coe (W. Coe 1970:87) on the subject of an Early Classic version of the Mendez Causeway.

Special Deposits

CACHE 151

LOCATION

Close to the NW corner of St. 21

CONTENT AND ARRANGEMENT

One cache vessel, 9 flint eccentrics, 9 incised obsidians, smashed pottery. A few other items probably not part of the cache are included (Table 5.1b, TR. 27A:fig. 42f).

PROBLEMATICAL DEPOSIT 168

LOCATION

On central axis of Str. 6F-27-2nd, cut through Fl. 3 (Fig. 55, 59a).

CONTENT AND ARRANGEMENT

Note: Items listed below are identified by Tikal Project catalogue numbers.

One jade bead (Cat. 53C-71); 1 shell bead (Cat. 53-72); 1 flint (Cat. 53-73); and metate fragments (Cat. 53-74).

DISCUSSION

Since the deposit was sealed by a stone lid and not by a floor, it probably was made at a time when the floor it intruded through was no longer in use. Most likely this would have been during construction of Str. 6F-27-1st. Possibly PD. 168 might have been part of a termination ritual for Str. 6F-27-2nd.

PROBLEMATICAL DEPOSIT 170

LOCATION

On the central axis of Str. 6F-27-1st about 8 m W of the foot of the stair, sealed by Fl. 5 and dedicatory to Str. 6F-27-2nd (Fig. 47b, 50, 64–67).

CONTENT AND ARRANGEMENT

Ceramic vessels of the Manik Complex (previously published in Tikal Report 25A:fig. 149–151) and osseous material (to be published in Tikal Report 30) mixed with stone, gravel, and mortar, extends through approximately 2 m, both vertically and horizontally, under Fl. 5 in no obvious pattern. Descriptions below include Tikal Project Op. 53C/Lot 9 catalogue numbers.

VESSEL 1 (Cat. 53C-57a)

Found at 216.70 m; this is in three pieces (Fig. 66a).

VESSEL 2

Lies above vessel 4 (Fig. 66a).

VESSEL 3 (Cat. 53C-31a)

Found at 137.70 m; inverted, in a bed of mortar (Fig. 65b, 66a; TR. 25A:fig. 150b).

VESSEL 4 (Cat. 53C-35a)

Lies directly below vessel 3 (Fig. 65b; TR. 25A:-fig. 150e).

VESSEL 5 (Cat. 53C-35b)

Found at 216.90 m; inverted, in four pieces, partly under a bedrock ledge in a mortar bed (Fig. 65b).

VESSEL 6

No data are available (Fig. 66a).

VESSEL 7 (Cat. 53-31a)

This contains skull fragments with inlaid teeth (Cat. 53C-32) and a mandible, molar, and bits of charcoal (Fig. 65b, 66a,b).

VESSEL 8 (Cat. 53C-40a)

Found at 216.80 m; it is a lid for vessel 13, partly beneath vessel 3 (Fig. 65b; TR. 25A:fig. 150f).

VESSEL 9

This vessel is not illustrated.

VESSEL 10

This is not illustrated; it probably comprises sherds of 53C-13.

VESSEL 11

This is not illustrated.

VESSEL 12 (Cat. 53C-41)

Beneath the bottom of vessel 12, and part of Cat. 53C-41, is a fragmented skull; not illustrated are teeth: 11 molars and part of a 12th; 1 lower first molar with occlusal caries; 6 premolars including all 4 uppers, attrition slight; 3 canines; 3 incisors, including 2 upper central with minimal caries and minimal abrasion (there is no evidence of notching or inlays). There is also one fragment of the second cervical vertebra.

Age: Adult; Sex: ?

VESSEL 13 (Cat. 53C-40a)

This is at 216.70 m and was covered by vessel 8; it contains a mandible and skull (Cat. 53C-41), 27 teeth, and charcoal (Fig. 65b, 66a, 67b; TR. 25A:fig. 150f).

VESSEL 14 (Cat. 53C-50a)

This is at 216.60 m; below vessel 53, upright, and very fragmented (Fig. 65b, 66a; TR. 25A:fig. 150h).

VESSEL 15

Illustrated in Fig. 66a.

VESSEL 16 (Cat. 53C-46a)

Found at 216.70 m; inverted over vessel 26 (Fig. 65b, 67b,c; TR. 25A:fig. 150d).

VESSEL 17 (Cat. 53C-46b)

This is a fragment, inverted over vessel 26, partly beneath vessel 16 (Fig. 66a, 67b,c).

VESSEL 18

This is not illustrated.

VESSEL 19

This is not illustrated.

VESSEL 20

This is not illustrated; found mixed with sherds of 53C-35a.

VESSEL 21 (Cat. 53C-35a)

This vessel is at 216.70 m; it is overlain by vessel 5 and contains a skull (Cat. 53C-36), facing SE, with most teeth in place (Fig. 65b, 66a; TR. 25A:fig. 150e).

VESSEL 22 (Cat. 53C-51a)

This is at 216.60 m and is in two fragments, containing loose skull fragments, loose teeth (Cat. 53C-52), and an obsidian fragment (Cat. 53C-33; Fig. 65b, 67c; TR. 25A:fig. 150c).

VESSEL 23 (Cat. 53C-51b)

This is at 216.70 m and is nearly vertical (Fig. 65b; TR. 25A:fig. 150c).

VESSEL 24 (Cat. 53C-57b)

This is preserved in fragments only (Fig. 67c).

VESSEL 25 (Cat. 53C-57b)

This is preserved in fragments only, at 216.30 m (Fig. 67c).

VESSEL 26 (Cat. 53C-46a)

Found beneath vessels 16 and 17, upright, containing small stones, a skull (Cat. 53C-47), with maxilla in place, teeth in mandible, and an obsidian flake (Fig. 66c, 67c; TR. 25A:fig. 150d).

VESSEL 27 (CAT. 53C-54A)

This is at 216.30 m, inverted over vessel 28 (Fig. 66a; TR. 25A:fig. 149f).

VESSEL 28 (Cat. 53C-54a)

This is at 216.20 m and contains bone and tooth fragments (Cat. 53C-55) in loose soil (contents of the vessel had air pockets and were not tightly packed; see Fig. 66a; TR. 25A:fig. 149f).

VESSEL 29 (Cat. 53C-57b)

Fragments of this vessel are at 216.30 m (Fig. 65b).

VESSEL 30 (Cat. 53C-62a)

This vessel is at 216.70 m and contains a skull (Cat. 53C-62a,b), face up (Fig. 65b, 67d; TR. 25A:fig. 149a).

VESSEL 31 (Cat. 53C-37a)

This is at 216.40 m and is inverted over vessel 35 (Fig. 65b, 66a; TR. 25A:fig. 149e).

VESSEL 32 (Cat. 53C-56a)

This vessel lies at 216.20 m with skull fragments (Fig. 66a; TR. 25A:fig. 149d).

VESSEL 33 (Cat. 53C-57a)

This vessel is at 216.30 m, in two parts, and contains (50) skull fragments not catalogued and unmentioned on the catalogue card (Fig. 65b, 66a; TR. 25A:fig. 149c).

VESSEL 34

This is at 216.20 m (Fig. 66a).

VESSEL 35 (Cat. 53C-37a)

This is at 216.30 m, beneath vessel 31 and above vessel 33, and a skull (Cat. 53C-38); 3 obsidian flake-blade fragments; and bone fragments on top (Fig. 66a,e; TR. 25A:fig. 149e).

VESSEL 36 (Cat. 53C-59)

At 216.40 m, this vessel is not illustrated, but is possibly paired with 53C-46 and 53C-4 (TR. 25A:fig. 150i).

VESSEL 37 (Cat. 53C-56a)

This is in fragments (with 53C-48, 43, 38) at 216.50 m.

VESSEL 38 (Cat. 53C-56a)

This is at 216.60 m; fragments are illustrated in Fig. 65b, 66a (also TR. 25A:fig. 149d).

VESSEL 39 (Cat. 53C-34a)

This is at 216.20 m, partly beneath vessel 40 (Fig. 66a; TR. 25A:fig. 149b).

VESSEL 40 (Cat. 53C-34b)

This is at 216.20 m (Fig. 66a; TR. 25A:fig. 149b).

VESSEL 41 (Cat. 53C-46b)

This is a fragment at 216.20 m.

VESSEL 42 (Cat. 53C-56b)

This is in fragments at 216.10 m.

VESSEL 43 (Cat. 53C-56a)

This is in fragments at 216.20 m (Fig. 66a).

VESSEL 44

This is at 216.40 m (Fig. 66a).

VESSEL 45 (Cat. 53C-44a)

This is at 216.30 m, with vessel 52 (Fig. 66b; TR. 25A:fig. 150a).

VESSEL 46 (Cat. 53C-60)

This is at 216.50 m and may have combined with vessel 36 (Fig. 66a; TR. 25A:fig. 151a3).

VESSEL 47

This is at 216.50 m with a skull fragment that has no evident deformation. Two teeth are present, heavily worn upper-lateral incisors.

VESSEL 48 (Cat. 53C-56a)

This is in fragments at 216.10 m (Fig. 66a).

VESSEL 49 (Cat. 53C-57b)

This is at 216 m; fragments (50) occur partly beneath a skull (Fig. 66a).

SKULL 50

This is upright, facing NW, deformed, and well packed with small stones, at 216.20 m (Fig. 66a).

SKULL 51

This is at 216 m and is upside-down; not illustrated.

VESSEL 52 (Cat. 53C-44a)

This contains a skull (Cat. 53C-45a) with 1 large,

shovel-shaped incisor; 1 inlaid tooth, 4 drilled for inlay; and 1 finger-bone fragment (Cat. 53C-45b). Vessel 45 may have been placed as a cover, at 216 m (Fig. 65b, 66a; TR. 25A:fig. 150a).

VESSEL 53 (Cat. 53C-50a)

This may have been inverted, possibly associated with vessels 14 and 56; there were no contents (Fig. 65b; TR. 25A:fig. 150h).

VESSEL 54

No data are available for this vessel.

VESSEL 55 (Cat. 53C-61)

This was in fragments, possibly associated with vessel 54; it probably is one of two paired vessels (TR. 25A:fig. 150j).

VESSEL 56 (Cat. 53C-50a)

Found in fragments, this vessel is not illustrated.

VESSEL 57 (Cat. 53C-56b)

Fragments of this vessel are located at 216.20 m (Fig. 65b).

VESSEL 58

This is at 216 m and is not illustrated.

VESSEL 59 (Cat. 53C-42a)

This is at 217 m and functions as a lid for vessel 60 (Fig. 65b, 66d; TR. 25A:fig. 150g).

VESSEL 60 (Cat. 53C-42a)

This is at 216.70 m and contained a very pitted skull, part of a vertebra, and teeth (Fig. 66d, 67a).

VESSEL 61 (Cat. 53C-80)

This is at 217 m and was crushed by large stones; there were no contents (Fig. 65b, 66d; TR. 25A:fig. 151a2).

VESSEL 62 (Cat. 53C-58)

This is at 216.80 m and associated with vessel 61 (Fig. 65b, 66d; TR. 25A:fig. 151a1).

SKULL (Cat. 53C-38)

This skull is extremely fragmented: the lambdoid suture is closed; the masto-occipital is well developed (mature individual?), with small mastoids. The teeth consist of 3 premolars; 2 molars (attrition moderate); 2 first incisors; 1 canine; 4 incisors with hematite inlays (photo 66-4-1616, 98-18-H[17A]).

The mandible is badly fragmented, with left third molar in place (attrition slight); molar and 2 premolars lost postmortem; first premolar root still in place; canine lost postmortem; periodontitis evident on anterior labial surface.

Age: Old adult, possibly in 60s. Sex: Female?

SKULL (Cat. 53C-43)

This skull is possibly female, but this is not definite. Teeth include 1 canine inlaid, with caries (photo 66-4-1619, 98-18-14A); 1 barrel-shaped incisor inlaid (same photo). Other teeth are badly fragmented and include at least 10 molars, 6 lower, 4 upper (one lower has severe root-surface caries); 4 premolars, 2 upper, 2 lower; 2 incisors.

Age: Adult.

SKULL (Cat. 53C-45a)

This skull is fragmented along suture lines; it is possibly young, with slight flattening of a gracile occipital and has sharp orbital margins. The teeth include 3 incisors, 2 inlaid (photo 66-4-1615, 98-18-BC7a); 2 inlaid canines (same photo); 5 premolars, 3 upper, 2 lower; 3 molars, 1 third molar not fully erupted, 2 probably lower.

Sex: Female?

TEETH (Cat. 53C-45b)

These occur with skull 45a and represent two individuals, one in late teens and one older child, ca. 9 years of age.

SKULL (Cat. 53C-47)

This skull has no evident deformation. The teeth include 2 upper lateral incisors heavily worn; 1 upper right canine inlaid with iron pyrite (photo 66-4-1620, 98-18-CC13); 2 other canines; 8 premolars; 9 molars, 3 possibly incompletely erupted, 3 with occlusal caries, 1 with distal caries. A portion of the mandible preserves the left first premolar and right second premolar and first molar; periodontitis is advanced.

Age: Adult. Sex: Female?

SKULL (Cat. 53C-36)

A skull (not illustrated) with coronal and sagit-

tal sutures closed; adult male. Teeth include 2 inlaid lower canines (photo 66-4-1619, 98-18-B[19A]); 1 upper left canine not inlaid; 1 upper right first incisor not inlaid; 1 upper left second incisor; 1 lower right incisor; 4 upper premolars; 3 lower premolars; 13 molars (which may indicate that there was more than one individual here since 12 is the normal total number of molars for an individual). Periodontitis is moderate and attrition slight. An inlaid canine may not belong with this skull.

Four vertebral fragments are preserved, including the odontoid process of the second cervical vertebra.

Age: Adult.

TEETH (Cat. 53C-63)

These (not illustrated) teeth include 5 molars: 2 upper and 1 possible upper; 2 lower show moderate wear; 1 lower and 1 upper show generalized root-surface caries; 3 upper premolars and fragments of other teeth; 1 right central incisor inlaid with pyrite; and 1 left first premolar inlaid.

SKULL (Cat. 53C-64)

Fragment of adult skull (not illustrated).

SKULL (Cat. 53C-65)

This skull appears deformed (and is not illustrated). The teeth include 3 inlaid incisors (photo 66-4-1620, 98-18-DC13), 2 upper inlaid centrals and 1 upper right second inlaid incisor; an inlaid tooth fragment; and 1 left upper central incisor, not inlaid (photo 10-21-98).

SKULLS (Cat. 53C-32)

These two fragmented skulls are at 216.20 m (Fig. 66a). The teeth include fragments of 4 molars; 1 premolar; 3 incisors; and 1 canine (the canine and 1 incisor are inlaid). The right and left second and third molars remain in place on one badly broken mandible; the third right molar is badly impacted; periodontitis is advanced (photo 66-4-1618 and 98-18-11[21A]).

Age: Adult?

TEETH (Cat. 53C-52)

Teeth are at 216 m and include an incomplete upper left canine inlaid (photo 66-4-1619, 98-18-C[36]), which corresponds to that of the upper right canine at the center of vessel 47/a; 3 canines are not inlaid; other teeth include 3 incisors, 2 upper central, 1 upper left second; 4 premolars, 2 upper and 2 lower; 9 molars, first and second in the left mandible, 6 lower, 3 upper, with straight wear.

Vessel 45 may have been placed as a cover (Fig. 65b, 66a).

Age: Adult. Sex: Unknown.

SKULL (Cat. 53C-55)

The skull is fragmented. Teeth comprise 4 lower molars, possibly erupted, and 4 upper molars, 1 surely erupted. These include 2 lower first molars erupted; 3 erupting second molars (ca. 11 years) with caries; and 3 are third molars. Also found were 5 canines (which may indicate that there was more than one individual here since 4 is the normal total number of canines for an individual) and 6 incisors. This is possibly associated with vessel 54.

Age: Child of 10 or 11 years. Sex: Unknown.

DISCUSSION

Breaks in Fl. 4 and 5 initially invited investigation; as it turned out, however, both had been caused by tree-root action (Fig. 47b). Excavation proved difficult because of backdirt from earlier clearing in the building and looseness of the material surrounding the deposit. Bedrock was encountered at the S and E edges of the problematical deposit, but not at the N. Some vessels had been tucked under a bedrock ledge that may have been part of a chultun (see below).

The deposit appears to have been made while workers assembled core masonry for Str. 6F-27-2nd, an unknown architectural feature underlying 6F-27-1st. The lowest vessels had been deposited in a rough hole cut into bedrock, possibly a partially collapsed chultun catalogued as Ch. 6F-6 (Fig. 65a). Others were in core masonry above bedrock. Rubble stones, boulders, blocks, and gravelly matrix overlie the vessels. Many had been smashed, presumably during masonry placement. Some vessels were bedded in blue-gray mortar.

Figure 65b and 66a show locations of some vessels at various levels. Some are illustrated separately. Excavation limits at N and W edges are arbitrary. The lateral extent of the deposit was not fully determined. Above bedrock there was no evident pit in the basal platform core. Vertical position of some vessels is recorded as meters above sea level, however

the point measured on each vessel for level datum is not consistent. Elevations noted below may be taken as general-level indicators. Individual vessels, illustrated in TR. 25A, are identified as of the Manik Ceramic Complex, that is, centuries earlier than Str. 6F-27-1st, but potentially contemporaneous with Str. 6F-27-2nd.

The deposit is clearly an offering of severed heads. Cervical vertebrae provide evidence for decapitation in some cases. Others may lack this due to poor preservation. Many of the teeth have dental inlays, something not common at Tikal, though rulers numbered 22, 23, and 24 had these inlays. They fall between the defeat of Double Bird (ruler 21, aka Wak Chan K'awiil, AD 537?–562) and accession of Shield Skull (ruler 25, aka Nuun Ujol Chaak, AD 657–679 [Martin 2003:table 1.1]). This may provide a tentative date for the deposit, sometime between mid-6th and mid-7th centuries.

Provenance of skulls, whether from Tikal or elsewhere, has not yet been established. If from "away," they might be trophy heads. It may not be coincidence that the date suggested above falls in a time of considerable conflict for Tikal, including wars with Caracol, Dos Pilas, and Calakmul (Martin and Grube 2000:39–43). Within a century, Tikal triumphed when Jasaw Chan K'awiil, the 26th ruler, "brought down the flint and shield" of Yich'aak K'ahk' (aka Jaguar Paw) of Calakmul (Schele and Freidel 1990:205–9; Martin and Grube 2000:44–45).

Chultun 6F-6

This small chultun has been cut into bedrock on the central axial line of Str. 6F-27-1st, immediately W of PD. 170 (Fig. 65a). It appears to have been filled at the time PD. 170 was deposited and the basal platform of Str. 6F-17-1st was installed. Some of the fill material looks like cut stone and may be from Str. 6F-27-2nd.

Architecture

Structure 6F-27 is usually included among the Tikal Great Temples as Great Temple VI. Although much smaller than Temples I-V, its hieroglyphic texts admit it into this exalted company (Fig. 68a,b, 69a,b).

Aside from dimensional uniqueness, 6F-27 differs noticeably from Temples I-IV in the absence of side insets and presence of triple doorways. Great Temple V also lacks side insets. The relatively large roofcomb chamber is equally anomalous within this group of structures.

The distinction between stair-side terraces and stair-side outsets made above (see MSP) may reveal something about design intentions. The stair-side elements have the profiles of typical stair-side outsets but with return faces angled like terrace faces. As a result they ally morphologically with both stair and terracing. It seems unlikely that this could have been done by accident or without direction. Authorities responsible for the design of the structure may have been engaged in some kind of philosophical speculation about the significance of terraces and stairs. The MSP may have been necessary in order to cover up an earlier fabric. But at the same time this part of the structure surely must have possessed some conceptual value of its own. Perhaps the thinking was that the stair embodied the same significance as the terracing, while retaining some degree of distinctness. Stairs, for example, may have served as the setting for particular ritual performances.

The basal platform is an architectural element rare at Tikal. Great Temple IV has a very large one. The other great temples have none. In part it may have served to level uneven bedrock. It may also have been inherited from the largely unknown earlier feature that it apparently overlies. Frontal extension of the basal platform provides a surface analogous to the North Terrace in front of the North Acropolis. This may act like a transition between the plaza space to the W and the building on its major substructure platform and building platform. Stela 21 and Alt. 9 are elements of this transitional space. Perhaps some individuals could use the stelae and altars in the plaza below while only certain others had access to the basal platform.

Absence of wall-top plaster is unusual in Tikal structures that have preplastered capstones. It may be that wall-top plaster was simply not observed. Vault-soffit plaster feathering down onto the wall often overlaps the point where wall plaster turns onto the wall top.

A remarkable feature of 6F-27 is the placement of vault beams at course levels. This does not rule out the presence of a timber falsework completely, but it

seems unlikely that vault beams could have been set (on a timber frame) prior to vault masonry and yet coincide with course levels in the soffit facings. The vault beams must have been set after the masonry had reached the desired level. This would have eliminated the need to cut soffit-facing stones around the beams. A timber framework may still have been set up, with poles projecting through the gap between half-vaults, to establish the vault-top level.

Associated Monuments

The text on the rear axial outset of the roofcomb and portions of the upper zone is long, complex, and badly damaged in most areas (Fig. 51, 60). As Berlin first noted, it bears a terminal date of 9.16.15.0.0 (Jones 1977:fig. 18), whereas the Dedicatory Date of St. 21 is 9.15.5.0.0 (TR. 33A:46). The difference, more than 30 tuns, led Satterthwaite and Jones (1965) to speculate that the text, and indeed the whole roofcomb, may be a secondary addition to the structure. Architectural features do not support this hypothesis. A plaster surface running under the roofcomb (Fig. 55) is most likely the roof surface. As such, it is no more than a construction-stage marker. As it happens, this is the only clear separation between construction stages in the structure. On completing the building, however, it would be no more than good standard Tikal practice to plaster the roof surface immediately. The plaster seal protects the otherwise vulnerable interior plaster finishes, particularly the vault-soffit plaster. Roofcomb construction could then proceed on this sustaining surface.

More recent examinations of the inscription have complicated matters, since there is an earlier, and much longer account of construction activity in columns E-F on the E facade (Stuart 2007). There is good reason to believe that the relevant dates need to be moved from the Early Classic positions (AD 528) in Jones (1977:53–55) to others in the Late Classic (AD 735), during the reign of Yik'in Chan K'awiil (Martin 2015). The association of St. 21 with Fl. 4 would be consistent with a construction date for 6F-27-1st in AD 735 (Martin 2015). The 28th ruler may have been involved with addition of the text, he certainly added Panel Z on the N Upper Zone and presumably was responsible for at least Panels U, V, and Y. As Table 5.2 shows, Str. 6F-27-1st underwent modifications at some point, mainly filling in the ends of Rm. 2 either to make the space smaller, or in response to perceived structural weakness associated with the large roofcomb chamber above Rm. 2.

The dating of the little-known 6F-27-2nd, that underlies it remains unclear (Fl. 3, Fig. 55, and Fl. 5, Fig. 47b). If it is associated with the Manik ceramics in P.D. 170 in the basal platform, then it would be an Early Classic construction, but without a deeper exploration this will remain unknown.

Sherds and Artifacts

Twelve lot groups representing sherds from construction cores and collapse (Table 5.1a,b,c,d) all produced Cauac assessments (from TR 27B:app. C). PD. 168 and 170, and Ca. 151, on the other hand, yielded Imix assessments. These latter probably represent ceramics current at the time of deposition, whereas the Cauac sherds must have come from earlier deposits swept up for use in later construction. The artifact collection includes material from Lot Group 5, PD. 170, a large skull burial in a former chultun (detailed above). Lot Group 5 is heavy in human skulls, vessels, including vessel fragments and a few other items. The usual flint and obsidian fragments are absent from Lot Group 5 but show up in the other groups.

Absolute Dates

Two samples were taken from vault beams, outer surfaces including bark of *Piscidia piscipula*. Two and three runs were done on the samples with averaged results: AD 437±51 years, and AD 668±44 years (^{14}C Dates for Tikal Samples, September 10, 1965, Tikal Project Archives, ^{14}C Lab Reports). Jones (1991) gives AD 766 as the construction date for Temple VI, hence the ^{14}C results appear centuries too early. Salvaging of wood members from demolished structures so that they could be re-used in later construction may account for these early ^{14}C dates.

Simon Martin (2015) has re-analyzed parts of the inscription on the E facade, integrating observations from other epigraphers and archaeologists to reach a tentative conclusion that the surface feature, 6F-27-1st, was rapidly built during the reign of Yik'in Chan K'awiil, the 27th Tikal ruler in the years AD 734–35, though uncertainty remains as to whether the roofcomb with its inscription is primary or secondary. Further uncertainty is cited concerning plaster cover of glyphs in the upper zones. Since it was standard practice for ancient Maya builders to always cover facing stone with plaster, the instances cited here may well reflect this usual treatment rather than revision of the text.

Shirley Mock (1998) reports on a skull burial at Colha, Belize, that bears a superficial resemblance to our skull pit here. Mock interprets the skull burial as a termination ritual and as an inducement for supernatural powers to inhabit the fabric of the temple. Termination ritual seems unlikely for 6F-27 but a skull cache, as interpreted by David Pendergast in the same volume (1998), would fit the bill admirably.

Stuart (1998) describes "och k'ahk'" as a fire ritual meant to accomplish the same thing as the skull burial, that is, to bring the structure to life, so to speak, or perhaps we could say to establish a supernatural power within its fabric. The ritual Stuart describes is one that would be done on completion of construction and, without attempting to be specific, its purpose would be to enable the structure to function as intended. In other words, the fire entering ritual and the skull burial reinforce each other as devices supportive of the reason for construction in the first place.

Megan O'Neil (2009) develops a theory concerning the buried sculptures and sculpture fragments at Tikal and other sites. She contends that, for the ancient Maya, burial enabled the items to retain their power. This argument applied to the PD. 170 skull burial suggests that the act of burial may have been as important as the items buried. Although the skulls may have possessed some form of power, burial on the axial of the structure not only focused that power onto Temple VI but also ensured that it would remain potent.

TABLE 5.1a
Lot Groups: Str. 6F-27
Op.53A

Lot Groups	Lot	Provenience	Ceramic Evaluation
1	1	Ca. 151	Imix
2	2,3	Near Stela 21	n.d.

TABLE 5.1b
Str. 6F-27: Distribution of Sherds and Artifacts by Lot Groups
Op. 53A

Study Group	Object	Lot Groups 1	2
Pottery	Sherds to Nearest LB		
Other Pottery	Cache vessel	1	
Chipped Flint	Eccentrics Irregular biface	9	1
Chipped Obsidian	Incised	9	
Ground Stone	Quartzite mano fragment		1
Shell and Bone			
Other	Stela fragments		*

* indicates quantity not specified

TABLE 5.1c
Lot Groups: Str. 6F-27
Op.53B

Lot Groups	Lot	Provenience	Ceramic Evaluation
1	1,2	Surface	Cauac

TABLE 5.1d
Str. 6F-27: Distribution of Sherds and Artifacts by Lot Groups
Op. 53B

Study Group	Object	Lot Groups 1
Other Pottery	Figurine fragments	1
Other	Glyph fragments	*

* indicates quantity not specified.

TABLE 5.1e
Lot Groups: Str. 6F-27
Op. 53C

Lot Groups	Lot	Provenience	Ceramic Evaluation
1	1,8,12	Surface	Cauac
2	2	Axial trench building platform level	E.C. and Cauac
3	3,4,5,6	Axial trench at foot of stair	E.C. and Cauac
4	7	NS trench of Stela 21	n.d.
5	9	PD. 170	E.C. and Imix
6	10	Trench, SE corner, basal platform	E.C. and Cauac
7	11	Trench, SW corner, basal platform	n.d.
8	13,15	Central Rm 1, on floor	Late Cauac
9	14	PD. 168	E.C. and Imix

TABLE 5.1f
Str. 6F-27: Distribution of Sherds and Artifacts by Lot Groups
Op. 53C

Study Group	Object	Lot Groups								
		1	2	3	4	5	6	7	8	9
Pottery	Sherds to Nearest LB	1	1	20	6		*	*	1	
Other Pottery	Censer fragments			5		1				
	Reworked sherd			1						
	Complete vessel				28					
	Vessel Fragment				37					
Chipped Flint	Used flake		3	8	3					
	Unused flake	3		6	2	3	1			
	Unmodified core	1		1						
	Elongated biface fragment			2			1			
	Unused chip			1						
	Retouched flake			1						
	Core fragment	1					1			
	Blade fragment					3				
Chipped Obsidian	Flake			2		2		*		
	Blade fragment			5		4				
Ground Stone	Arkose metate fragment			1						
	Quartzite metate fragment			1						
Shell and Bone	Skull					12				
	Land snail					14				
	Rodent canine					3				
	Finger bone					1				
	Human teeth					2				
	Human bone									*
	Shell bead									8
	Bird bone	1								
Other	Jade bead	2		1		1				1
	Monument fragment			2						
	Mask fragment			2						
	Carved stucco fragment			2						
	Charcoal sample					5				
	Stone bead									1

TABLE 5.2
Structure 6F-27-1st: Time Spans

Time Span	Construction Stage	Special Deposit			Lot	Other Data
		Fl.	Ca.	PD.		
1	˒					Abandonment of 6F-27-1st.
2						Use of 1st as modified by Rm. 2 reduction.
3			151			Use of 1st as initially built; St. 21, Alt. 9.
4	1,2	1,2,4,6		168,170		Construction of 1st; 2,200 m^3.
5					53A1–3,B1–2, C1–15,D1	Use of 2nd.
6		3,7				Construction of 2nd, volume unknown.

VI

Conclusions

Chronology

In the absence of a single stratigraphic column, inscriptions, ^{14}C dates, and architectural attributes provide estimates for chronological sequence. On the basis of the latter, Great Temple V is identified as the earliest of the structures reported here. Masonry attributes suggest this: facing stones are of the block type most common in Middle Classic times at Tikal. Rounded terrace corners on the pyramid may provide support for this dating. Suggested is a 7th-century date for construction. The fake building platform may mark the earliest appearance of this feature at Tikal, more common in Late Classic work.

If inscriptions on the building and roofcomb of Great Temple VI do indeed refer to its construction by Yik'in Chan K'awiil in AD 735, this would place it next in line, the second of the four reported here. Exceptionally, Temple VI has veneer facings on building walls, something common at Tikal on range-type buildings but not on temples.

Radiocarbon results for Great Temple IV place its construction sometime after the mid-8th century. This would be a good fit with its two carved lintels that celebrate the 27th king Yik'in Chan K'awiil, who ruled between AD 734 and ca. 761. Thus, this may be the third temple in the TR. 23B series.

Great Temple III has been associated with a ruler named Dark Sun and, assuming it was built after his death, construction must have taken place well into the 9th century. Almost certainly, this must be the last, chronologically, of the four described here.

Temple

The term "temple" has been applied throughout this volume without any qualification (for visual comparison of great temples, see Figures 70, 71, and 72). Indeed, this is how the term is generally used. Maler, in the 1890s, designated five of the Great Temples this way (he missed Great Temple VI), also with no qualifications or explicitly stated meanings. He was simply continuing a tradition that goes back to the earliest investigations of ancient Maya ruins.

The Great Temples of Tikal seem to demand a "temple" designation. The epithet "great" reflects the magnitude of Temples I through V (Maler's Great Temples). Temple VI has been admitted to the fold on account of the extraordinary inscriptions on its roofcomb and upper-zone surfaces.

Sometimes only the building part is considered to be the "temple"; pyramids or substructure platforms are regarded simply as devices to elevate the "temple" into an exalted and commanding, dominant position. Then too, structures of this sort are often understood as funerary monuments (M. Coe 1956). Great Temple I, built over a spectacular tomb (Bu. 116), appears definitely associated with the Late Classic ruler Jasaw Chan K'awiil and strongly supports the funerary interpretation. Since this author does not entirely agree with these views, I would like to propose my own.

It is very evident that non-material forces played a central part in ancient natural philosophy. When they looked at the night sky, for example–so much more vivid than it is for most of us city dwellers–they had to account for the brilliant lights. They certainly did not think of them as gigantic balls of flaming gas: they were convinced that those mysterious lights could somehow affect their every action and that, therefore, it was incumbent upon them to ensure that the influences impinging upon them would be as positive as possible. Rulers had a particular responsibility for this and could draw on the resources of the community to this effect.

Bringing this nebulous argument into focus with the Great Temples, and assuming that the date suggested here for Temple V is correct, the following is proposed: after a period of military reversals during the 6th and early 7th centuries, theoretical natural philosophers in the community decided that building a really high ceremonial structure might improve their position. Not long after construction of Temple V, near the end of the 7th century, Tikal triumphed over Calakmul, their former conqueror and rival. This must have convinced them that the Great Temple format really did work and so building more of them would make sense.

If this speculative reconstruction is at all accurate, it follows that the structures we call Great Temples were built to secure positive influences coming from such natural phenomena as the stars, planets, sun, moon, wind, lightning, and thunder. My guess is that appropriate architecture would encourage the forces influencing human outcomes to inhabit the fabric of the structures at times of ceremonial performance. In this sense, the temples could be said to be alive. A temple, then, could be defined as a work of architecture designed to attract the forces evident in natural phenomena.

A deceased ruler could be understood as one of these forces. His or her tomb, together with various caches, the burning of offerings, and ritual performances, could be seen as elements of the temple intended to enhance its primary function. The masks on temple facades might act as ways of naming the forces in question and, thus, calling to them.

Of course, this still leaves open the question of how we can identify structures designed according to the criteria mentioned above. It is possible that we can be fairly certain about some, uncertain about others, and probably there are a few that we cannot identify.

Wall Facings

A persistent pattern in the masonry of these structures that might be Tikal temples appears in the type of masonry facings applied to different parts of the fabric. For example, Early Classic structures on the North Acropolis, which might be temples, have veneer facings on substructure terraces, but cobble or rubble facings on building walls. In Late Classic temple work, veneer facings continue to be used on terraces, while wall facings are done with brick-like units. In Great Temple IV this pattern persists, although the wall-facing units are larger and on III they are quite large headers. Temple VI presents an exception, with veneer facings on building walls.

How this pattern, not visible in completed structures, might relate to intentions that temples should attract natural forces is certainly speculative but may have something to do with "house" metaphors. The most obvious temples at Tikal have building units formed as house images, unusually paired images, one in front of the other. Specialized masonry for their walls might have been seen as a way to reinforce the sense of house in the perceptions of the forces that the architecture was designed to invite. Veneer facings in building walls may have been regarded as not consistent with house construction. Where this leaves Temple VI remains problematic.

Pyramid

High pyramidal substructures posed the most demanding challenges of all ancient Maya construction at Tikal, much more demanding than vaulting. This is so because much of their mortar was low in quality, not very adhesive, and prone to revert to mere earth over time. The problem is that granular material piled at an angle much greater than its natural angle of repose is certain to spread in time. Only the adhesive quality of the mortar works against this, unless other strategies are employed. An obvious way to prevent spread would be to erect retaining walls at the outer edges. But this is an approach that runs counter to ancient Maya ideas about stability in masonry construction.

They always built masonry structures as assemblages of independently stable units. Their vaults demonstrate this most clearly. Over long, narrow rooms they built half-vaults, one on each side, not touching each other and, therefore, not exerting outward thrusts on the walls. Capstones span the gap but do not act as keystones in vaults, such as the Romans built. Roman vaults require buttresses. Maya vaults do not.

When builders at Tikal contemplated high pyramidal substructure platforms, they applied the same strategy that had worked for centuries in vault construction. Structure 5D-33-1st demonstrates their method. Wall-like units, nested against each other, form the inner core of the pyramid, each independently stable (TR 14:fig. 170, 171). At different terrace levels these core walls follow different paths so that their joints do not coincide. Clearly they understood the structural value of staggered jointing. We do not see this in facing masonry and this is because the facings were not expected to act as retaining walls. As 5D-33-1st slowly eroded over centuries of abandonment nearly all facing masonry sloughed off, but the inner core walls were able to withstand the ravages of weather and vegetation.

We know how Str. 5D-33-1st was built, but we lack this information for the four Great Temples III, IV, V, and VI, since their substructure platforms have not been sectioned. Since they remain standing, the high pyramidal platforms, except for Temple VI, must have been built using techniques similar to Str. 5D-33-1st.

Alignments

Great Temples I, II, III, and IV established an E-W alignment in the form of a narrow fan. From the doorway of Temple I the three others are seen against the western horizon like the marks on a scale. They define seven sunset positions moving from S to N: S of III, directly behind III, between III and II, directly behind II, between II and IV, directly behind IV, and N of IV. These solar stations could establish a series of festivals or ceremonials running throughout the year, as sunset positions move N and again as they move S. This procession defines thirteen ritual periods (since either the N or S position would only be counted once). At Tikal, sunset

positions are much clearer than sunrises because of morning mist generated by the great Santa Fe Bajo E of the city center.

This arrangement means that morning sunlight falls on the front facades of Temples II, III, and IV, with their sculptural features and masks. From the ancient Maya viewpoint, the morning sun would see these images while the evening sun would see the imagery on Temple I. This may explain why we see imagery only on frontal parts of temples. If Temples II, III, and IV were sited along a single line, Temple II would block morning sun from the other two and Temple IV would block evening sun from Temple I.

Great Temple V, facing toward the N, forms part of a N-S alignment with the North Acropolis and the North Group. The line passes immediately in front of the Temple I building, E of the North Acropolis center, but on alignment with Str. 3D-43 in the North Zone. These two alignments formed by Great Temples establish a "cross format" embedding the four directions conspicuously in the most prominent features of the epicenter. This would likely have been very satisfying to ancient Maya natural philosophers.

A contrivance that might have been similarly satisfying concerns Great Temple V. During part of the year, sunlight falls on its front facade so that the sun sees the imagery there. Perhaps this would establish a ritual period specific to this Temple during this time.

Harrison (1999:191) includes Temple V in a right-angle alignment with Temples I and IV assuming that Temple V is the latest of the three great temples. Now that Temple V is known to be the earliest, Harrison's argument is simply reversed; the position of Temple IV was located by the right-angle rule. Harrison (1999:fig.122) illustrates a jade plaque as a model of a possible surveying instrument that could be used for turning right angles. Such a device would indeed be useful for layout of architectural structures and might explain how it is that most major constructions do appear "squared-up." However, the value of right-angle relationships between non-adjacent structures as a principal guiding the growth of the city is less clear. This would seem to imply that the right-angle possessed a meaningful value in itself. For individual structures accurate right-angled corners are intrinsically satisfying because they look strong and give an impression of solidity. Here it is not the right-angle that has value but the result of its accurate application in the production of ordered architectural form.

The putative surveying instrument cited above would use a right-angle set out at small scale to estimate right-angles at much larger scales. The small-scale angle inscribed on the plaque could be done accurately by eye. It is a type of device widespread in pre-modern times when eye-ball criteria were the only means available. Astrolabes, surveyor's cross-staffs, and quadrants employ essentially the same principles.

A mystical appreciation for the right-angle emerged in Classical Greece with the discovery of the mathematics of the right-angle (Crease 2008). This knowledge could support an intrinsic value for right-angles that would be appropriate for their embedding in large-scale geometry of an urban field. There is nothing in Maya mathematics (Closs 1986) to suggest the ancient Maya knew the math of the right-angle. So while a device such as the one illustrated by Harrison (cited above) may have been used for construction it might not have been used for urban development.

How, then, were locations for the Great Temples at Tikal determined? Temples I and II replace earlier structures on E and W sides of the Great Plaza. Carmack (1981:270–73) describes a similar situation at Utatlán. Here the sharply vertical Tojil temple stands on the E side of the plaza and the much lower, more horizontal Awilix temple occupies the W side. Similarly, Temple I is vertical on the E and Temple II, lower on the W. Tojil is masculine and Awilix feminine; gender is not so clear at Tikal due to lack of conquest era information.

Back to temple location and alignment. Temples I and II are placed directly opposite each other but not on the same axial line as defined by the center of the doorway and the center of the stair at its base. This line projected form Temple I meets Temple II at the center of its doorway, whereas the equivalent line from Temple II passes S of the Temple I stair; on azimuth 101 degrees 30 minutes (258/30) as measured on TR 14:fig. 61, reasonably close to winter solstice sunset (244 degrees 54 minutes at 21 degrees N, Aveni 1980:table 9). Thus, at about one winal before winter solstice sunset, the shadow of Temple II would fall directly on Temple I; this, I suggest, may be the type of alignment that would be of interest to the Tikal Maya.

The slight off-set of axes between Temple I and II can hardly have been accidental or unnoticed; the two are so close together. A proprietorial issue may have been at play; that is, each axis may have been regarded as belonging exclusively to each structure, as indicated by placement of axial burials and caches (Pendergast 1998). Positioning of Temples III and IV follow this reasoning. They clearly do not align with Temple I yet set up a strong EW alignment that forms a cross-axial arrangement with NS features like the South Acropolis, Temple V and the North Group dominated by Str. 3D-43 on its high pyramidal substructure (TR 23A:fig. 5, TR 11:North Zone Map Sheet).

Bassie-Sweet (1996) argues that the symbolism of cross-axial orders understood as cross-roads was fundamental to ancient Maya mythology and relations between human and supernatural forces. The Great Plaza itself presents a cross-axial order (TR 11 Great Plaza Map Sheet) with Temples I and II as the EW axis set against Str. 5D-33-1st and 5D-71 in the NS direction. If this idea is valid, then the Great Plaza was so planned to be recognized as an appropriate place for offerings and petitions to supernatural powers.

When Temple V was set up as the S marker for the larger cross-roads, order in the NS direction the choice of sites would have been limited. Natural contours fall off sharply to the S of the Tikal epicenter. The South Acropolis would have been in existence, as was the Lost World complex to its W. Placing Temple V E of the South Acropolis may have been the only option available. By good fortune the sight-line linking Temple V with Str. 3D-43 in the N falls just in front of the Temple I building; someone standing at the head of the Temple I stair is well aware of the Temple V-Str. 3D-43 NS axis and the EW one established by Temples I, II, III, and IV. So the Great Temples were built to make fundamental Maya mythology a concrete experiential part of the Tikal epicenter, but that is not the only reason for their construction.

Bassie-Sweet (2008:44–46) describes contemporary corn-planting rituals that suggest a more fundamental reason for building large-scale pyramidal temples. She relates how the present-day farmer regards seed corn as dead when planted, and the rituals involved in setting up the milpa and making offerings at its shrine as instrumental in enabling the corn to regain life, to sprout, and to produce a new crop. By analogy a deceased ruler could be "planted" in a tomb and the temple erected over it, together with rituals and offerings performed on and around it, enable the ruler to regain life as a power in the spirit world, a power benevolently inclined toward the community that has labored so mightily to assist his resurrection.

Temple V appears to have been built at a time when the political fortunes of Tikal had been adverse (Culbert 1991:134–40; Martin and Grube 2000:40–43; Martin 2003:24–30), probably at the same time that Str. 5D-22-1st on the North Acropolis was experiencing an intense episode of intrusive cache offerings (TR 14:fig. 99–104). No tomb has been found in Temple V but we have the example of Str. 5D-73, BU. 196, probably housing Yik'in Chan K'awiil, ruler 27, aka Ruler B, (Martin 2003:table 1.1) showing that a ruler associated with one structure (Temple IV) could be buried in another (5D-73). Yik'in Chan K'awiil, thus, seems to have had two temples built to support his career as a supernatural force, 5D-73 over his tomb, and 5C-4 (Temple IV) invoking the victorious battles over El Peru and Naranjo (described on Lintels 2 and 3). Temple V may have been inspired by a need for help to regain political power for Tikal while Temple IV may have had a quite different motivation celebrating a victory in hope of retaining power already gained.

Temple III has not been probed for a possible tomb containing the 29th ruler Nuun Yax Ahiin II aka Ruler C, 768–794, or either of the other rulers from this late time (Martin 2003:table 1.1). It is the steepest of the Great Temples at Tikal and retains more roofcomb imagery (Fig. 30). Its location takes advantage of relatively flat terrain S of the Tozzer Causeway (TR 11:Great Plaza Map Sheet). Temple IV, already in place, is aligned on azimuth 107 degrees, a line that passes well N of Temple I. So the Temple III location had to be S of Temple IV to set up a coherent EW lineament with the three Great Temples. A consideration here may have involved creation mythology associated with the number three (Freidel, Schele, and Parker 1995:94–95), since these temples do seem to form a distinct group within a W vista.

More puzzling is the location of Temple VI away off to the SE of the epicenter. There are hints of an earlier structure on the site but so scanty as to defy any attempt to even guess the nature and scale of it. Possibly it was an ancestor shrine containing ancient

relics and the skulls buried out in front after final construction of the extant fabric in AD 766 (Jones 1991:119). Presumably the Mendez Causeway (TR 11:Great Plaza Map Sheet and Temple of Inscriptions Map Sheet) was built specifically to connect the new Temple VI with the epicenter by means of continuous plaster paving. This causeway all by itself indicates the importance attached to plaster paving as a way to establish a recognizable temple precinct. The inscriptions on the rear axial outset, naming remote rulers, may stand as further evidence that Temple VI served an ancestor cult.

The first of the Great Temples at Tikal, as defined by presence of a high, pyramidal substructure, would be Str. 5D-5 (Great Temple V), built as mentioned above at a time of uncertainty for Tikal. Str. 5D-33-1st, was next, most likely started in AD 682, the inaugural date of Jasaw Chan K'awiil, and (perhaps) with Shield Skull, 25th ruler, aka Nuun Ujol Chaak in Bu. 23 (Jones 1991:119). If these suppositions are valid, then 5D-33-1st satisfies Bassie-Sweet's model of corn planting (cited above) as construction undertaken to assist in the revivification of Shield Skull. Incorporation of fragmented St. 31 within 33-1st core (and inside partially dismantled 33-2nd), with its list of dynastic precursors (TR 33A:fig. 52b) suggests that this structure too might have ancestor cult affinities. Together with Temple VI 33-1st lacks the side inset common to Temples I, II, III, and IV, and those on the summit of the North Acropolis. So perhaps 33-1st and Temple VI share a common cult focus.

Following 5D-33-1st the next Great Temple was II, known by means of floor connections to precede Temple I, and style dated to 9.13.0.0.0 or AD 692 (Jones 1991:118). Extensive tunneling found no tomb within the substructure at plaza level (TR 14:fig. 274) and there is no convenient ruler other than Jasaw Chan K'awiil at this time. So Temple II may be exception to the Bassie-Sweet "planting" theory. Proportions are so unlike those of 33-1st that a very different cult focus might be suspected in any case. The orientation discussed above was established prior to construction of Temple I and, therefore, must have been self-directed so to speak.

When construction began on Temple I layout was carefully managed so that the new axis aligned with the center of Temple II but on an axial line of its own. Only the builders would know this; it is not at all obvious. The two structures face each other squarely as though on the same axis, yet their individual axes do not coincide. Knowledge of this axial separation might have been important to ritual specialists who probably resided in the Central Acropolis and could read the hieroglyphic texts on stelae. They would know exactly what supernatural powers, or ancestors, were associated with each temple, and presumably the metaphysics of temple-building demanded separate lines for each temple axis.

Temple I, of course, built over Bu. 116 (TR 14:fig. 260) stands as a plausible case for Bassie-Sweet's corn-planting argument (cited above). The ruler Jasaw Chan K'awiil, 26th in the dynastic succession, also known as Ruler A, had presided over Tikal's re-emergence as a regional power. Presumably then, once deceased, he would be regarded as a potentially powerful supernatural ally amply worth the effort and investment represented by Temple I to assist his rise to power in the afterlife, in the same way that ritual performances in a milpa assist the germination of the corn.

A decision to build a Great Temple would have been politically strategic in the game of prestige played between rival polities. The US, in the 1960s, did a similar thing in undertaking to place a man on the moon within the decade in order to stay ahead of the USSR. While the political motive would have been relatively simple, design of a Great Temple would have been complex and multi-functional. Theological factors would have been important and equally there would have been considerations of everyday function. Houston (1998:361) mentions the role that various levels would have played in ritual performances, providing appropriate places for spectators, actors, and elite personages. The steps cut into side terraces of Temples I and II (TR 14:fig. 253c, 265c) show that this potentiality was indeed actualized, at least in these two structures. Presence/absence of similar stairs in Great Temples III, IV, and V has not been established and, indeed, it was the reconstruction program directed by Jorge Guillemin that uncovered the side terrace stairs in Great Temples I and II. Great Temple V does not command an obvious audience area but both III and IV face extensive open areas; these structures might have side terrace stairs not yet detected.

Recent re-dating of Lintel 3, Temple I (Kennett et al. 2013) has confirmed that the lintel was carved no later than AD 712, whereas the temple erected decades later after the death of ruler Jasaw Chan K'awiil. This shows clearly that Great Temple construction was an undertaking planned long in advance of implementation as a major state project.

References

Aveni, Anthony F.
1980   *Skywatchers of Ancient Mexico*. Austin: University of Texas Press.

Bassie-Sweet, Karen
1996   *At the Edge of the World: Caves and Late Classic Maya World View*. Norman: University of Oklahoma Press.
2008   *Maya Sacred Geometry and the Creator Deities*. Norman: University of Oklahoma Press.

Berlin, Heinrich
1951   El templo de las inscripciones–VI de Tikal. *Antropologia e Historia de Guatemala* 3(1):33–54.

Carmack, Robert M.
1981   *The Quiché Mayas of Utatlán: The Evolution of a Highland Guatemala Kingdom.* Norman: University of Oklahoma Press.

Carrasco, Dávid
1999   *City of Sacrifice: The Aztec Empire and the Role of Violence in Civilization*. Boston: Beacon Press.

Closs, Michael P.
1986   The Mathematical Notation of the Ancient Maya. In *Native American Mathematics*, edited by Michael P. Closs, pp. 291–369. Austin: University of Texas Press.

Coe, Michael
1956   The Funerary Temple Among the Classic Maya. *Southwestern Journal of Anthropology* 12:387–94.

Coe, William R.
1967   *Tikal, a Handbook of the Ancient Maya Ruins*. Philadelphia: The University of Pennsylvania Museum of Archaeology and Anthropology.
1970   *Tikal, a Handbook of the Ancient Maya Ruins; with a guide map*. [Second edition] Philadelphia: The University of Pennsylvania Museum of Archaeology and Anthropology.

Crease, Robert P.
2008   *The Great Equations*. New York: W.W. Norton & Co.

Culbert, T. Patrick
1991   Polities in the northeast Peten. In *Classic Maya Political History: Hieroglyphic and Archaeological*

Evidence, edited by T. Patrick Culbert, pp.128–46. School of American Research Advanced Seminar Series. Cambridge: Cambridge University Press.

Freidel, David, Linda Schele, and Joy Parker
1993   *Maya Cosmos: Three Thousand Years on the Shaman's Path*. New York: William Morrow.

Gómez, Oswaldo
1999   Excavaciones en el Interior del Templo V, Tikal. In *Simposio de Investigaciones Arqueológicas en Guatemala* (12 session), conference proceedings, pp. 187–94. www.asociaciontikal.com.
1998   Nuevas excavaciones en el Templo V, Tikal. In *XI Simposio de Investigaciones Arqueológicas en Guatemala, 1997,* edited by J.P. Laporte and H. Escobedo, pp.54–70. Guatemala: Museo Nacionalde Arqueología y Etnología.

Gómez, Oswaldo and Cristiana Vidal Lorenzo
1997   El Templo V de Tikal: Su excavación. In *X Simposio de Investigaciones Arqueológicas en Guatemala, 1996,* edited by J.P. Laporte and H. Escobedo, pp.315–31. Guatemala: Museo Nacional de Arqueología y Etnología.

Harrison, Peter D.
1999   *The Lords of Tikal*. London: Thames and Hudson.

Haviland, William A., and Anita de Laguna Haviland
1995   Glimpses of the Supernatural: Altered States of Consciousness and the Graffiti of Tikal, Guatemala. *Latin American Antiquity* 6(4):295–309.

Houston, Stephen, D.
1998   Classic Maya Depictions of the Built Environment. In *Function and Meaning in Classic Maya Architecture*, pp. 333–72, edited by Stephen D. Houston. Washington, DC: Dumbarton Oaks.

Jones, Christopher
1991   Cycles of Growth at Tikal. In *Classic Maya Political History*, pp. 102–27, edited by T. Patrick Culbert. New York: School of American Research.
1977   Inauguration Dates of Three Late Classic Rulers of Tikal, Guatemala. *American Antiquity* 42(4):28–60.

Kennett, D.J., Irka Hajdas, Brendan J. Culleton, Soumaya Belmecheri, Simon Martin, Hector Neff, Jaime Awe, Heather V. Graham, Katherine H. Freeman, Lee Newsom, David L. Lentz, Flavio S. Anselmetti, Mark Robinson, Norbert Marwan, John Southon, David A. Hodell, and Gerald H. Haug.
2013   Correlating the Ancient Maya and Modern European Calendars with High-Precision AMS[14]C Dating. *Scientific Reports* 3:1597; DOI:10.1038/srep01597.

Maler, Teobert
1911   *Explorations in the Department of Peten, Guatemala*. Memoirs of the Peabody Museum of Archaeology and Ethnology vol. 5 no. 1. Cambridge, MA: Peabody Museum of Archaeology and Ethnology, Harvard University.

Martin, Simon
1996   Tikal's "Star War" Against Naranjo. In *Eighth Palenque Round Table, 1993*, Vol. 10, edited by M.J. Macri and J. McHargue, pp. 223–36. San Francisco: The Pre-Columbian Art Research Institute.

2000   Nuevos Datos Epigráficos sobre la Guerra Maya del Clásico. In *La Guerra entre los Antiguos Mayas, Memoria de la Primera Mesa Redonda de Palenque 1995*, edited by Silvia Trejo. pp. 105–24. Mexico: Instituto Nacional de Antropología e Historia.

2003   In Line of the Founder: A View of Dynastic Politics at Tikal. In *Tikal: Dynasties, Foreigners, & Affairs of State*, pp. 3–45. New York: School of American Research.

2015   The Dedication of Tikal Temple VI: A Revised Chronology. *PARI Journal* 15(3):1–10.

Martin, Simon, and Nikolai Grube
2000   *Chronicle of the Maya Kings and Queens*. London: Thames and Hudson.

Mock, Shirley Boteler
1998   The Defaced and the Forgotten: Decapitation and Flaying/Mutilation as a Termination Ritual at Colha, Belize. In *The Sowing and the Dawning*, edited by Shirley Boteler Mock, pp. 113–24. Albuquerque: New Mexico.

Muñoz Cosme, Gaspar
1997   El Templo V de Tikal: Su arquitectura. In *X Simposio de Investigaciones Arqueológicas en Guatemala, 1996,* edited by J.P. Laporte and H. Escobedo, pp.300–314. Guatemala: Museo Nacional de Arqueología y Etnología.

O'Neil, Megan E.
2009   Ancient Maya Sculptures of Tikal, Seen and Unseen. *Res* 55/56:119–34.

Pendergast, David M.
1998   Intercession with the Gods: Caches and Their Significance at Altun Ha and Lamanai, Belize. In *The Sowing and the Dawning*, edited by Shirley Boteler Mock, pp. 55–63. Albuquerque: University of New Mexico Press.

Proskouriakoff, Tatiana
1950   *A Study of Classic Maya Sculpture*. Washington, DC: Carnegie Institution of Washington Publication 593.

Ralph, Elizabeth K.
1965   Review of Radiocarbon Dates from Tikal and the Maya Calendar Correlation Problem. *American Antiquity* 30(4):421–27.

Riese, Berthold
1979   The "Hel" Glyph. Paper Presented at the Symposium on Phoneticism in Mayan Hieroglyphic Writing. State University of New York, Albany.

Satterthwaite, Linton, and Christopher Jones
1965   Memoranda on the Text of Structure 6F27 at Tikal ("Temple of Inscription," "Temple VI"). Unpublished paper.

Schele, Linda and David Freidel
1990   *A Forest of Kings: The Untold Story of the Ancient Maya*. New York: William Morrow.

Stuart, David
1998   "Fire Enters His House": Architecture and Ritual in Classic Maya Texts. In *Function and Meaning in Classic Maya Architecture,* edited by Stephen D. Houston, pp. 373–425. Washington, DC:

            Dumbarton Oaks Research Library and Collection.
2007   "White Owl Jaguar": A Tikal Royal Ancestor. Maya Decipherment.
            https://decipherment.wordpress.com/2007/11/04/white-owl-jaguar-a-tikal-royal-ancestor/.
2012   Dating Tikal's Mendez Causeway. Maya Decipherment
            https://decipherment.wordpress.com/2012/02/16/dating-tikals-mendez-causeway/.

Taube, Karl
1998   The Jade Hearth. In *Function and Meaning in Classic Maya Architecture*, edited by S.D. Houston,
            pp. 427–78. Washington, DC: Dumbarton Oaks.

Tikal Project
1965 ^{14}C Dates for Tikal Samples, September 10, 1965. Tikal Project Archives, ^{14}C Lab Reports,
            Philadelphia: University of Pennsylvania Museum of Archaeology and Anthropology.

Tozzer, Alfred M.
1911   *Preliminary Study of the Ruins of Tikal, Guatemala*. Memoirs of the Peabody Museum of
            Archaeology and Ethnology vol.5 no. 2 . Cambridge, MA: Peabody Museum of Archaeology and
            Ethnology, Harvard University.

Tikal Reports (see TR. 12):

TR. 6:
Coe, William R., Edwin M. Shook, and Linton Satterthwaite
1986   The Carved Wooden Lintels of Tikal. In *Tikal Reports 1–11*, edited by E.M. Shook, W.R. Coe,
            V.L. Broman, and L. Satterthwaite, pp. 17–46. Facsimile Reissue of Original Reports Published
            1958–1961. Philadelphia: The University of Pennsylvania Museum of Archaeology and
            Anthropology.

TR. 11:
Carr, Robert F., and James E. Hazard
1961   Map of the Ruins of Tikal, El Peten, Guatemala. In *Tikal Reports 1–11*, edited by E.M. Shook,
            W.R. Coe, V.L. Broman, and L. Satterthwaite, pp. iii–26. Facsimile Reissue of 1986 of Original
            Reports Published 1958–1961. Philadelphia: The University of Pennsylvania Museum of
            Archaeology and Anthropology.

TR. 12:
Coe, William R., and William A. Haviland
1982   *Introduction to the Archaeology of Tikal, Guatemala. The University Museum*. Philadelphia: The
            University of Pennsylvania Museum of Archaeology and Anthropology.

TR. 14:
Coe, William R.
1990   *Excavations in the Great Plaza, North Terrace and North Acropolis of Tikal*, vols. 1–4. Philadelphia:
            The University of Pennsylvania Museum of Archaeology and Anthropology.

TR. 20A:
Haviland, William A.
2014   *Excavations in Residential Areas of Tikal: Non-elite Groups without Shrines: The Excavations*.
            Philadelphia: University of Pennsylvania Museum of Archaeology and Anthropology.

TR. 23A:
Loten, H. Stanley
2002   *Miscellaneous Investigations in Central Tikal.* Philadelphia: University of Pennsylvania Museum of
        Archaeology and Anthropology.

TR. 23C:
Loten, H. Stanley
n.d.   *Miscellaneous Investigations in Central Tikal: Structures 5D-91 to 5D-99.* Philadelphia:
        University of Pennsylvania Museum of Archaeology and Anthropology.

TR. 23D:
Loten, H. Stanley
n.d.   *Miscellaneous Investigations in Central Tikal: Structures* 5C-49, 5D-77, 5D-84, 5D-86,
        5D-87, and 6D-1. Philadelphia: University of Pennsylvania Museum of Archaeology and
        Anthropology.

TR. 25A:
Culbert, T. Patrick
1993   *The Ceramics of Tikal: Vessels from the Burials, Caches and Problematical Deposits.* Philadelphia:
        The University of Pennsylvania Museum of Archaeology and Anthropology.

TR. 27A:
Moholy-Nagy, Hattula, with William R. Coe
2008   *The Artifacts of Tikal: Ornamental and Ceremonial Artifacts and Unworked Material. Part A.*
        Philadelphia: University of Pennsylvania Museum of Archaeology and Anthropology.

TR. 27B:
Moholy-Nagy, Hattula
2002   *The Artifacts of Tikal: Utilitarian Artifacts and Unworked Material. Part B.* Philadelphia: University
        of Pennsylvania Museum of Archaeology and Anthropology.

TR. 33A:
Jones, Christopher, and Linton Satterthwaite
1982   *The Monuments and Inscriptions of Tikal: The Carved Monuments.* Philadelphia: The University
        of Pennsylvania Museum of Archaeology and Anthropology.

TR. 34B:
Loten, H. Stanley
n.d.   *The Architecture of Tikal, Guatemala.* Philadelphia: The University of Pennsylvania Museum of
        Archaeology and Anthropology.

Illustrations

FIGURE 1

a

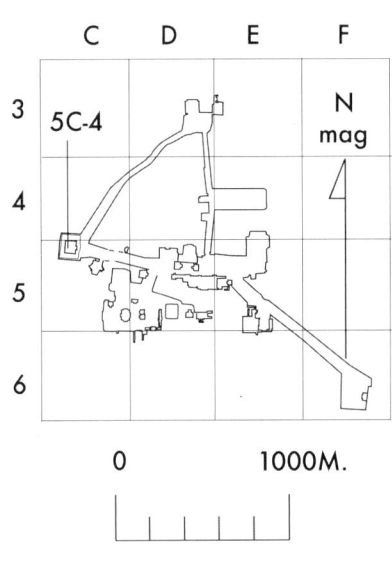

b

Str. 5C-4 Location.
a. View from doorway of Str. 5D-1 looking W. *b*. Location map after TR. 11 (scale 1:40,000).

FIGURE 2

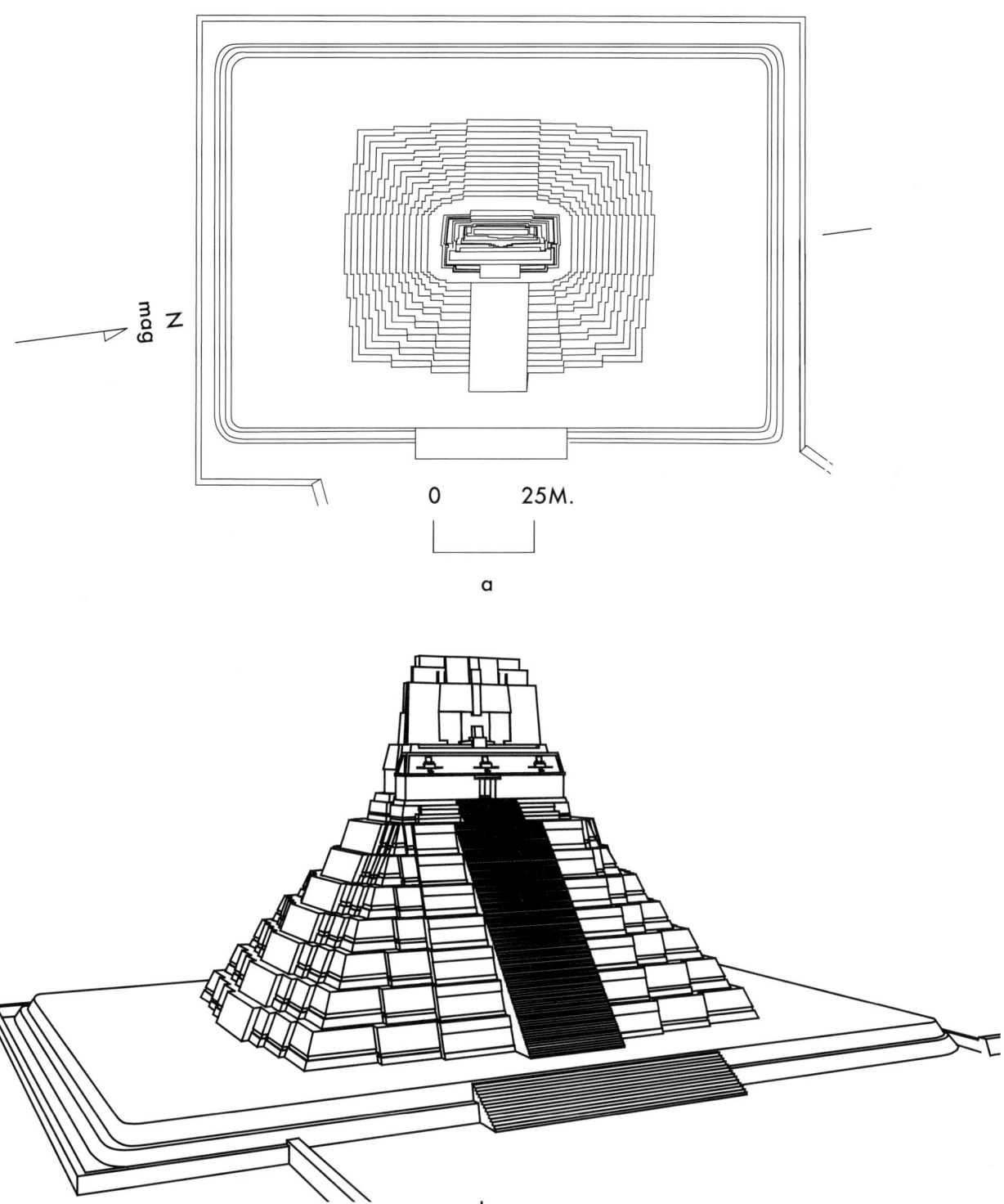

Str. 5C-4 Precinct.
a. Plan (scale 1:1,500). *b*. Perspective reconstruction view from SE (not to scale). Basal platform and precinct wall details estimated.

FIGURE 3

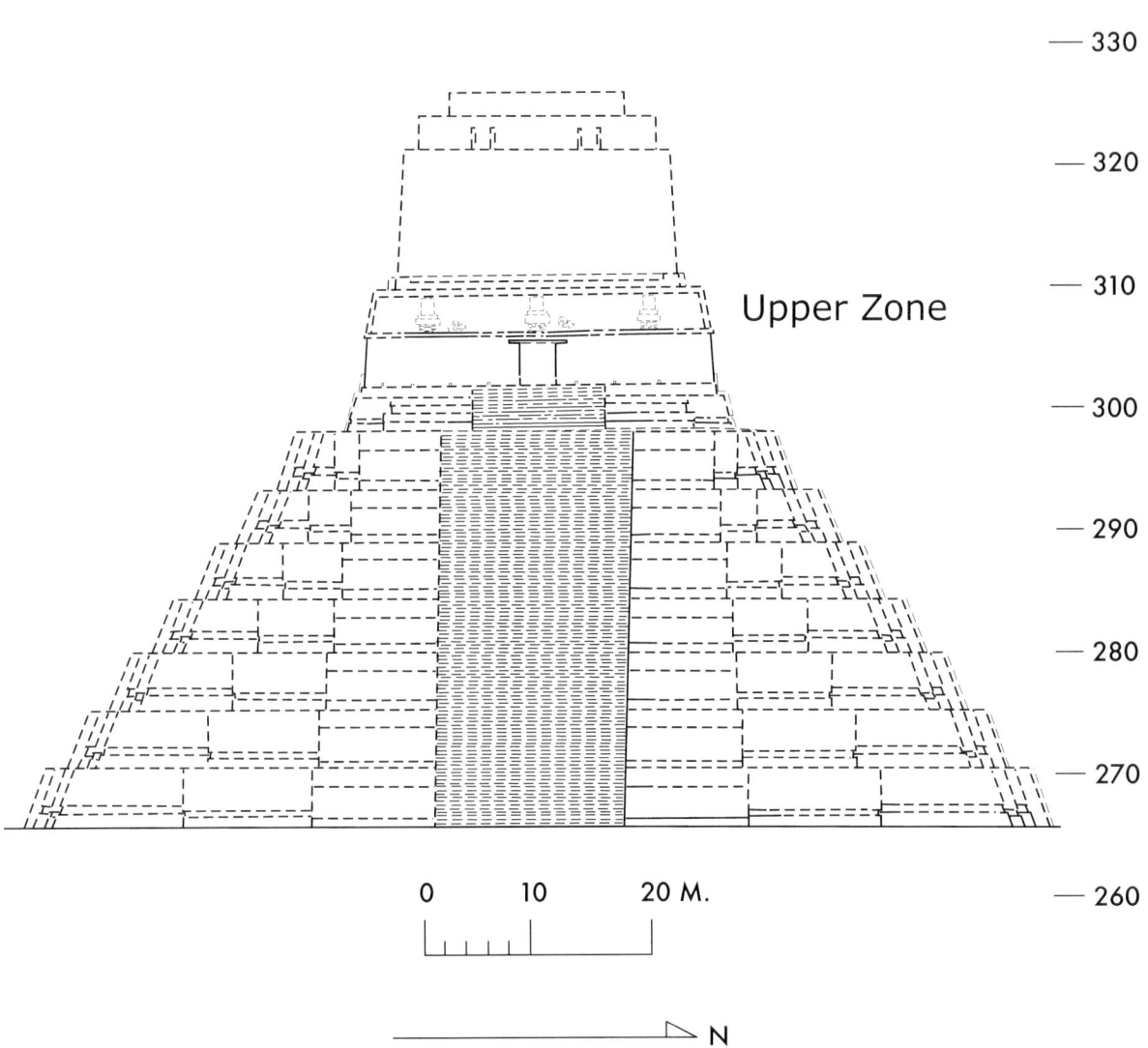

— 330

— 320

— 310

Upper Zone

— 300

— 290

— 280

— 270

0   10   20 M.

— 260

N

Str. 5C-4 Front Elevation (scale 1:600).

FIGURE 4

Str. 5C-4 Aerial View Looking SW.

FIGURE 5

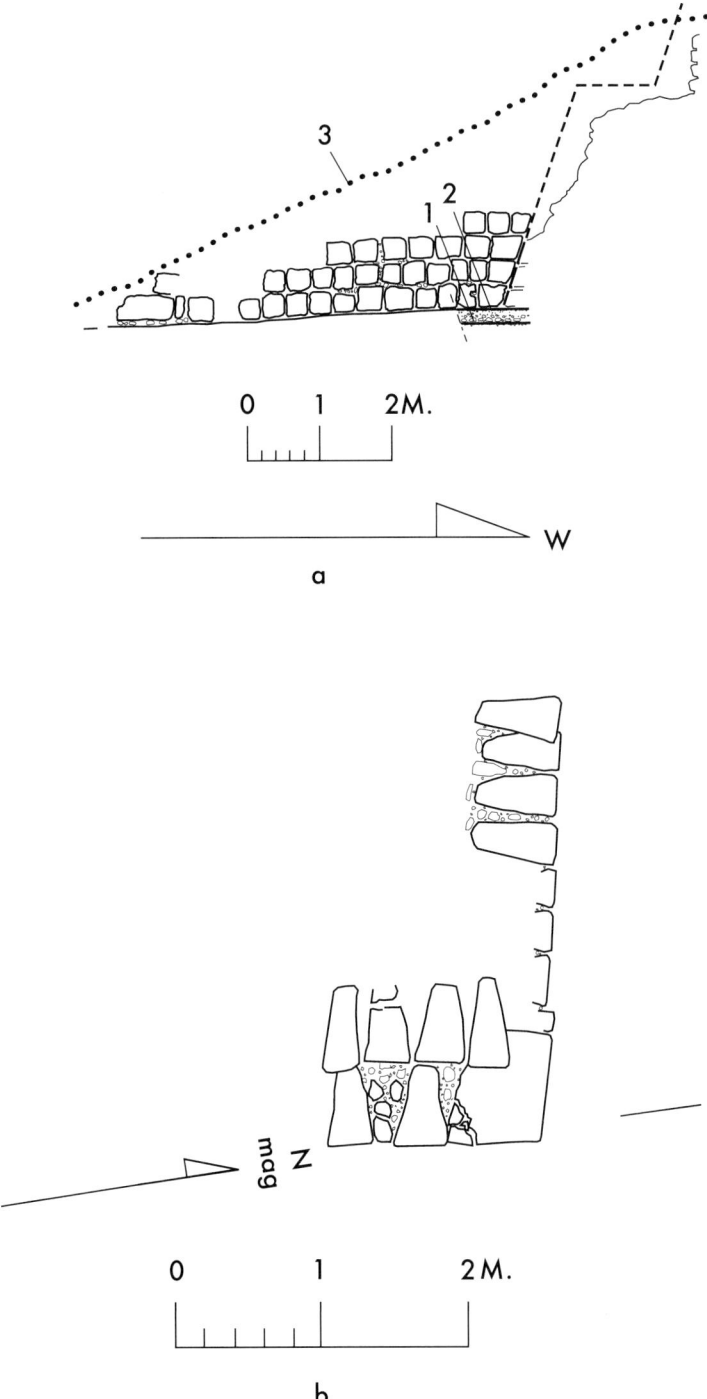

Str. 5C-4 Basal Platform Details.
a. Stair side. *1*, Hard floor. *2*, Hard floor. *3*, Debris line (scale 1:100). *b.* Stair masonry (scale 1:50).

FIGURE 6

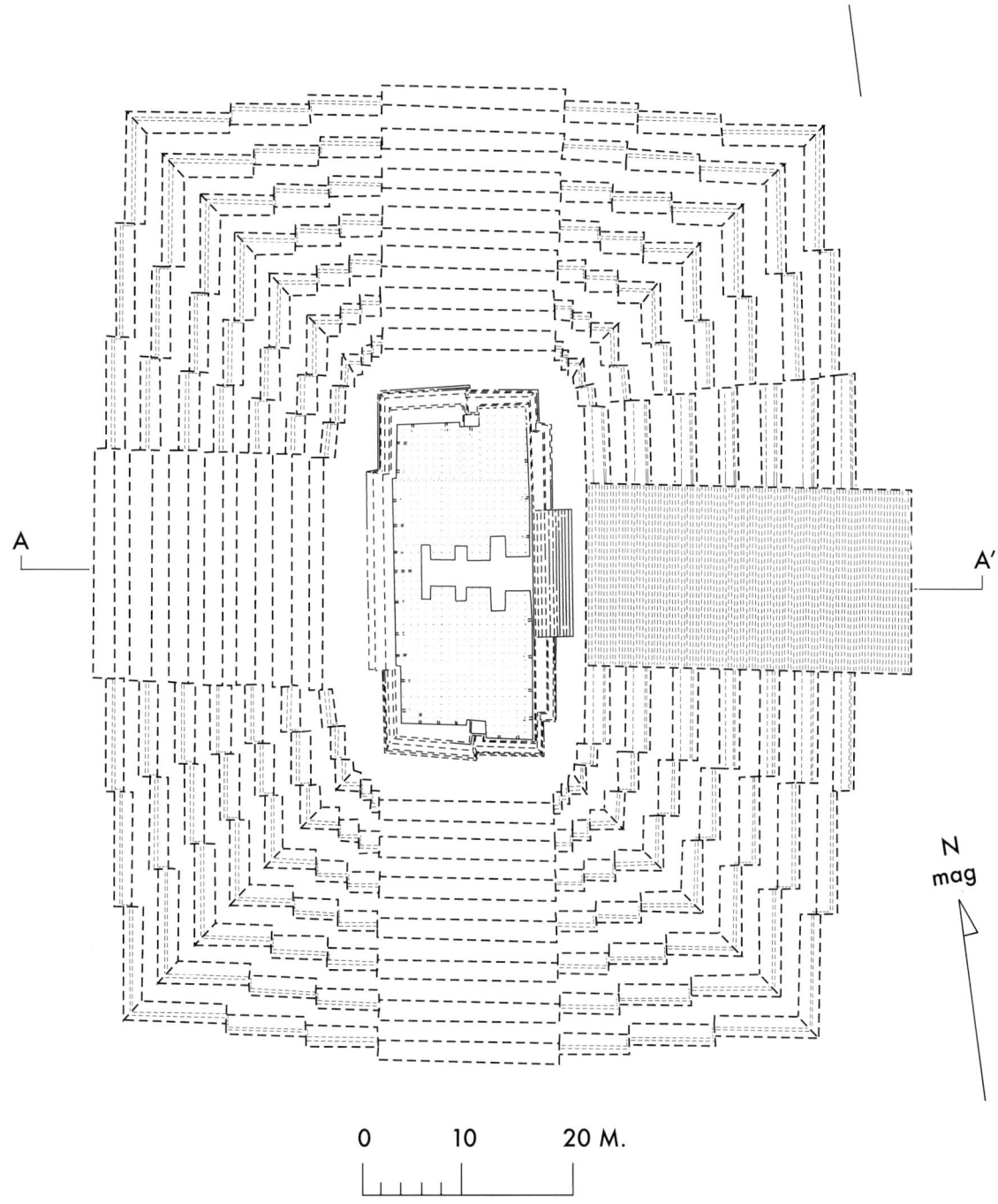

Str. 5C-4 Plan (scale 1:600).

FIGURE 7

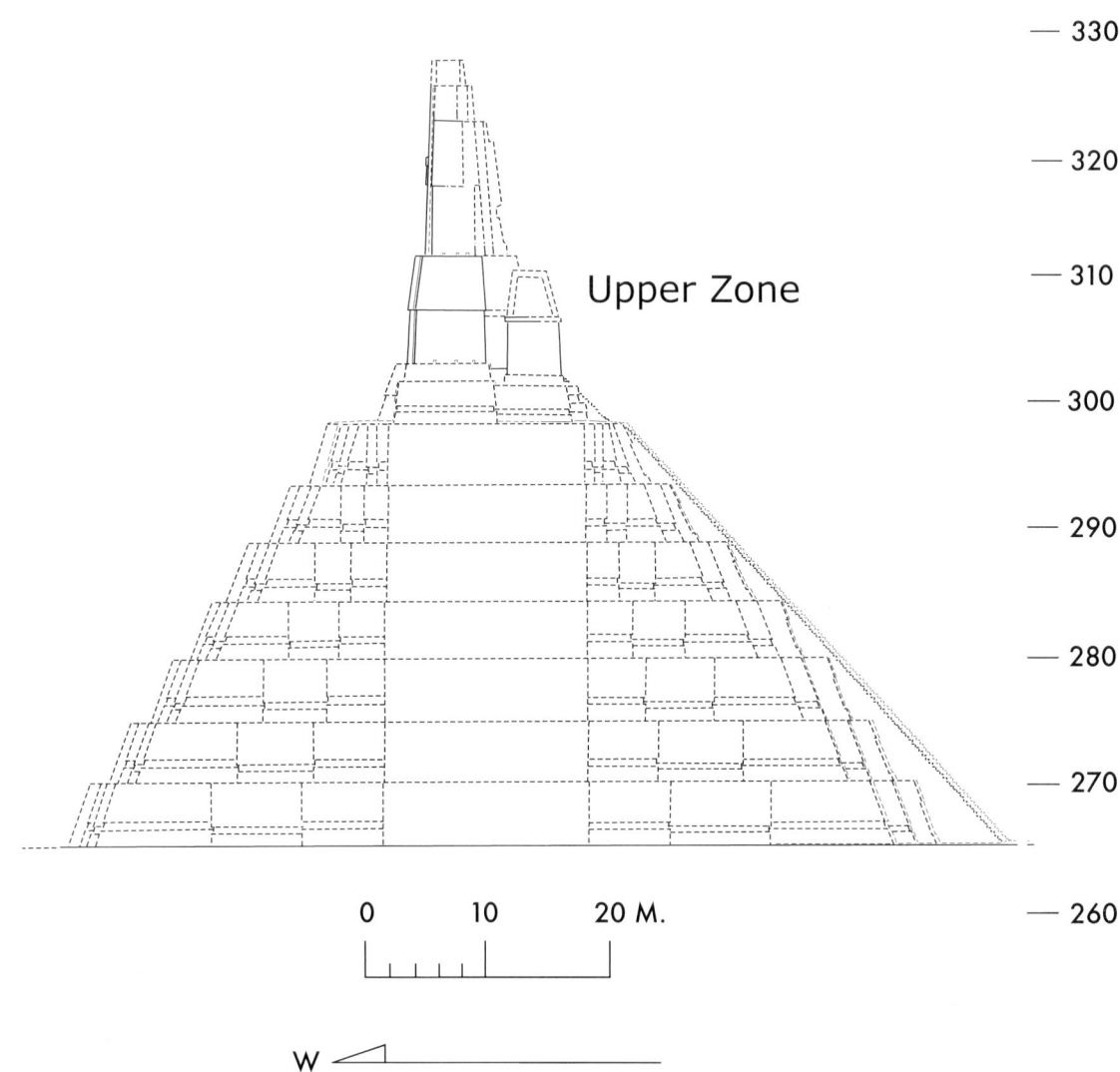

— 330

— 320

— 310

Upper Zone

— 300

— 290

— 280

— 270

0   10   20 M.

— 260

W

Str. 5C-4 S Elevation (scale 1:600).

FIGURE 8

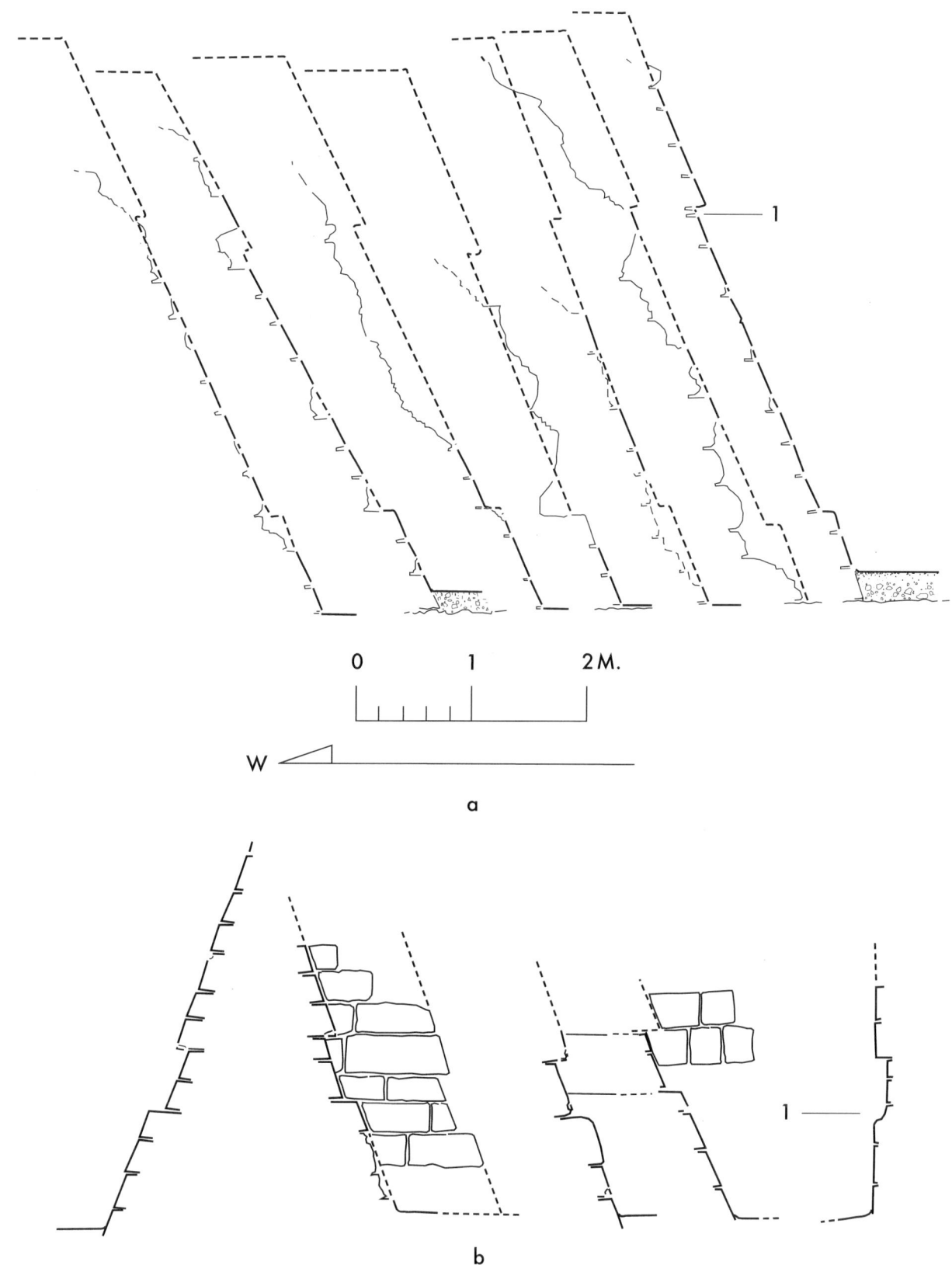

Str. 5C-4 Pyramid Profiles (scale 1:50).
a. Stair-side profiles. *1*, Leveling course. *b*. Terrace profiles. *1*, Molding cut below course level.

FIGURE 9

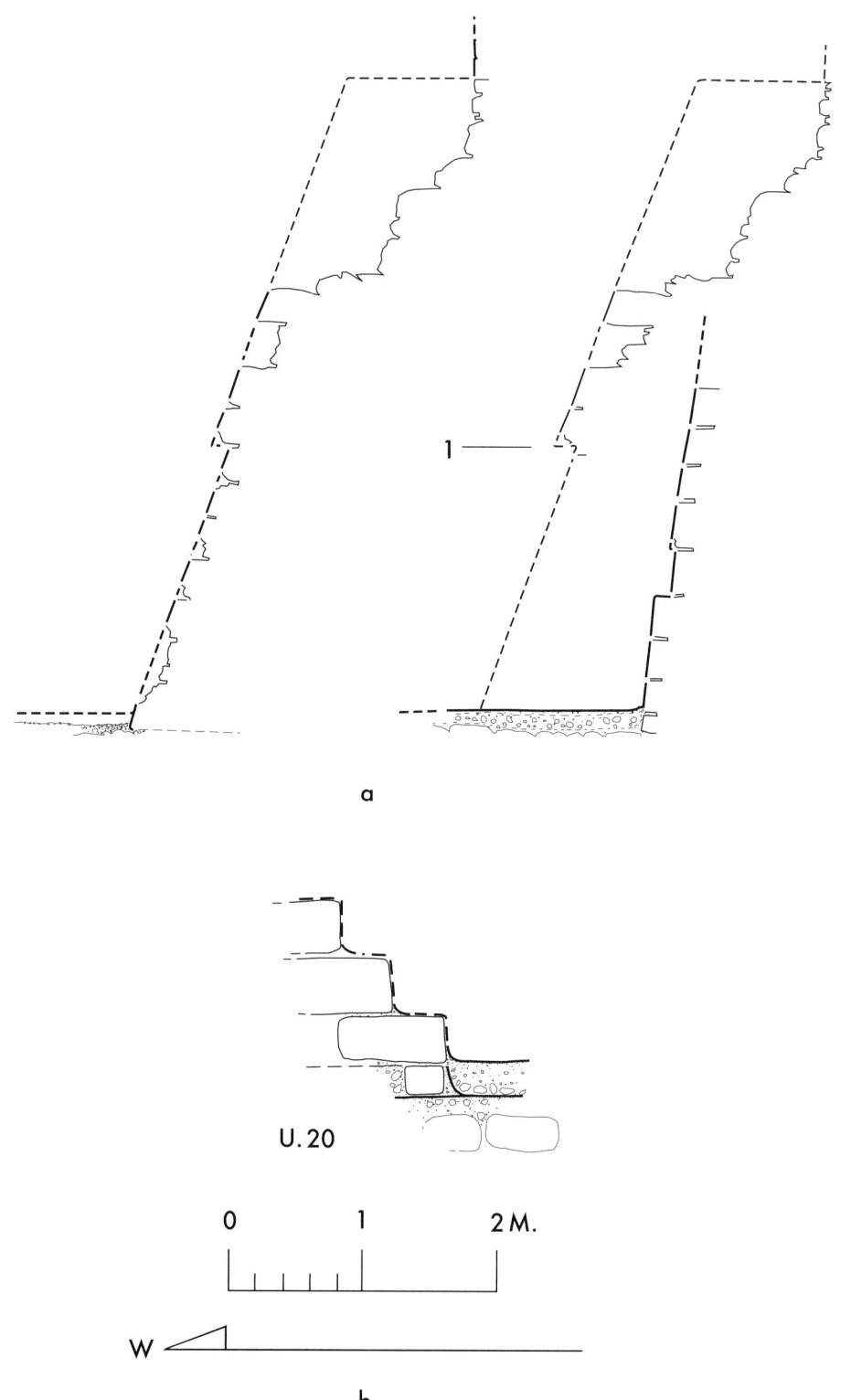

Str. 5C-4 Substructure Details (scale 1:50).
a. Rear axial outset profiles. *1*, Apron outset cut above course level. *b*. U. 20.

FIGURE 10

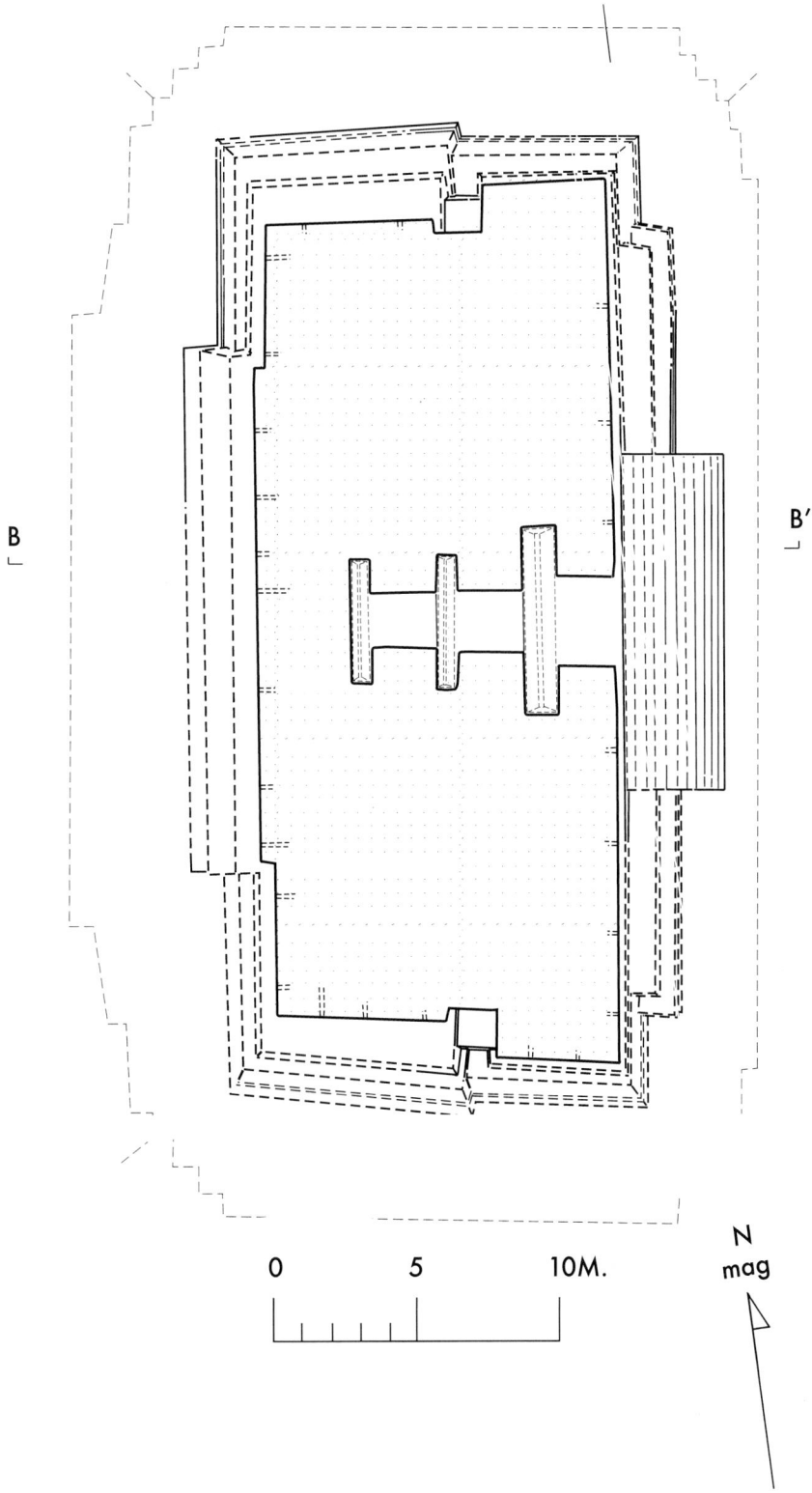

B

B'

0   5   10M.

N
mag

Str. 5C-4 Building Plan (scale 1:250).

FIGURE 11

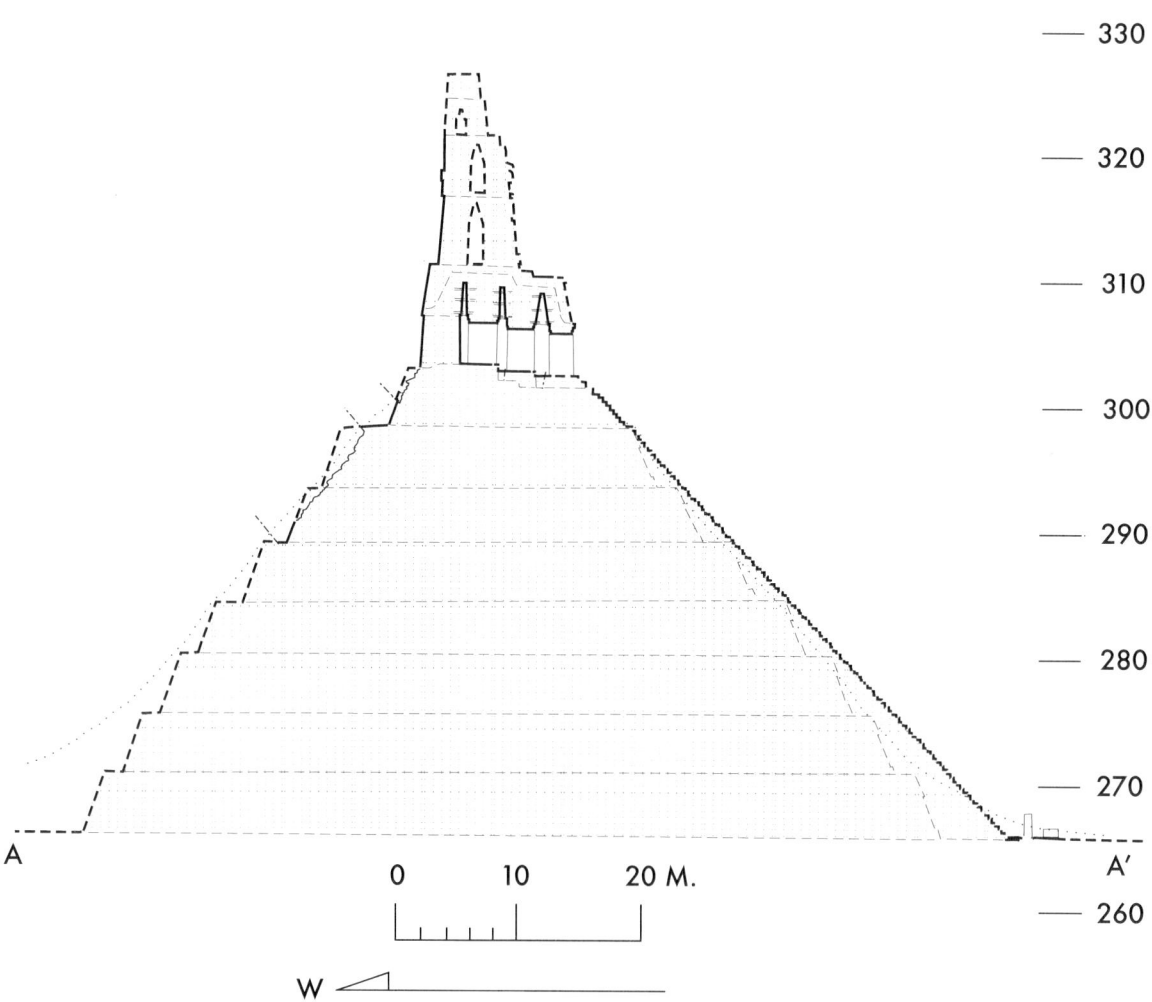

— 330

— 320

— 310

— 300

— 290

— 280

— 270

A   A′

0   10   20 M.

— 260

W

Str. 5C-4 Section A-A' (scale 1:600).

FIGURE 12

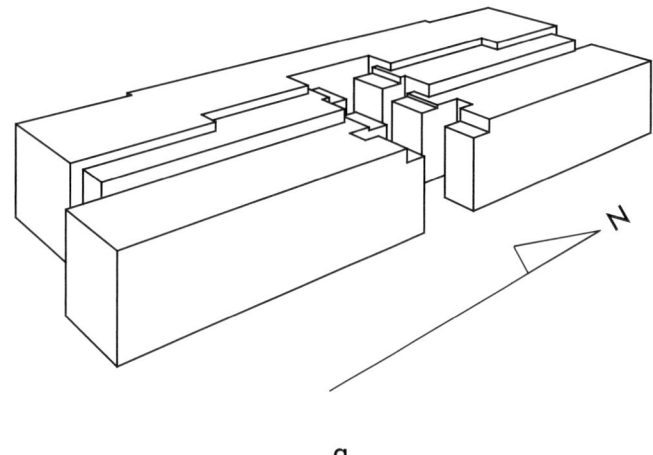

a

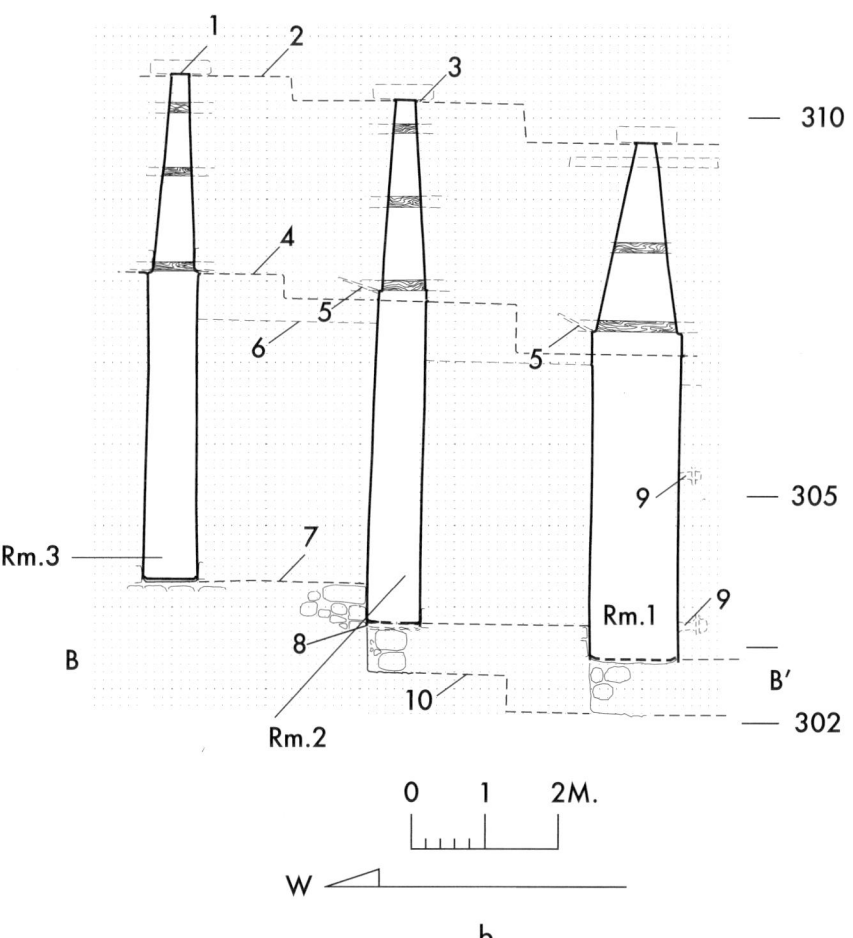

b

Str. 5C-4 Building Wall Data.
a. Wall schematic. *b*. Section B-B' (scale 1:100). *1*, Preplastered capstone. *2*, Estimated line of vault mass. *3*, Soffit plaster turns under capstone. *4*, Estimated line of wall top. *5*, Rod row socket. *6*, Level of lintel bed. *7*, Level of floor at centerline. *8*, Wall footing (subwall). *9*, Cord holder. *10*, Estimated line of Building Platform top surface (a rough level).

FIGURE 13

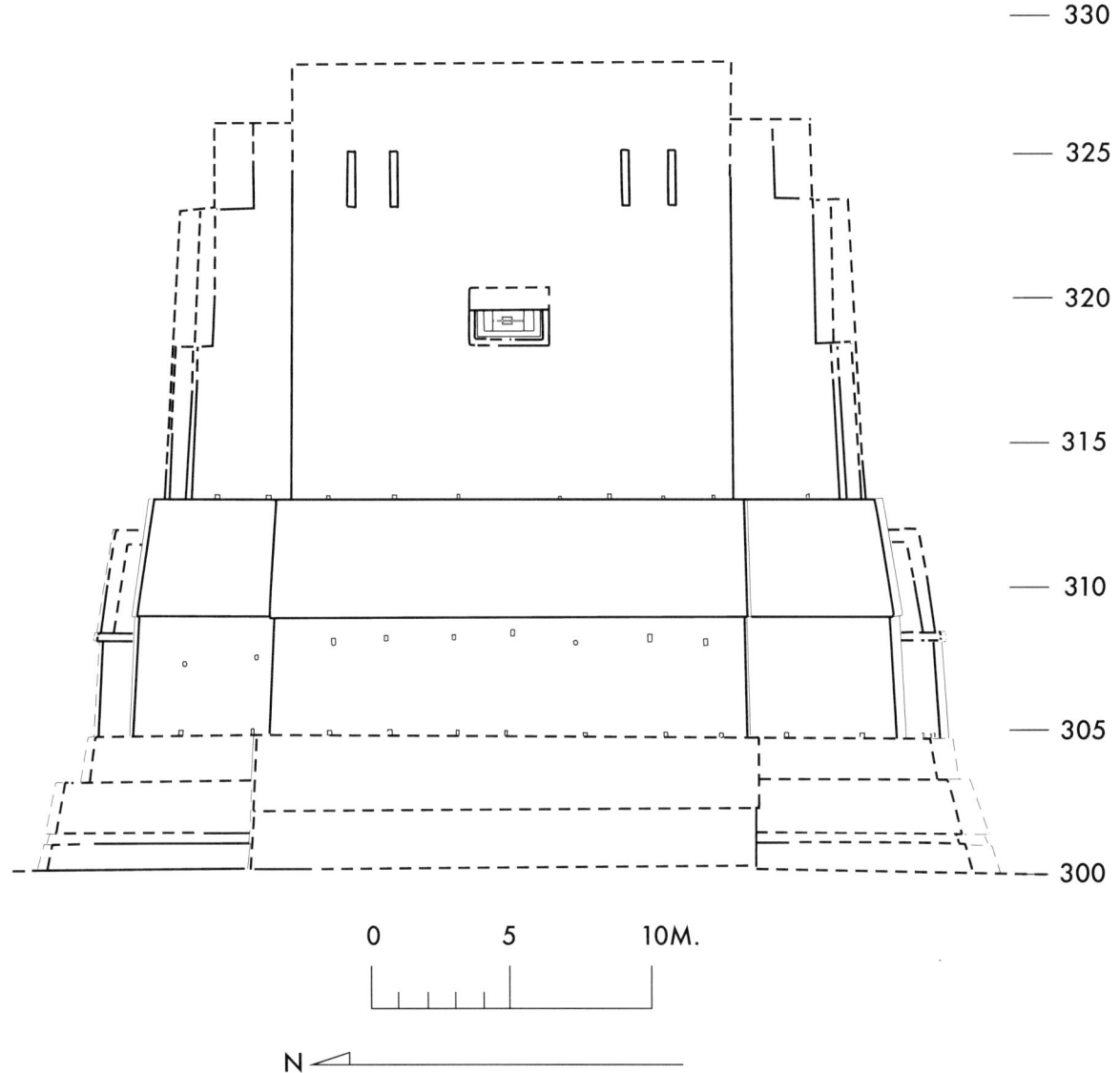

— 330

— 325

— 320

— 315

— 310

— 305

— 300

0 5 10M.

N

Str. 5C-4 Rear Elevation of Superstructure (scale 1:250).

FIGURE 13a

Str. 5C-4 Lintel 2. Courtesy of the Penn Museum; Tikal Project image 69-5-98.

FIGURE 13b

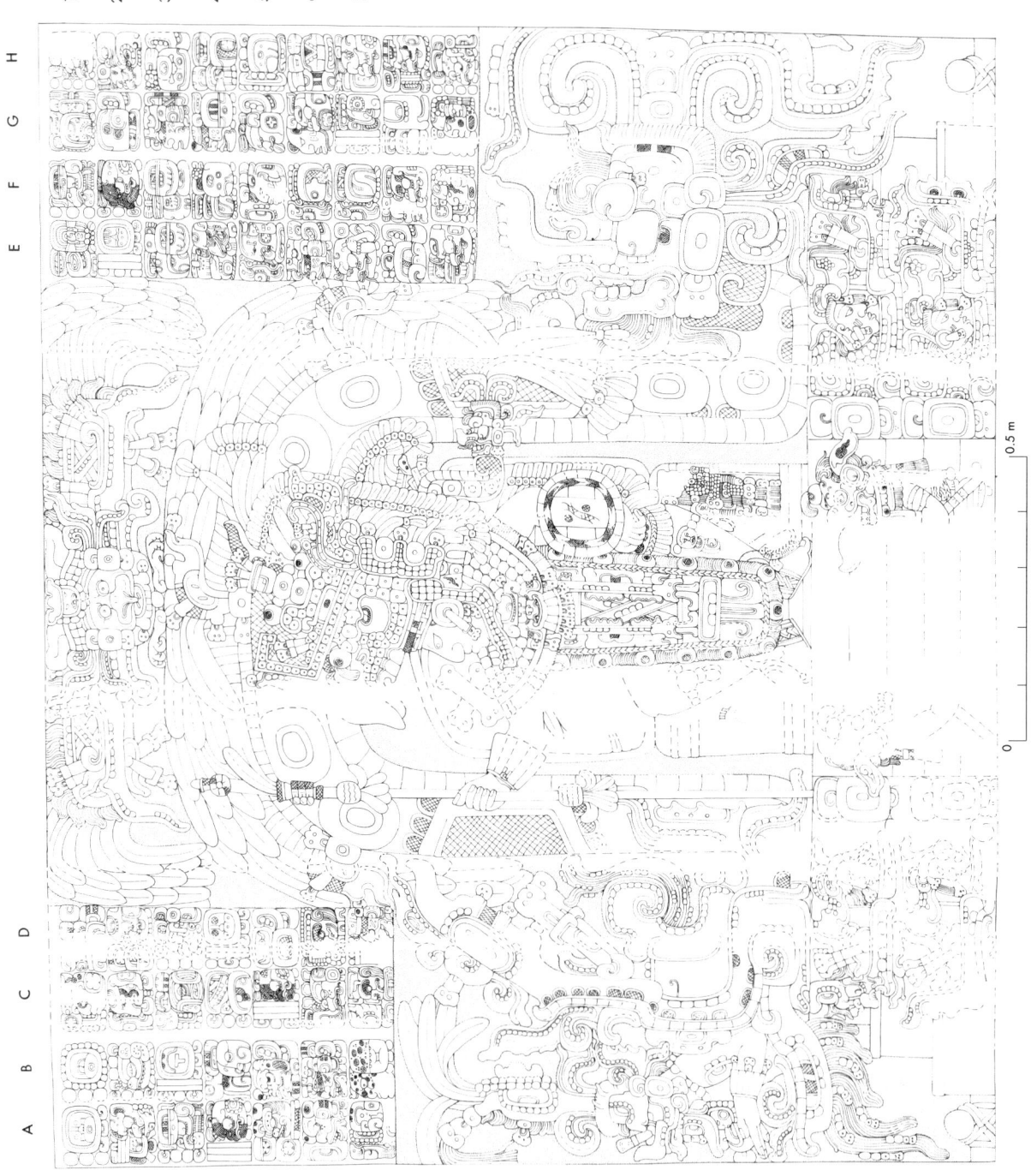

Str. 5C-4 Lintel 3. Courtesy of the Penn Museum; Tikal Project image 69-5-99.

FIGURE 14

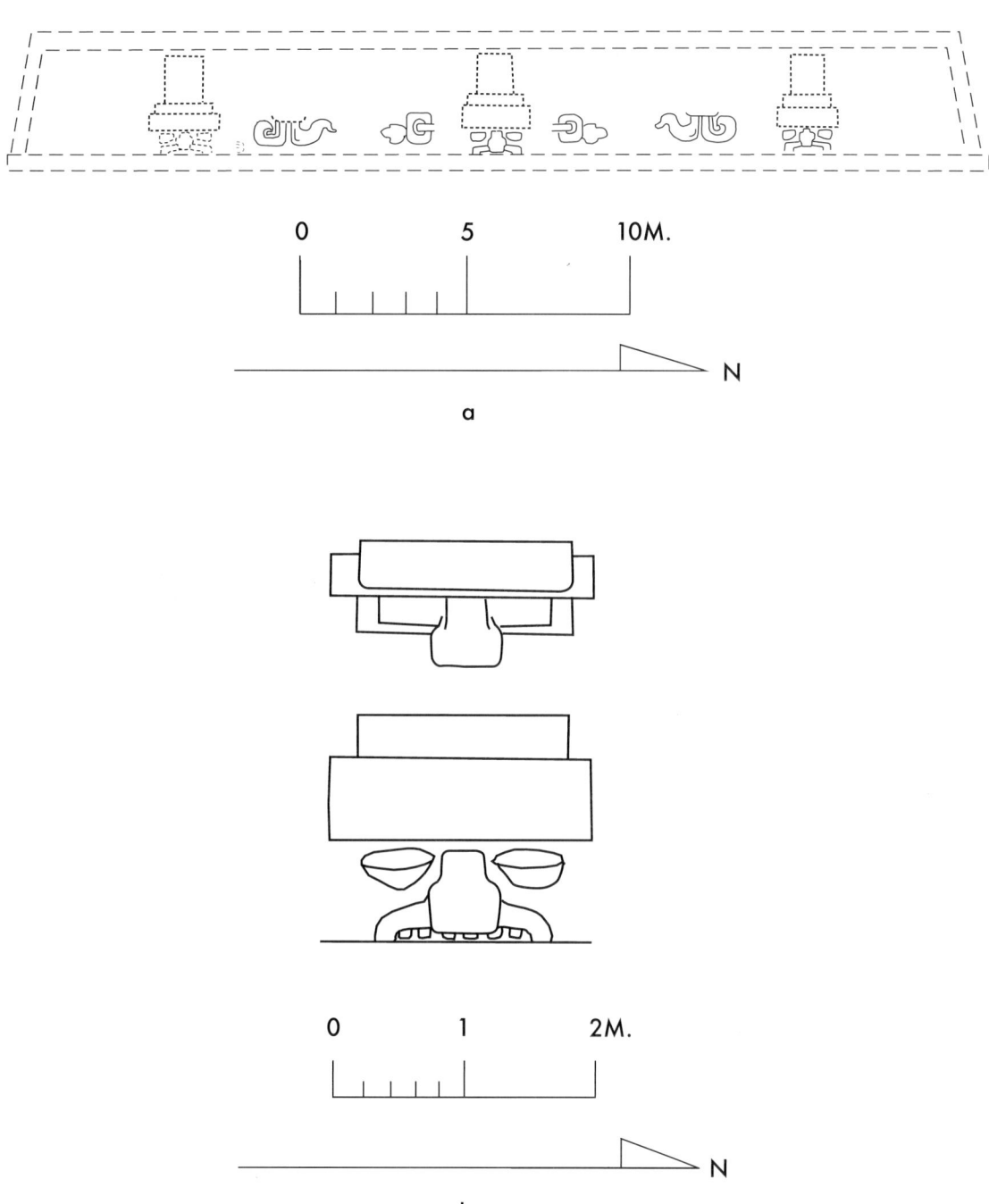

Str. 5C-4 Upper-Zone Details.
a. Sculpture locations on E facade (scale 1:200). *b*. Typical mask diagram (scale 1:50).

FIGURE 15

Str. 5C-4 View from Str. 5D-3.

FIGURE 16

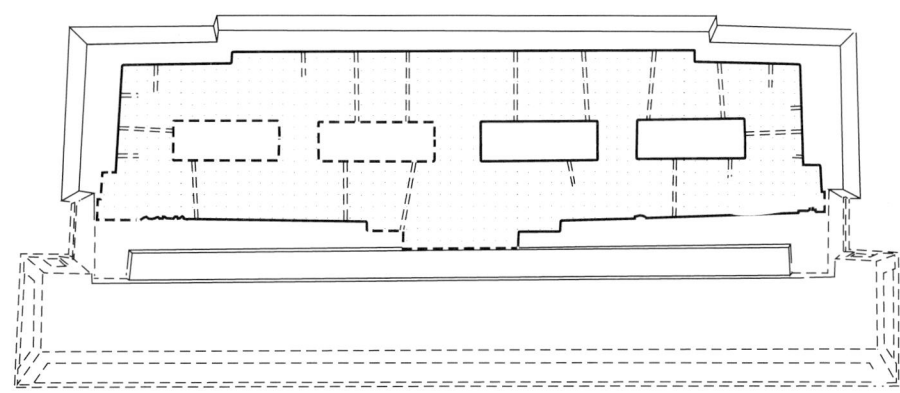

a

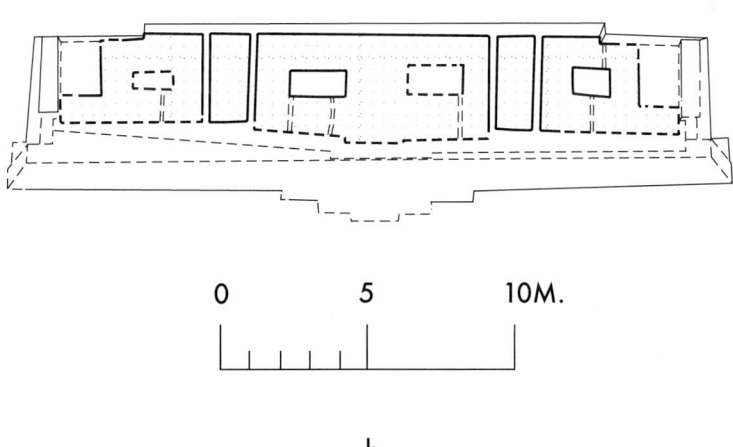

b

Str. 5C-4 Roofcomb Chambers (scale 1:250).
a. Plan at lower level. *b*. Plan at upper level.

FIGURE 17

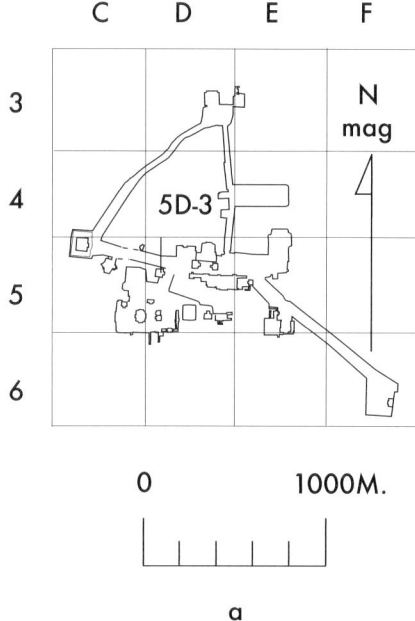

a

b

Str. 5D-3 Location.

a. Location map after TR. 11 (scale 1:40,000). *b.* Maler photograph taken in the 1890s showing 5D-2 in foreground, 5D-3 to left, 5C-4 to right.

FIGURE 18

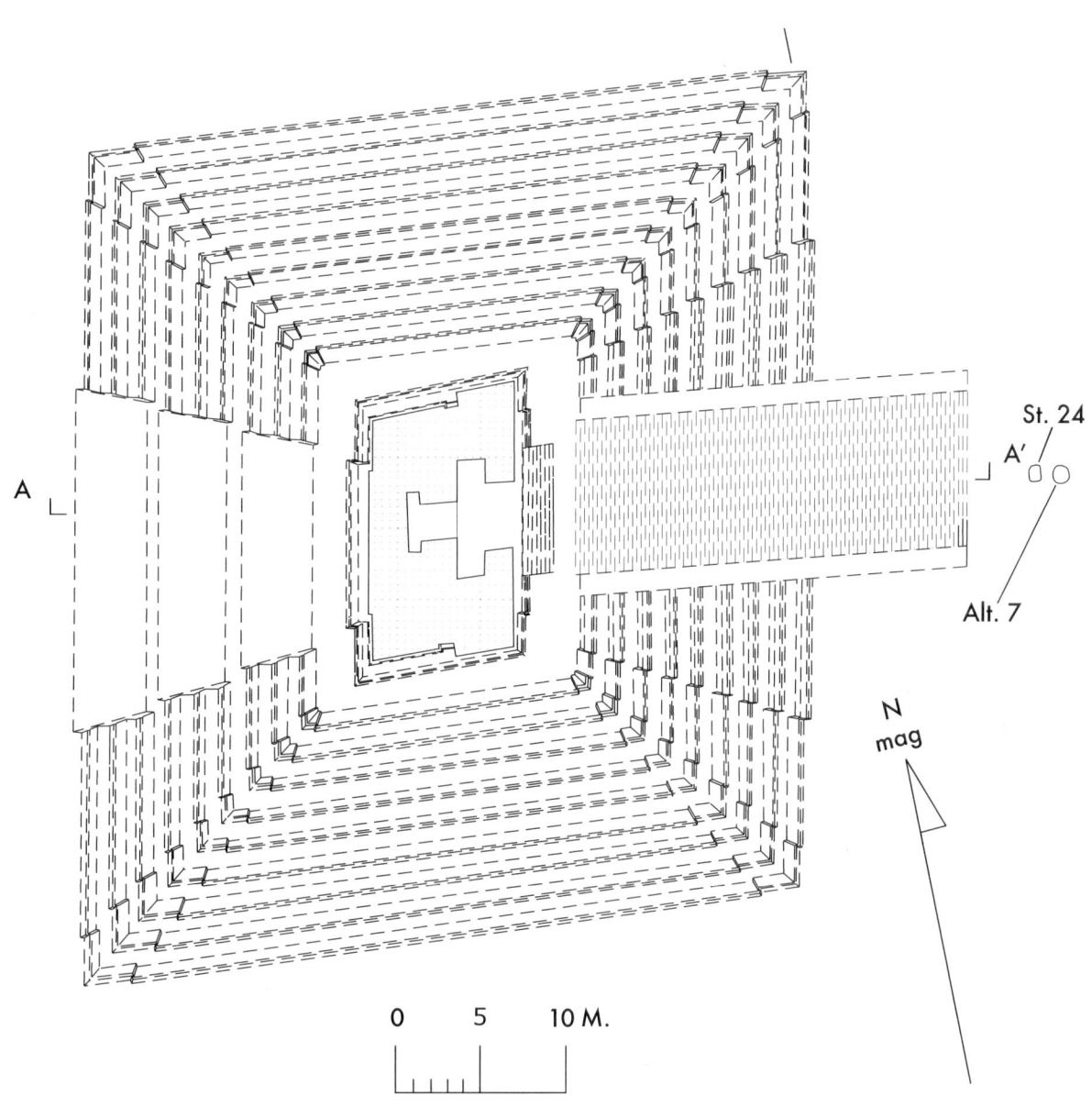

St. 24

A′

Alt. 7

A

N
mag

0   5   10 M.

Str. 5D-3 Plan (scale 1:400).

FIGURE 19

Str. 5D-3 in Maler Photograph taken in the 1890s. Looking NW.

FIGURE 20

A B E F C D

1
2
3
4
5
6
7
8
9
10
11
12
13
14
15
16
17
18
19

0   0.5 m

Str. 5D-3 Lintel 2. Drawing by Coe 1967. Courtesy of the Penn Museum; Tikal Project image 69-5-195.

FIGURE 21

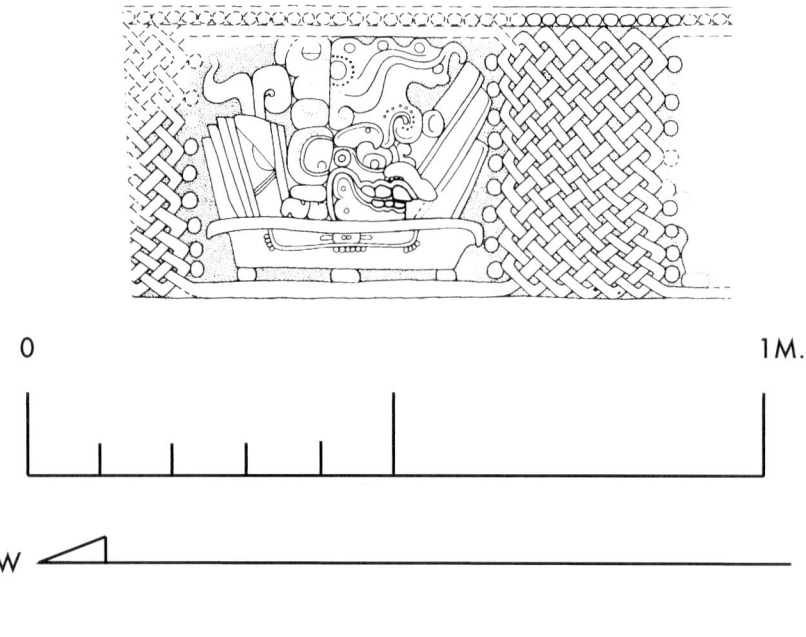

0   1M.

a

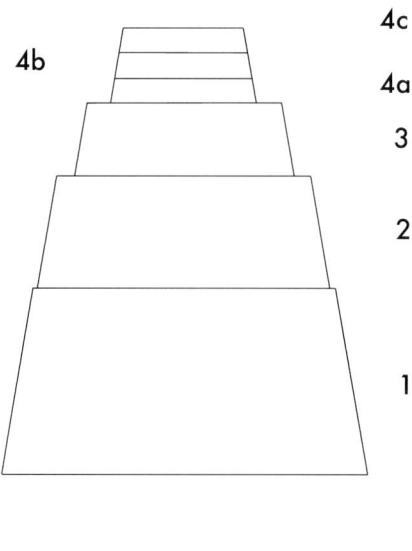

b

Str. 5D-3 Details.
a. Image on Alt. 7. Drawing by Coe (TR. 12:fig. 40b; scale 1:20). *b*. Construction-stage diagram (not to scale). *1*, Lower substructure. *2*, Building platform and
building walls. *3*, Vaults and upper zones. *4a*. First roofcomb stage. *4b*. Second
roofcomb stage. *4c*. Third roofcomb stage.

FIGURE 22

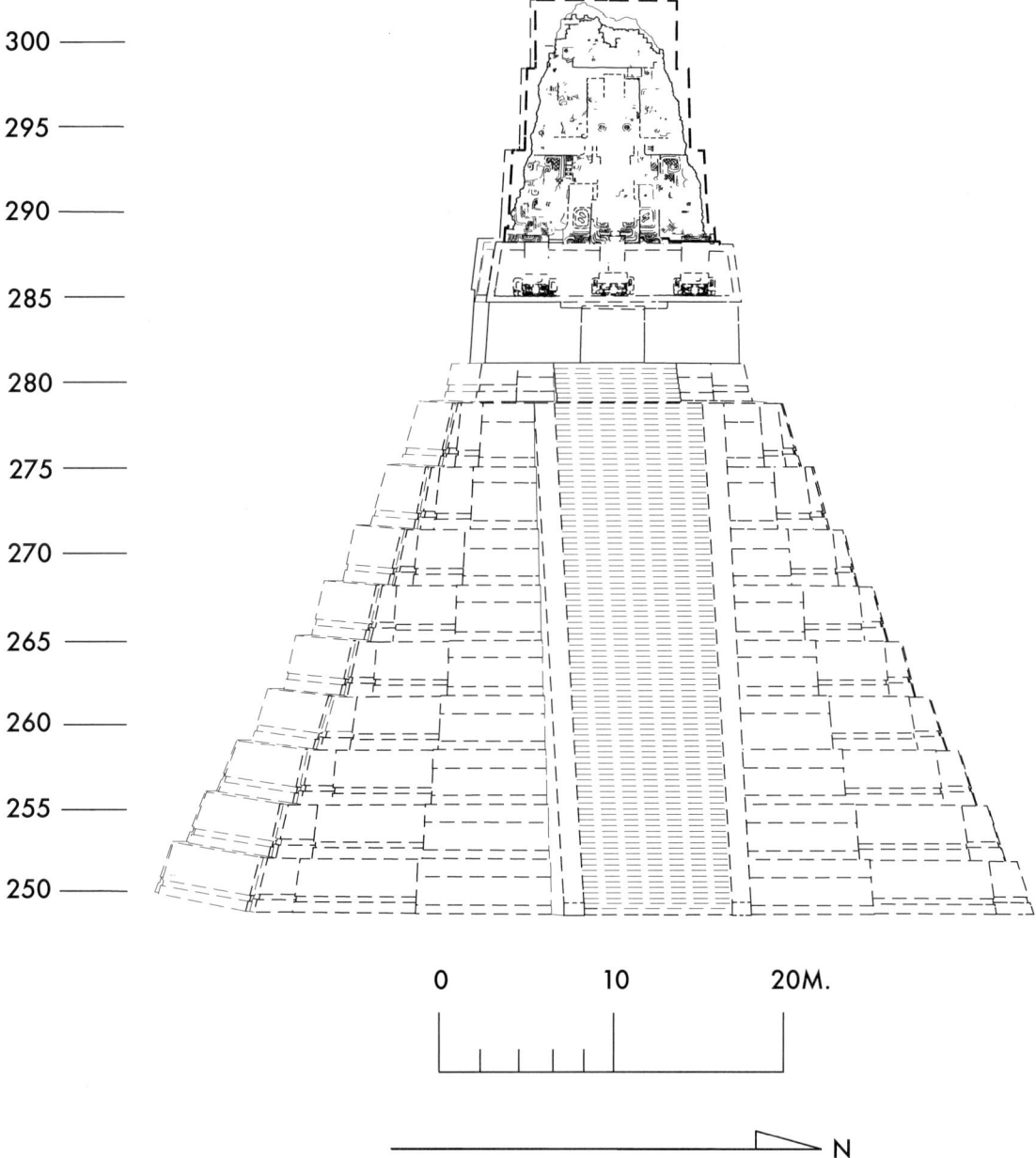

300 —

295 —

290 —

285 —

280 —

275 —

270 —

265 —

260 —

255 —

250 —

0   10   20M.

N

Str. 5D-3 E (Front) Elevation (scale 1:400).

FIGURE 23

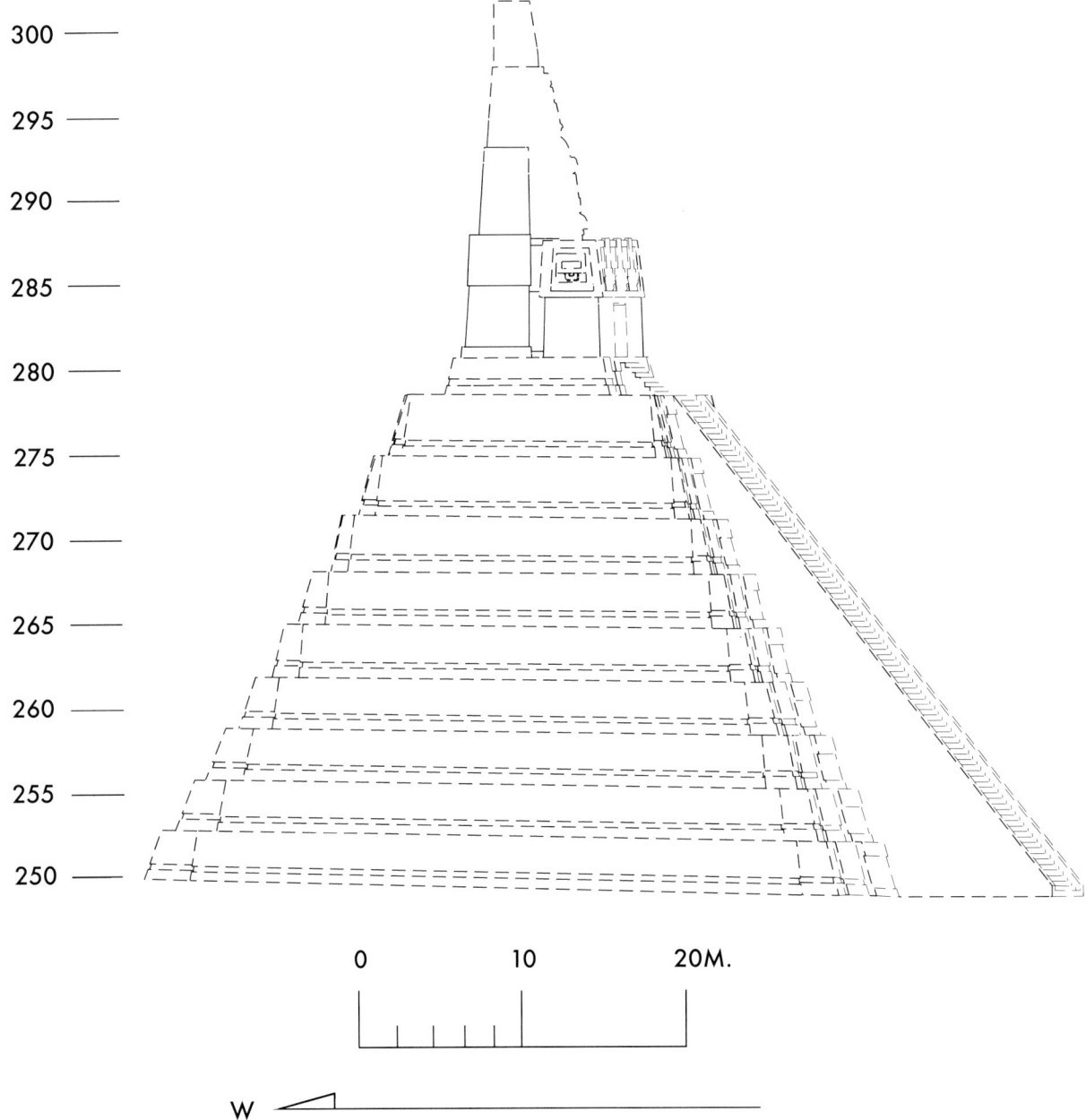

Str. 5D-3 S (Left Side) Elevation (scale 1:400).

FIGURE 24

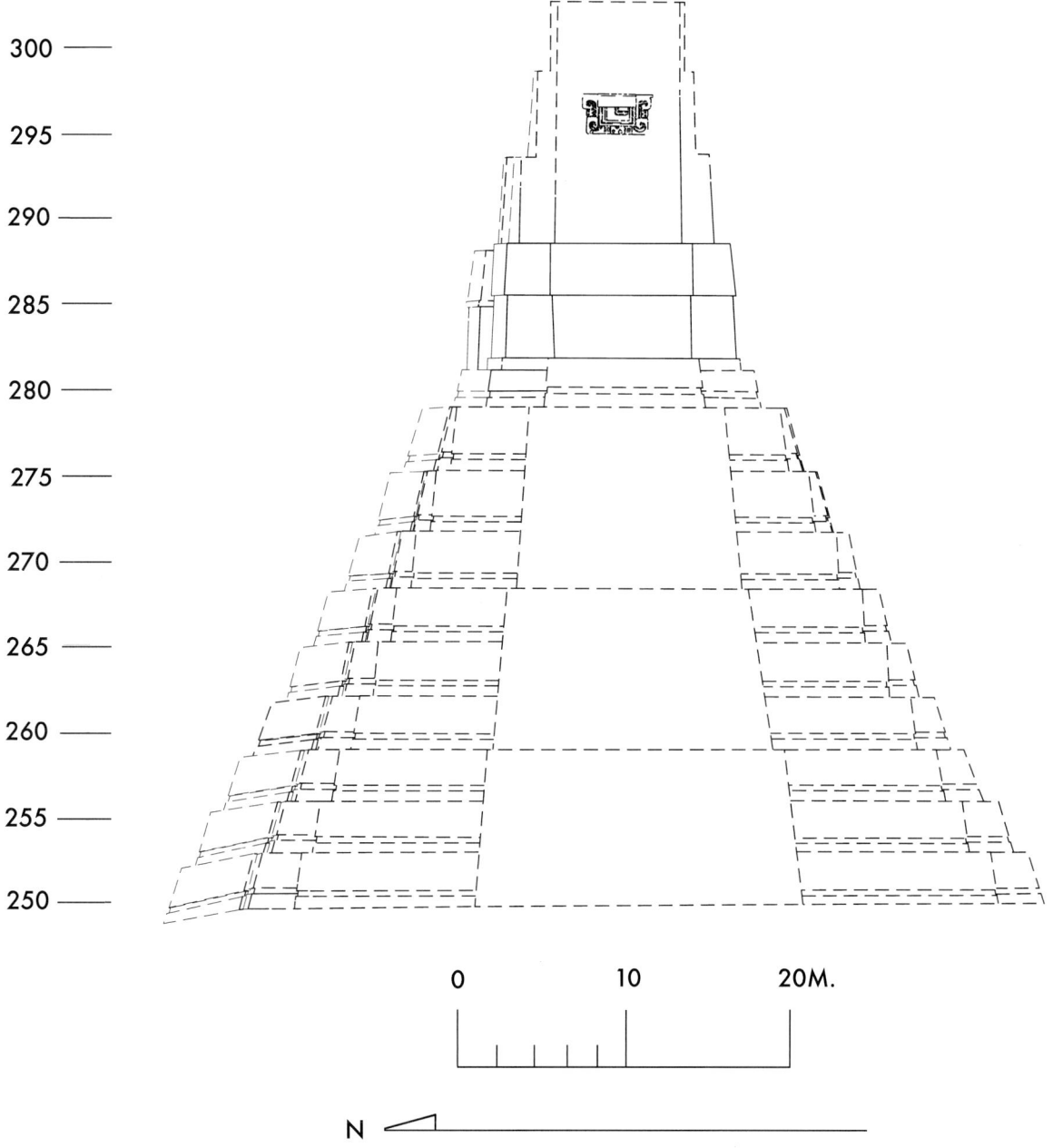

300 —

295 —

290 —

285 —

280 —

275 —

270 —

265 —

260 —

255 —

250 —

0   10   20M.

N

Str. 5D-3 W (Rear) Elevation (scale 1:400).

FIGURE 25

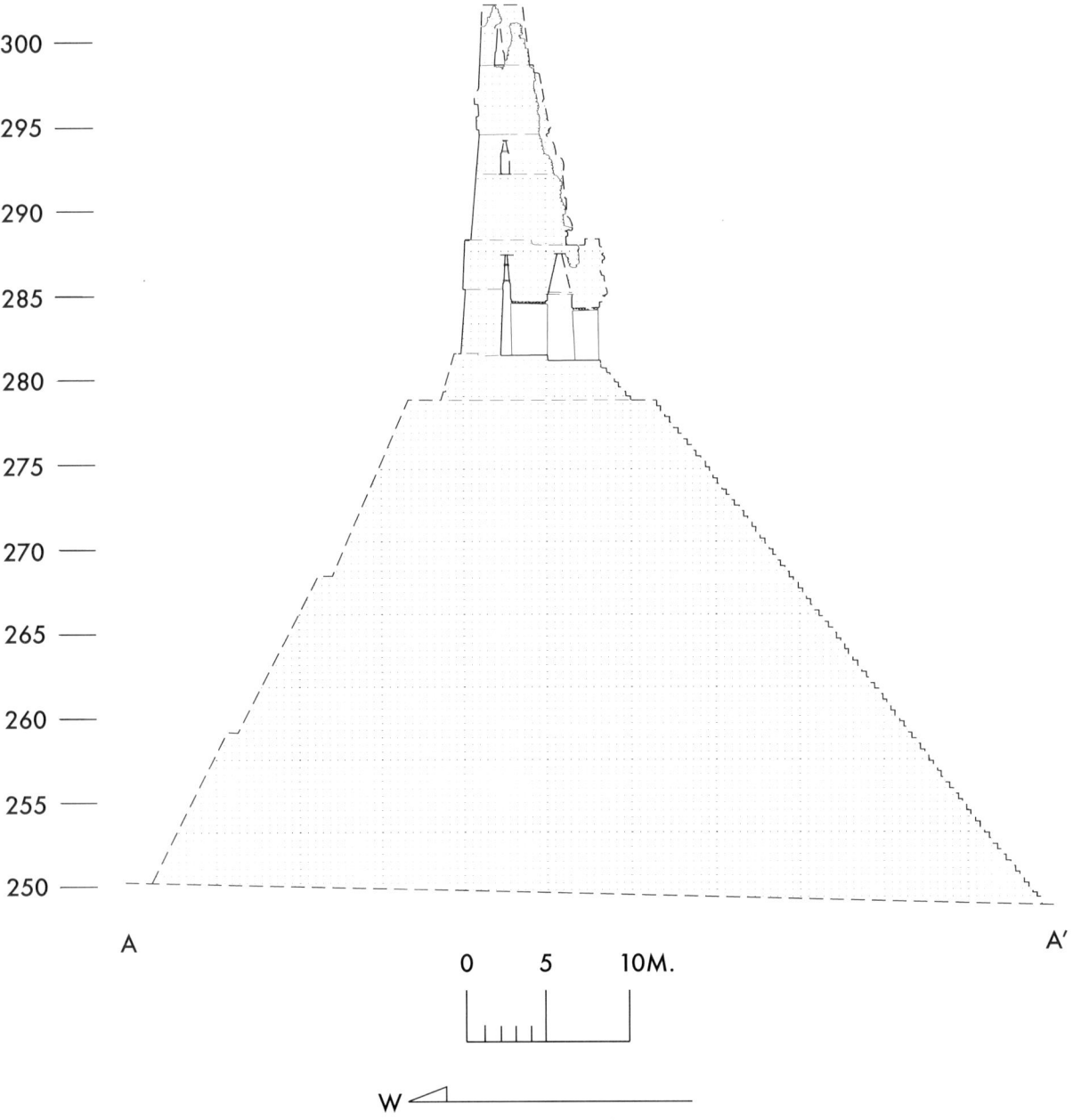

Str. 5D-3 Section/Profile A-A' (scale 1:400).

FIGURE 26

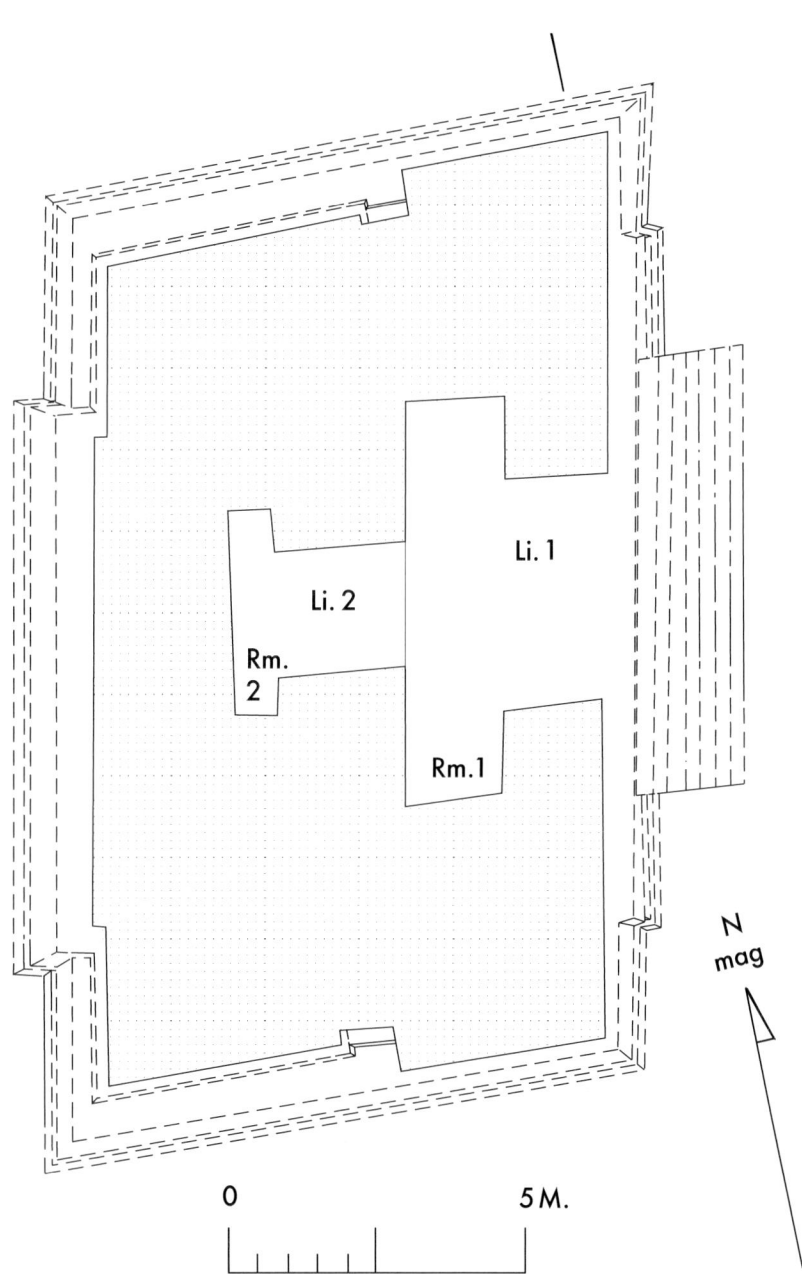

Str. 5D-3 Building Plan (scale 1:125).

FIGURE 27

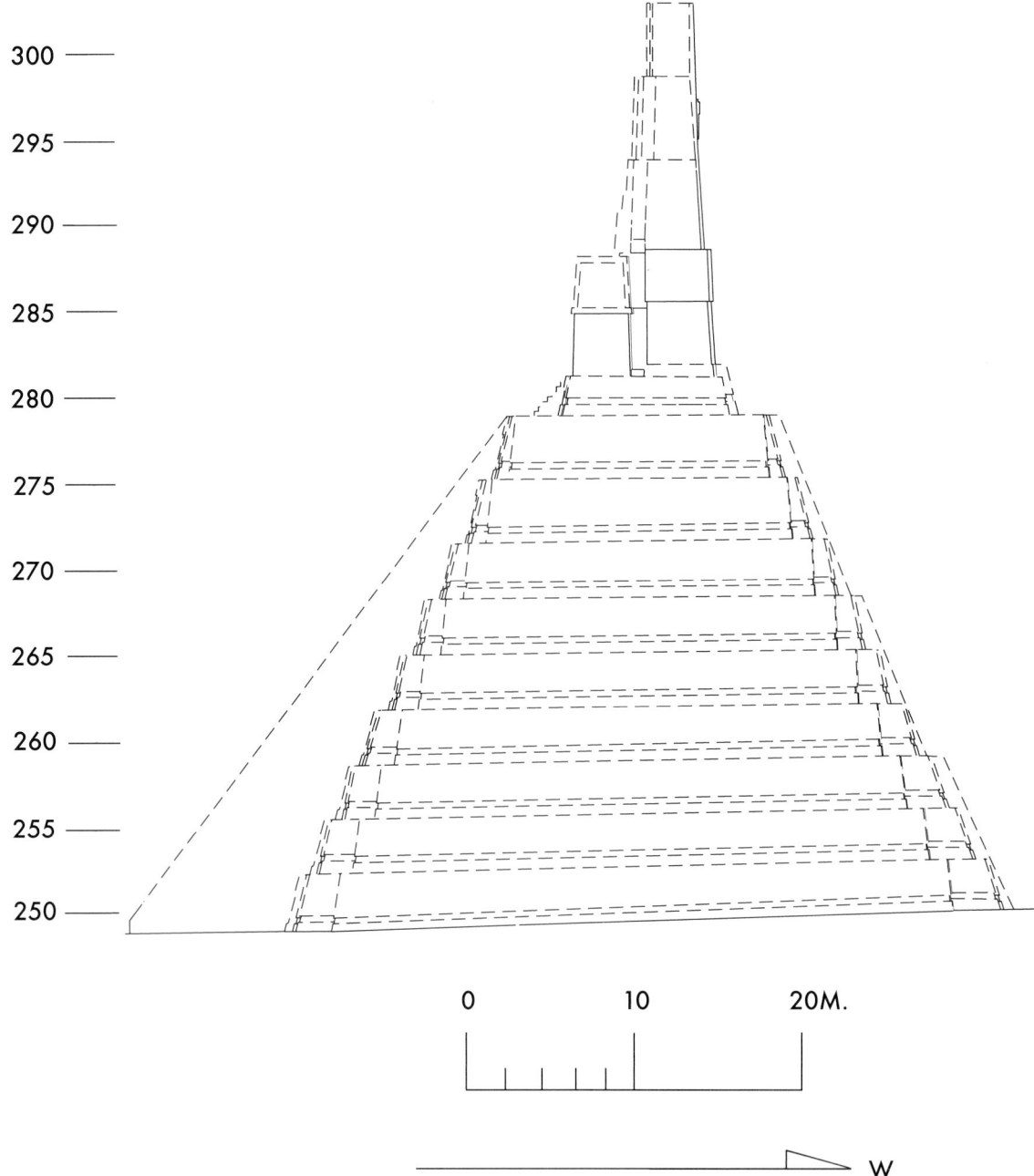

300 ——

295 ——

290 ——

285 ——

280 ——

275 ——

270 ——

265 ——

260 ——

255 ——

250 ——

0   10   20M.

W

Str. 5D-3 N (Right Side) Elevation (scale 1:400).

FIGURE 28

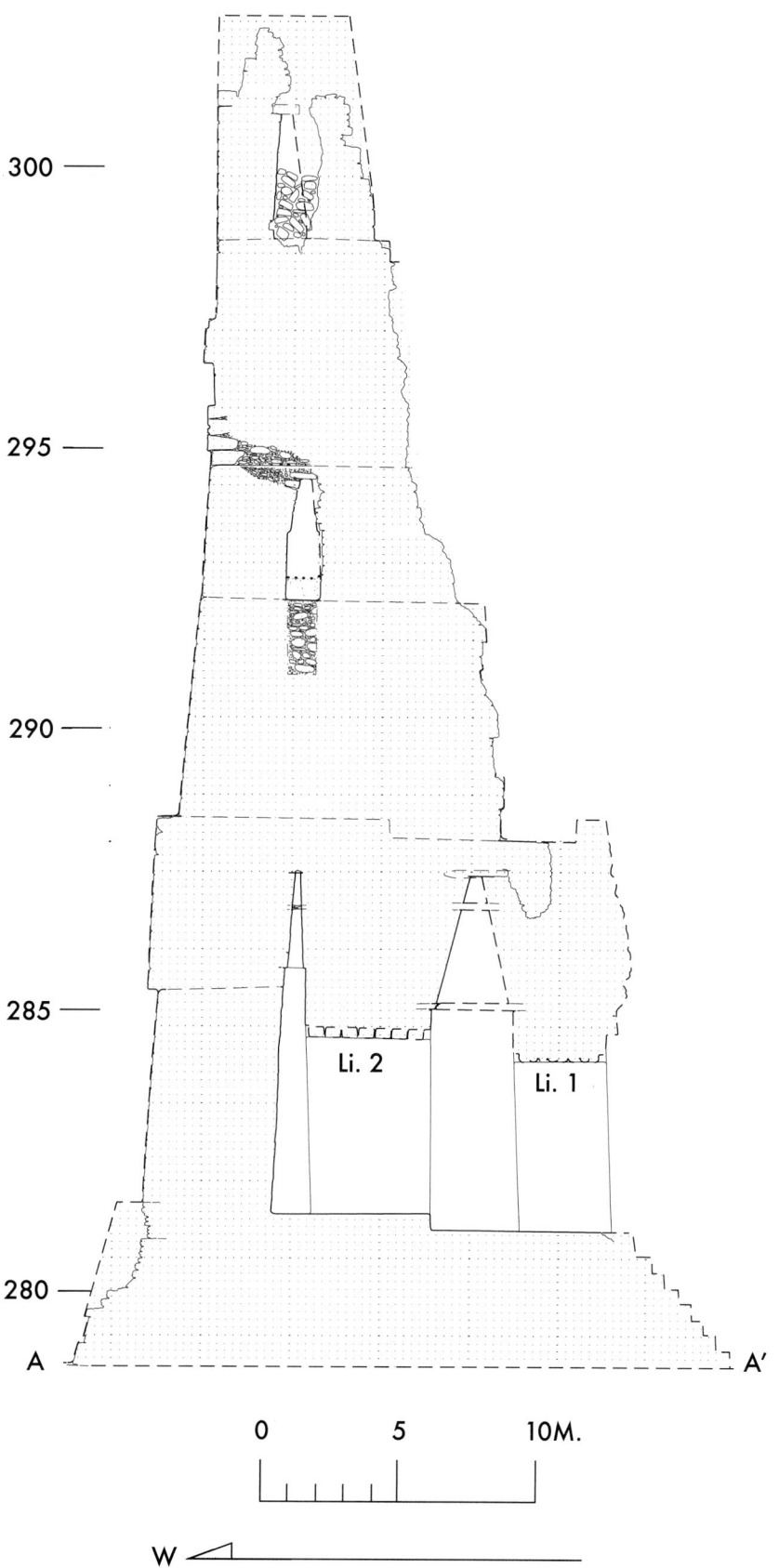

300 —

295 —

290 —

285 —

Li. 2

Li. 1

280 —

A

A'

0   5   10M.

W

Str. 5D-3 Section/Profile A-A' Superstructure (scale 1:125).

FIGURE 29

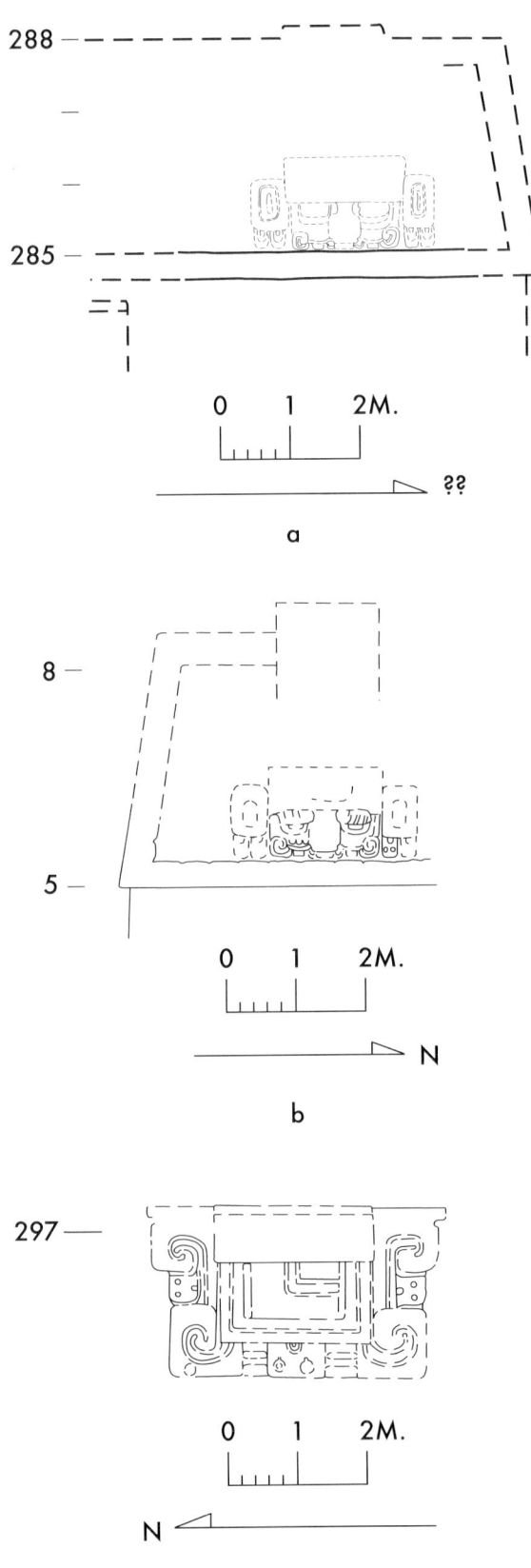

288 —

285 —

0 1 2M.

a

8 —

5 —

0 1 2M.

N

b

297 —

0 1 2M.

N

c

Str. 5D-3 Facade Sculpture (scale 1:100).
a. Upper-zone mask detail. *b*. Upper-zone mask detail. *c*. Sculpture panel W facade roofcomb.

FIGURE 30

305 —

300 —

295 —

290 —

288 —

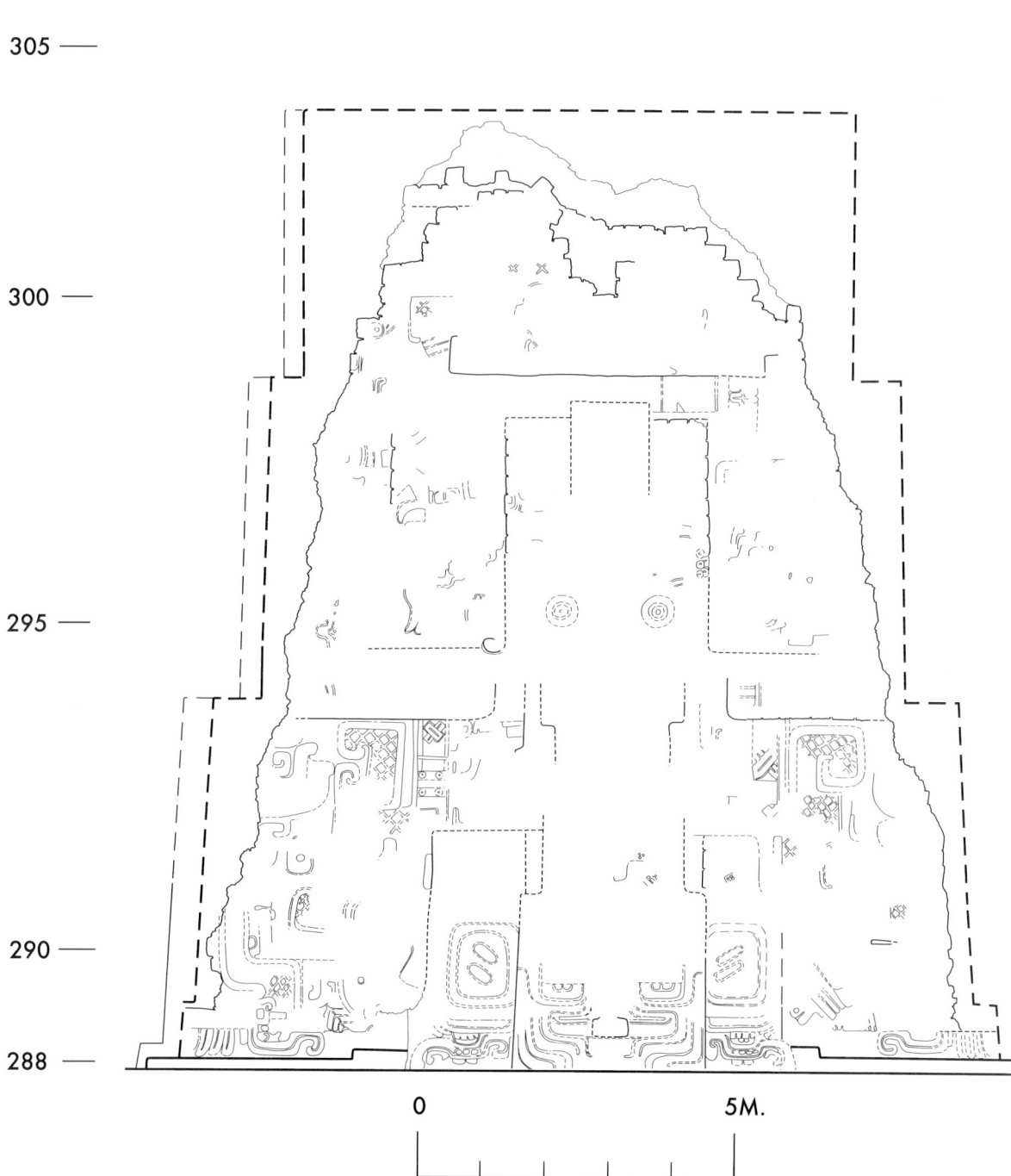

0   5M.

N

Str. 5D-3 E (Front) Elevation Roofcomb (scale 1:100).

FIGURE 31

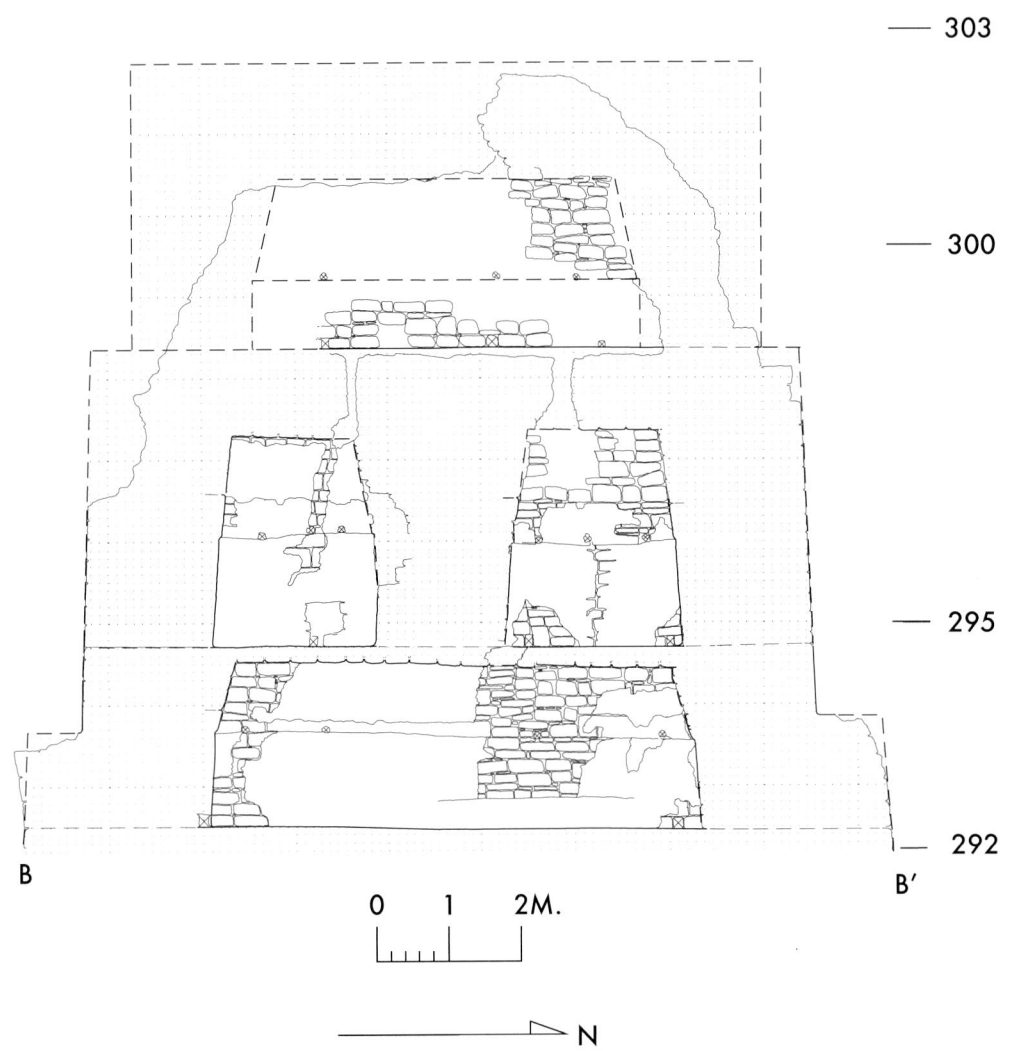

—— 303

—— 300

—— 295

—— 292

B

B'

0   1   2M.

N

Str. 5D-3 Section/Profile B-B' Roofcomb (scale 1:100).

FIGURE 32

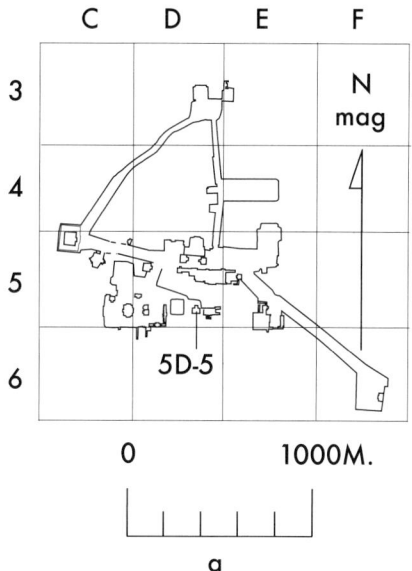

a

b   c

Str. 5D-5 Location and Photographs.
a. Location map after TR. 11 (scale 1:40,000). *b*. Photograph looking S from Central Acropolis. *c*. Photo looking N (part of Str. 5D-5 roofcomb in foreground).

FIGURE 33

310 —

305 —

300 —

295 —

290 —

0   1   2M.

N

Str. 5D-5 Superstructure W (Right Side) Elevation (scale 1:120).

FIGURE 34

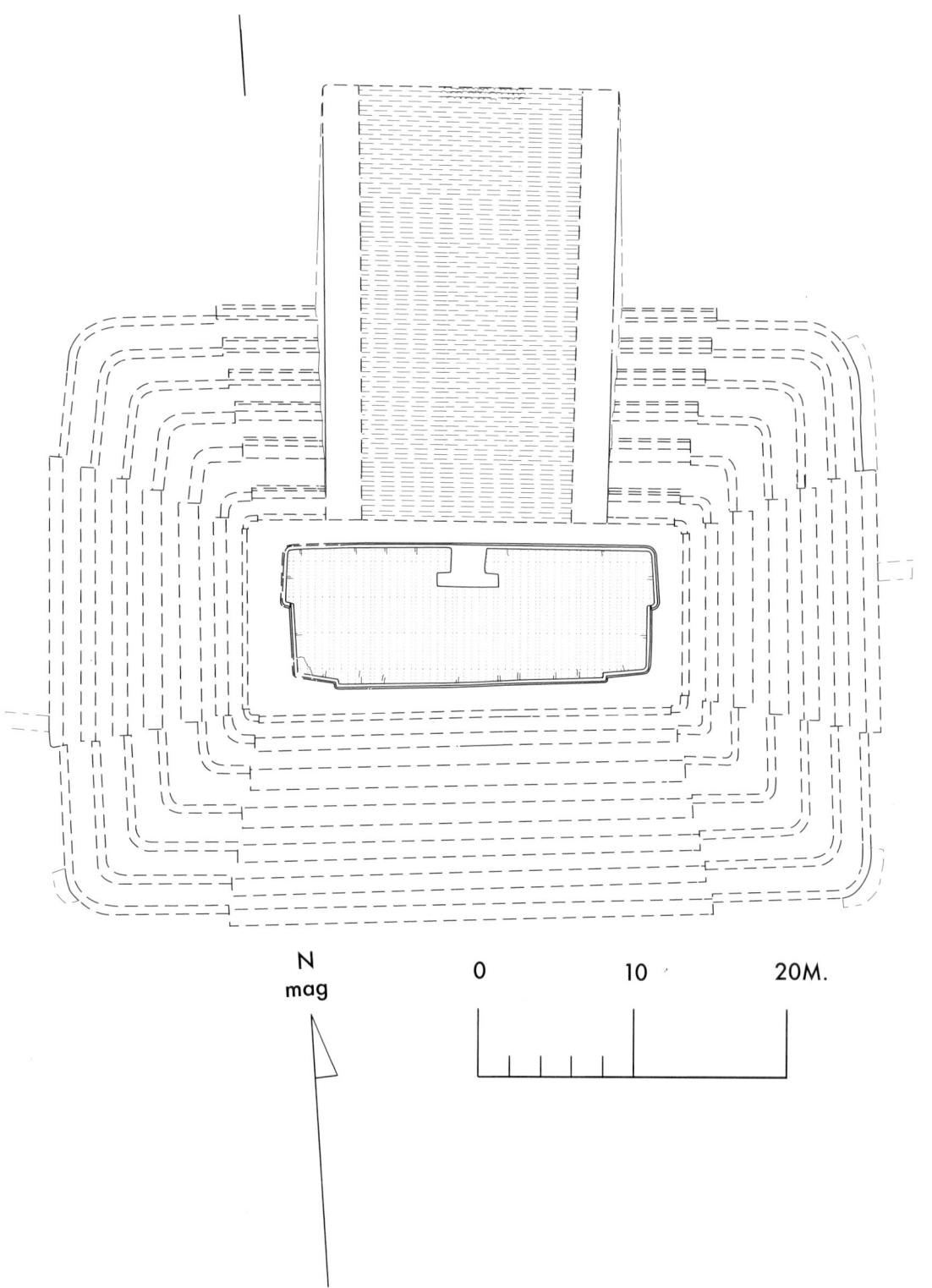

N
mag

| 0 | | 10 | | 20M. |

Str. 5D-5 Plan (scale 1:400).

FIGURE 35

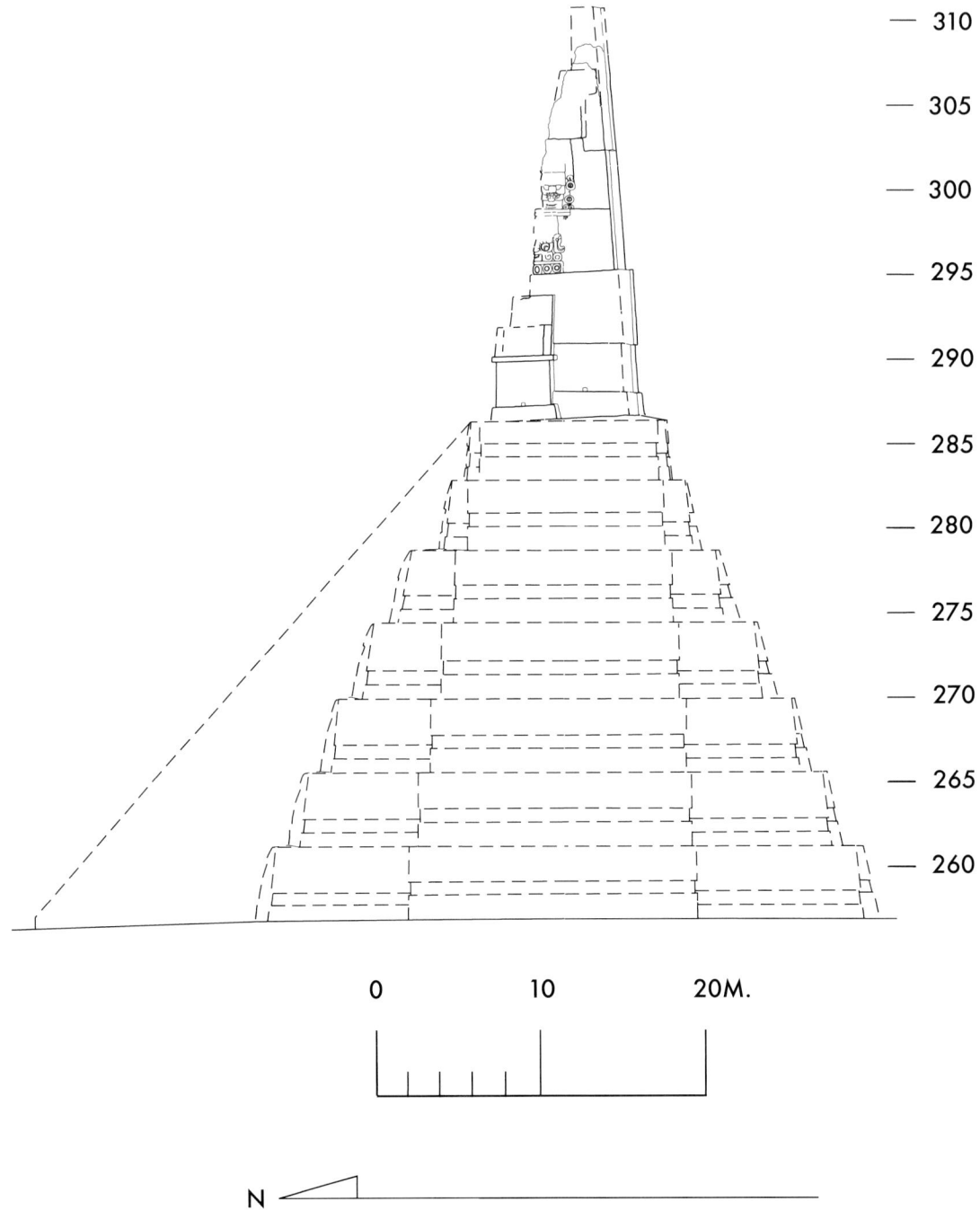

— 310

— 305

— 300

— 295

— 290

— 285

— 280

— 275

— 270

— 265

— 260

0   10   20M.

N

Str. 5D-5 W (Right Side) Elevation (scale 1:400).

FIGURE 36

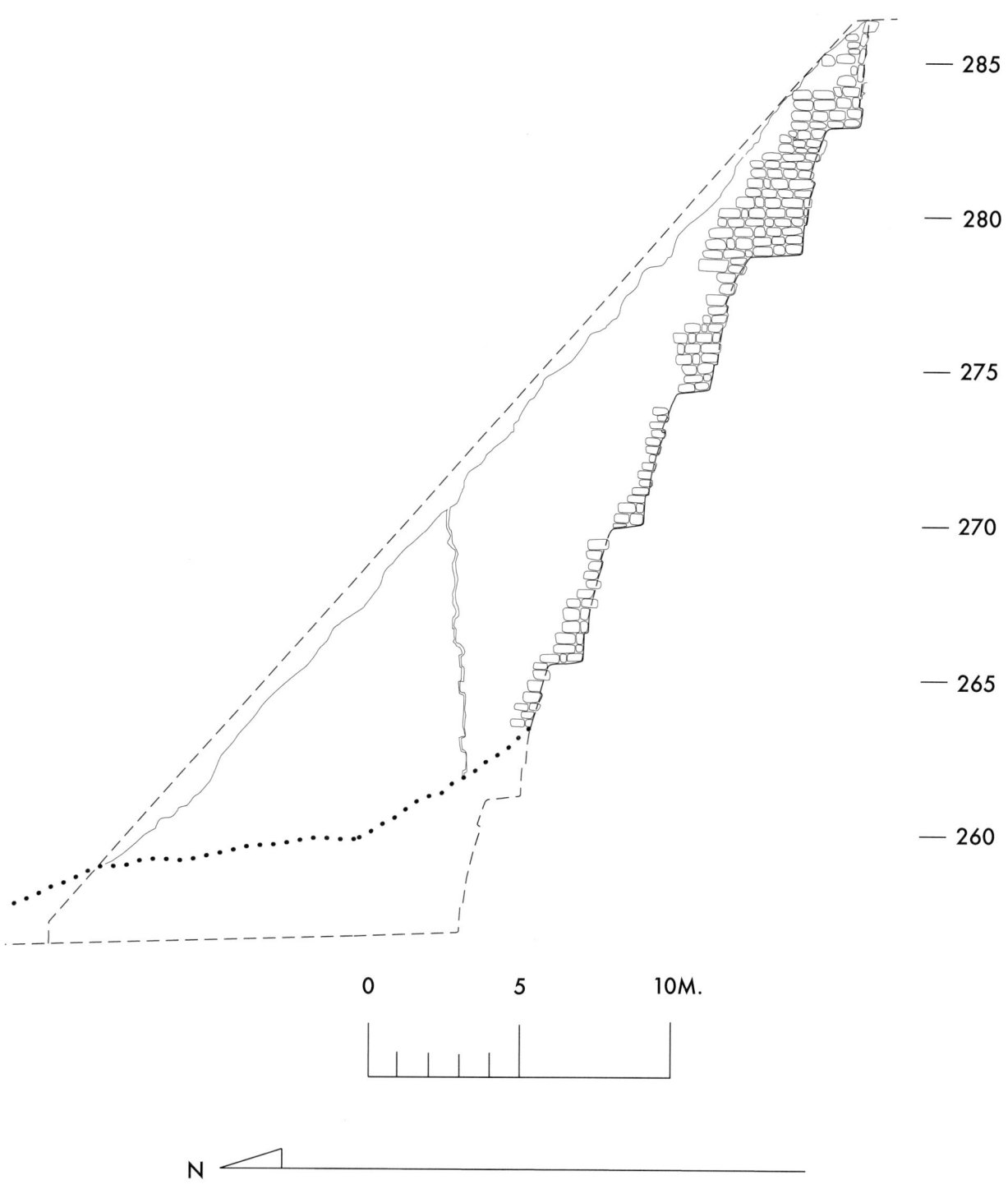

— 285

— 280

— 275

— 270

— 265

— 260

0   5   10M.

N

Str. 5D-5 Stair-side Outset Profile (scale 1:200).

FIGURE 37

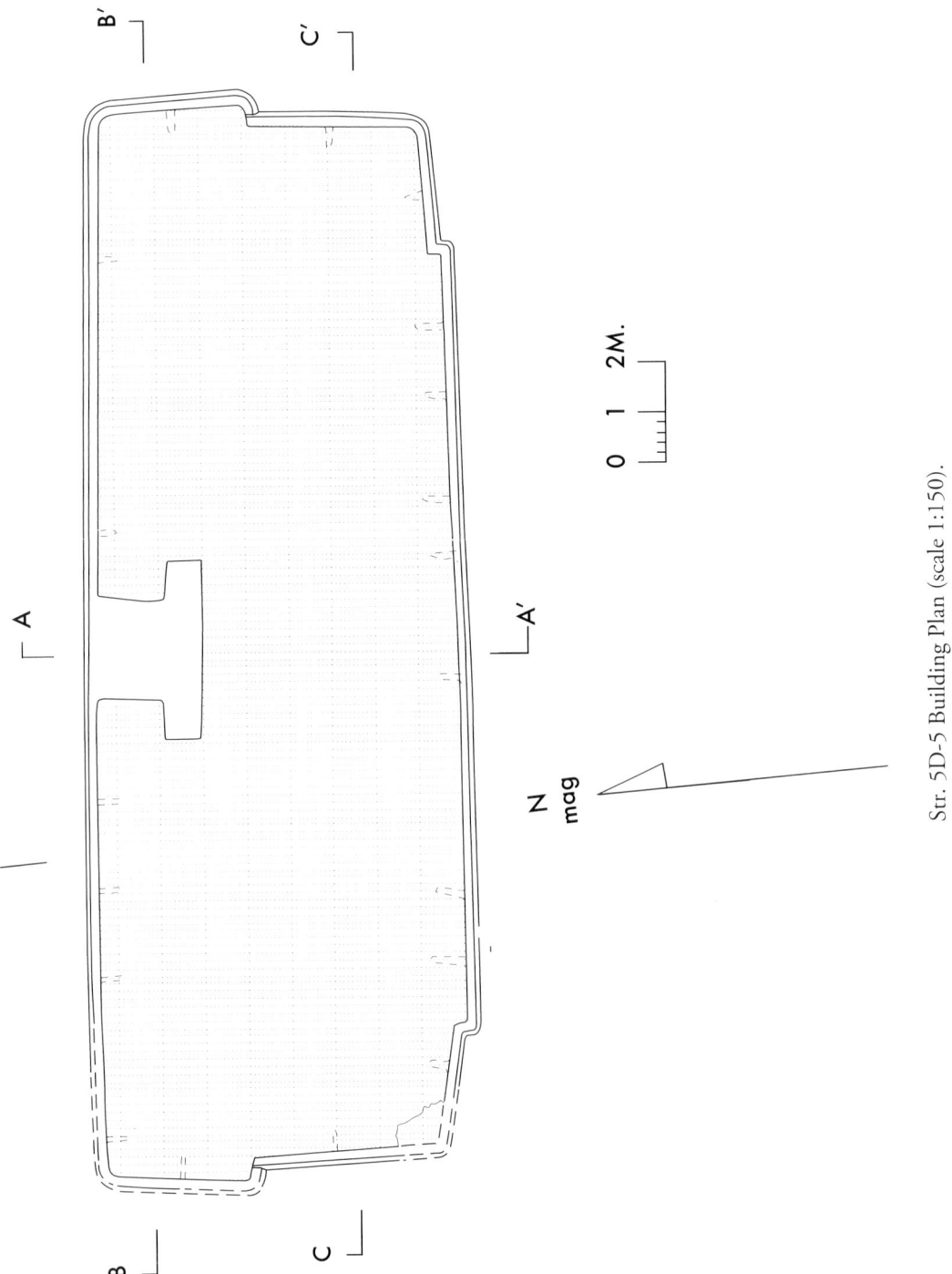

Str. 5D-5 Building Plan (scale 1:150).

FIGURE 38

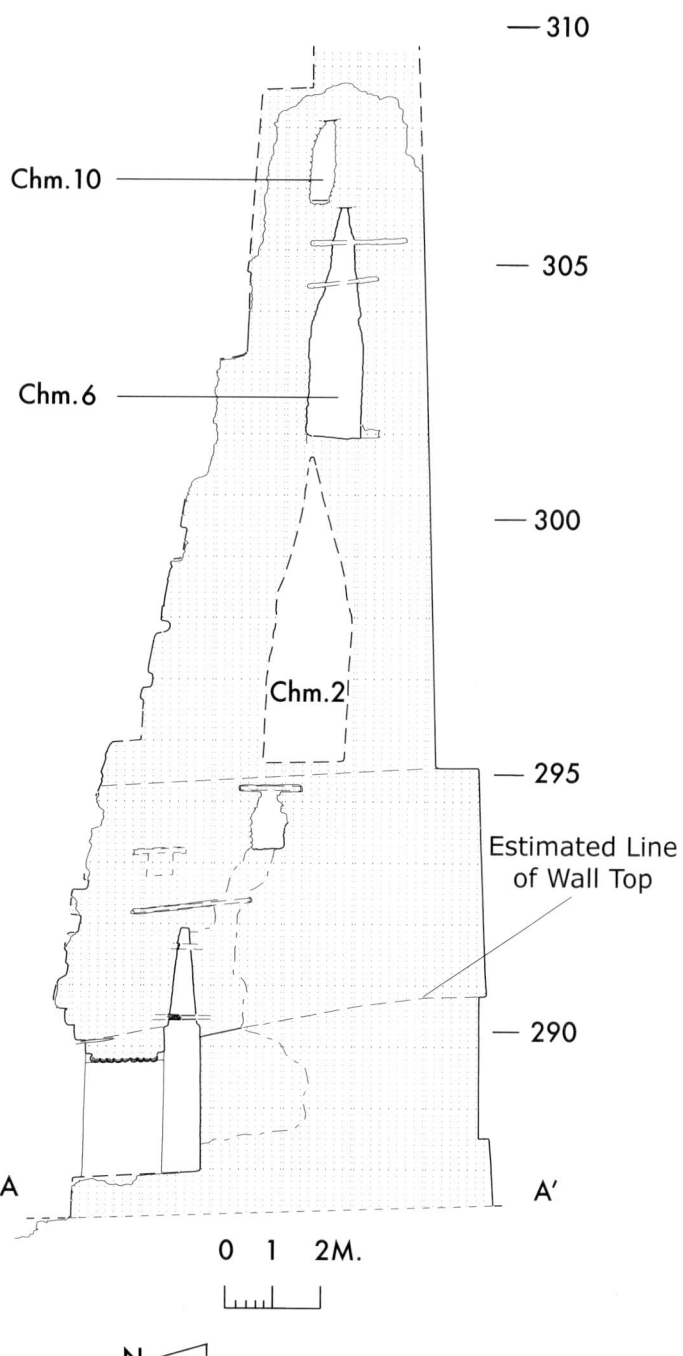

—310

Chm.10

—305

Chm.6

—300

Chm.2

—295

Estimated Line
of Wall Top

—290

A   A'

0 1 2M.

N

Str. 5D-5 Section/Profile A-A' Superstructure (scale 1:150).

FIGURE 39

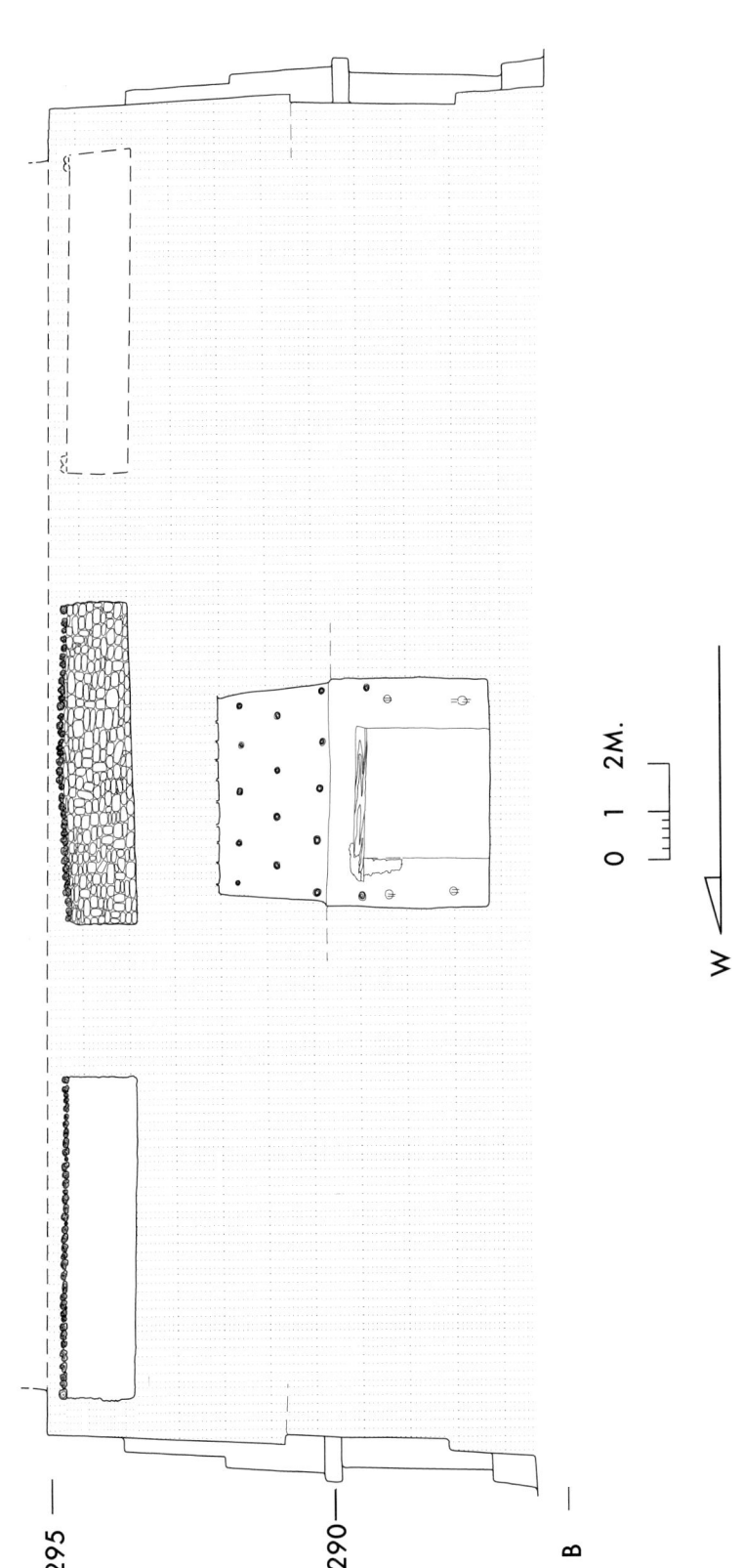

Str. 5D-5 Section/Profile B-B' Building (scale 1:125).

FIGURE 40

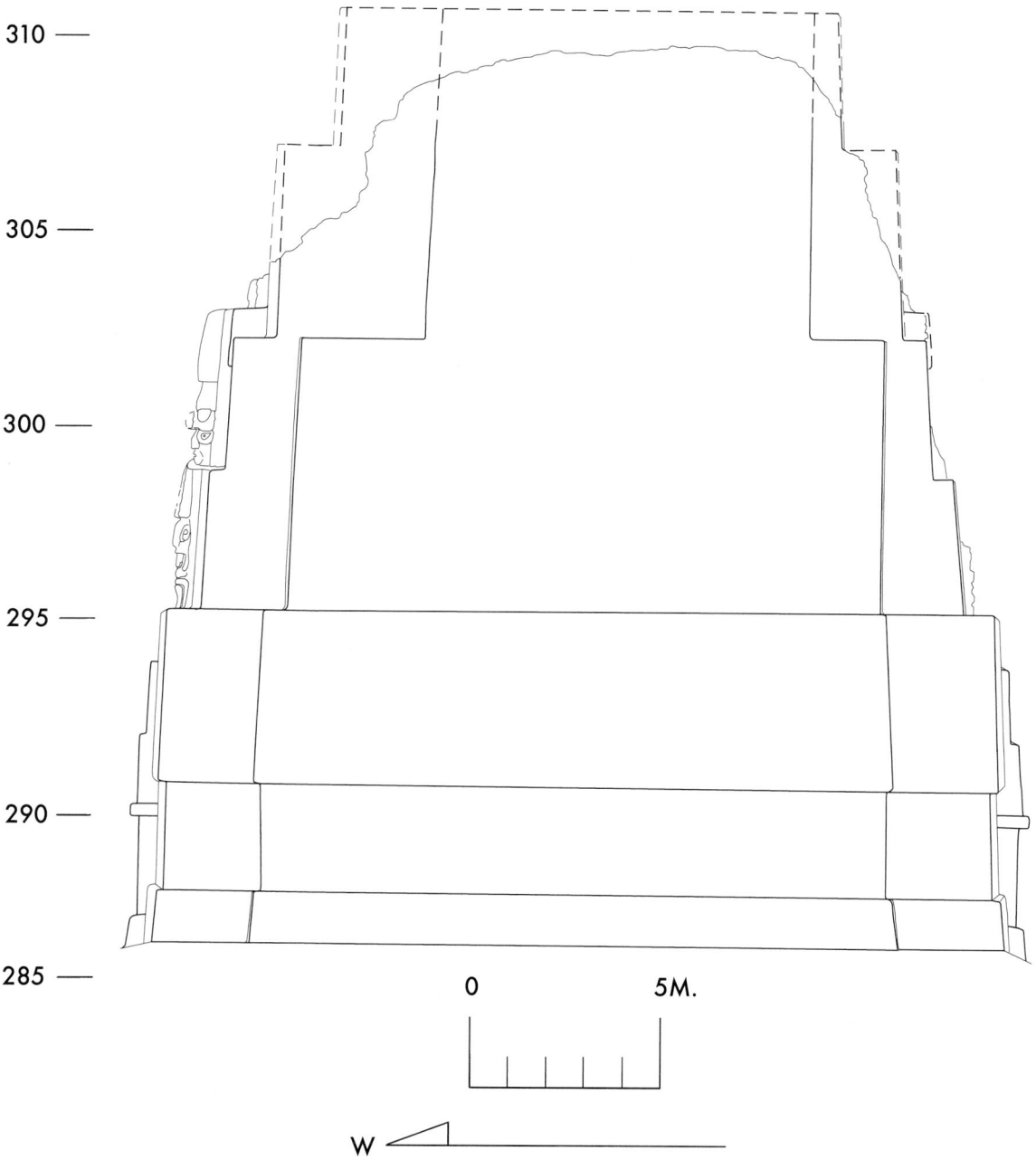

310 —

305 —

300 —

295 —

290 —

285 —

0   5M.

W

Str. 5D-5 S (Rear) Elevation Superstructure (scale 1:175).

FIGURE 41

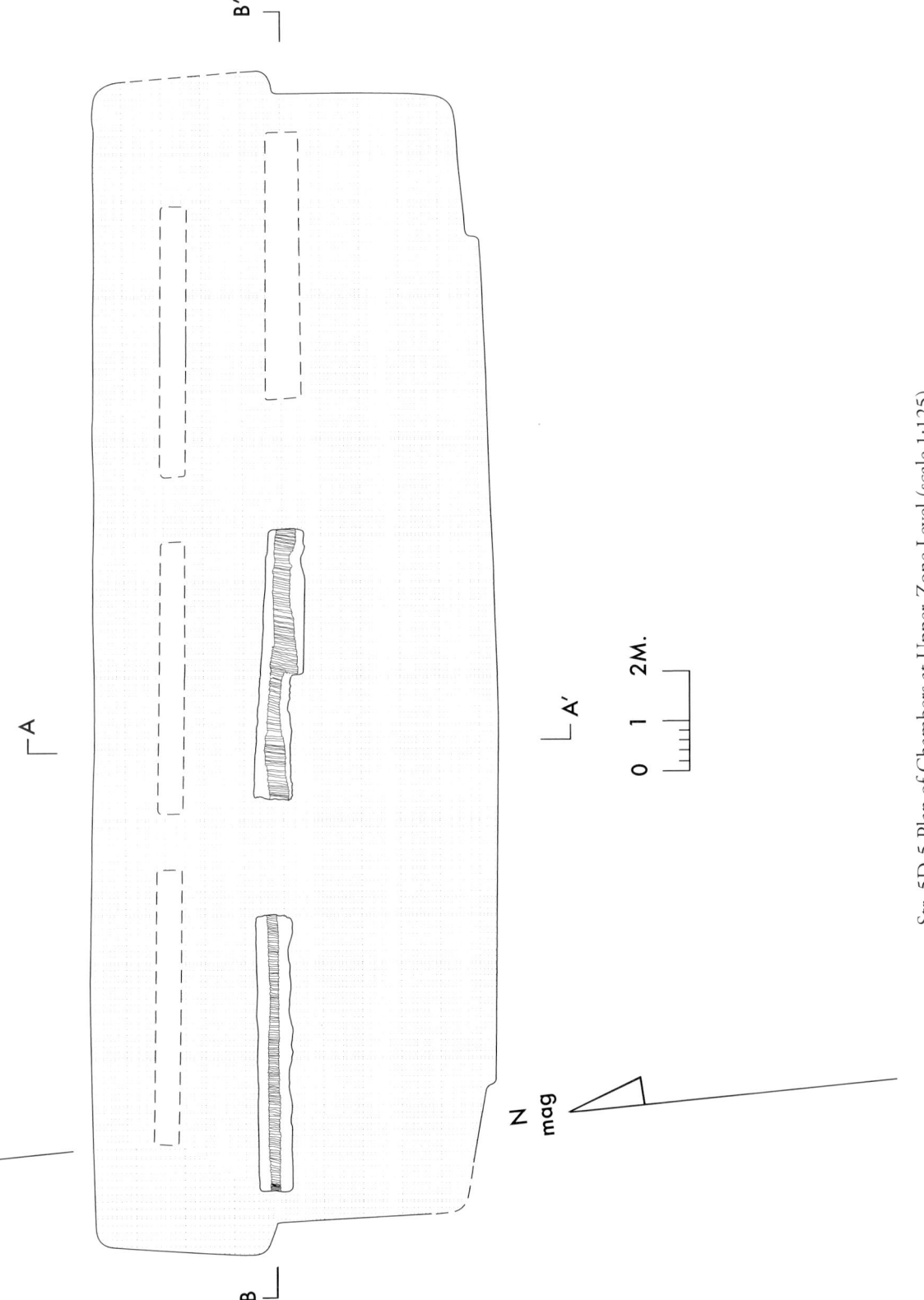

Str. 5D-5 Plan of Chambers at Upper-Zone Level (scale 1:125).

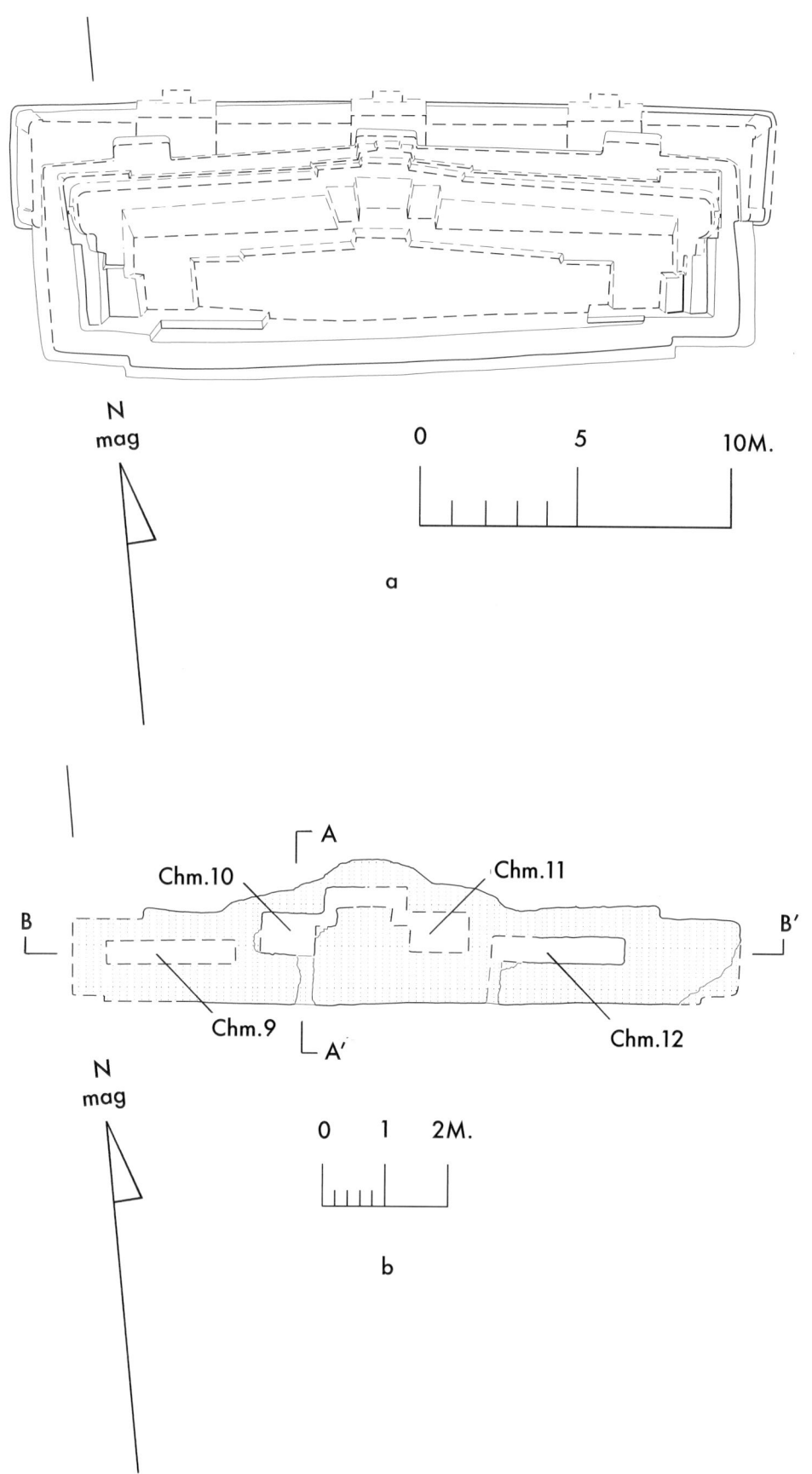

FIGURE 42

N
mag

0   5   10M.

a

A

Chm.10   Chm.11

B   B'

Chm.9   A'   Chm.12

N
mag

0   1   2M.

b

Str. 5D-5 Roofcomb Details.
a. Bird's-eye reconstructed roofcomb (scale 1:200). *b*. Plan of upper-level roofcomb chambers (scale 1:125).

FIGURE 43

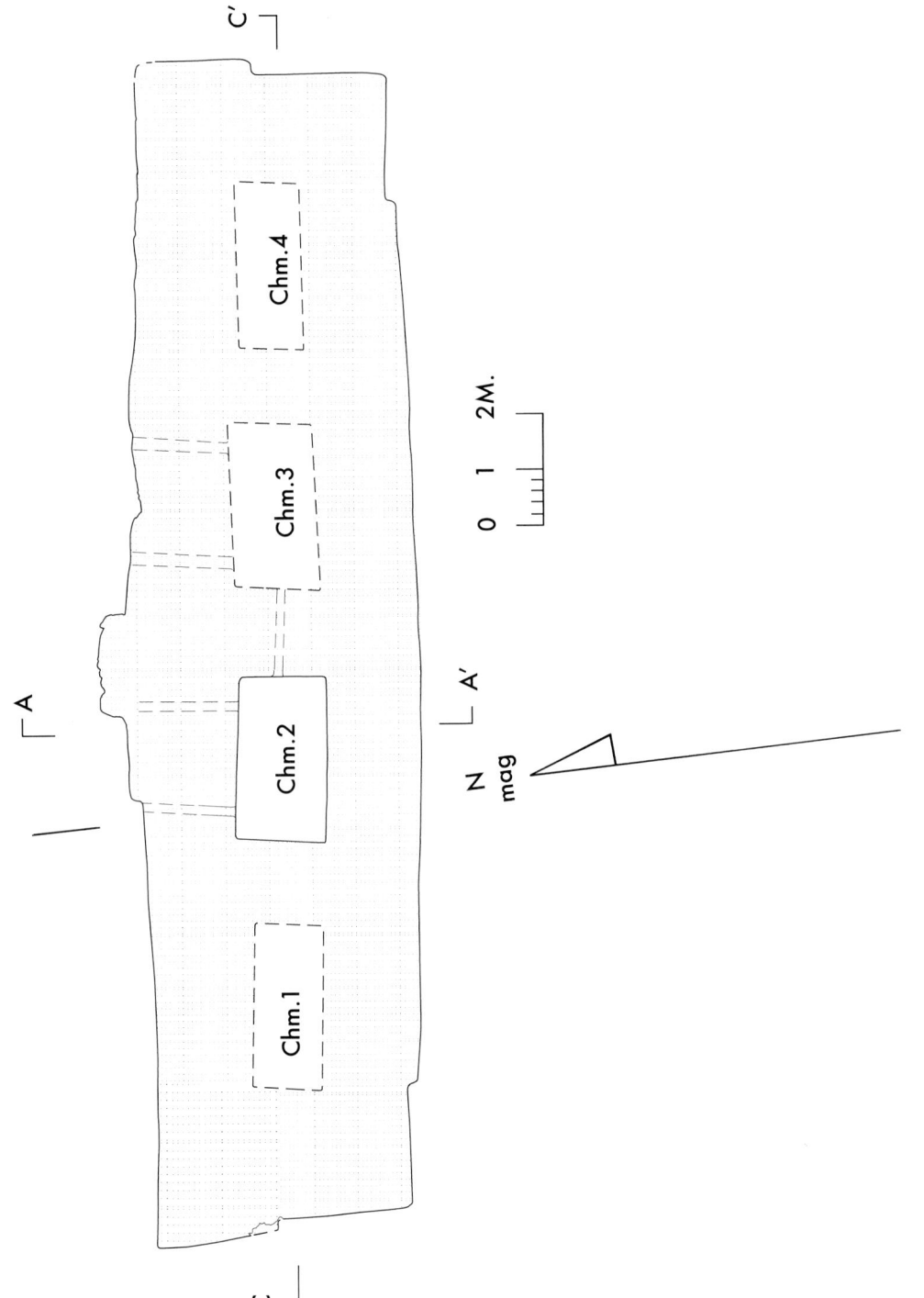

Str. 5D-5 Plan of Lower Roofcomb Chambers (scale 1:125).

FIGURE 44

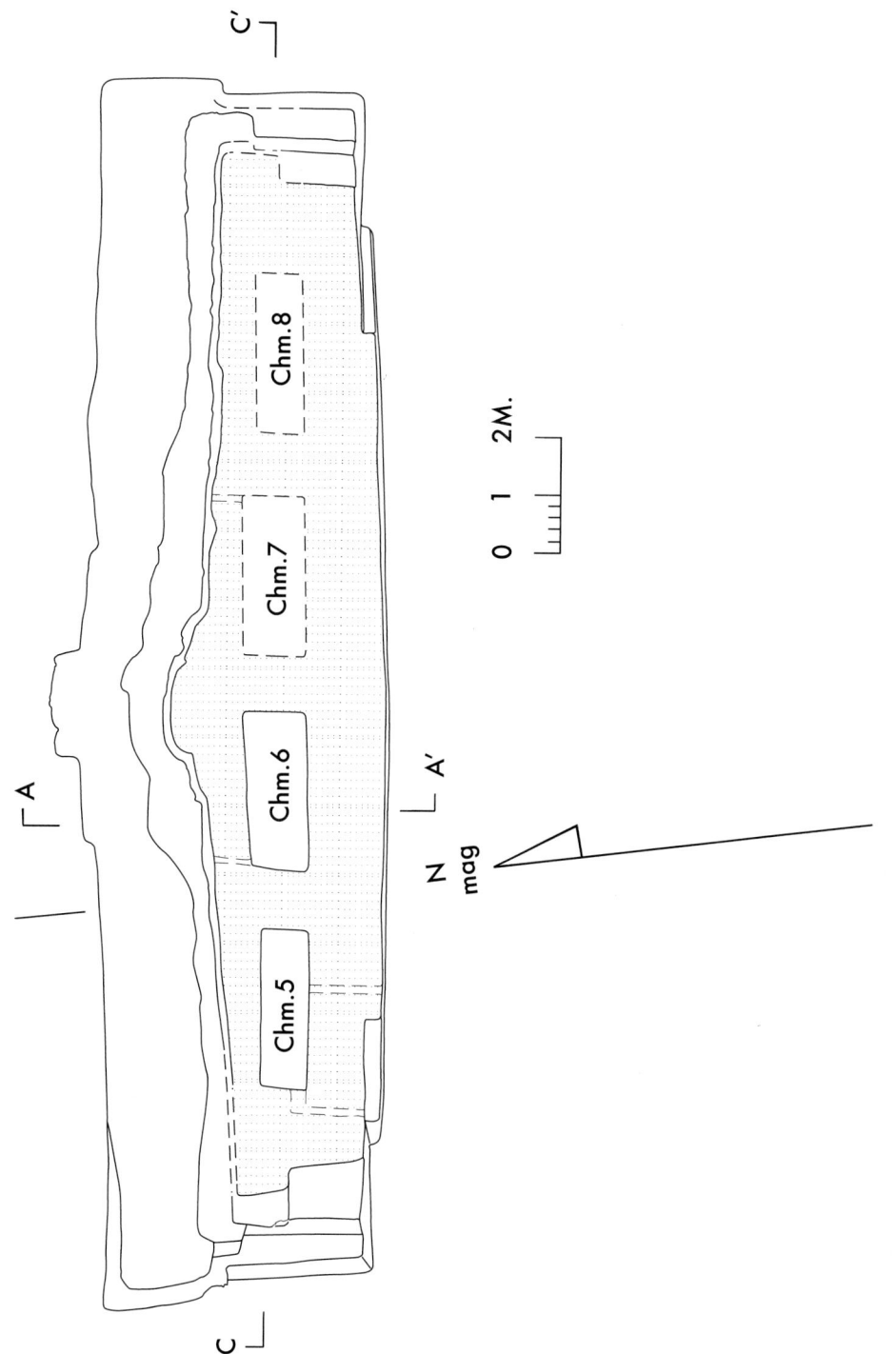

Str. 5D-5 Plan of Mid-Level Roofcomb Chambers (scale 1:125).

FIGURE 45

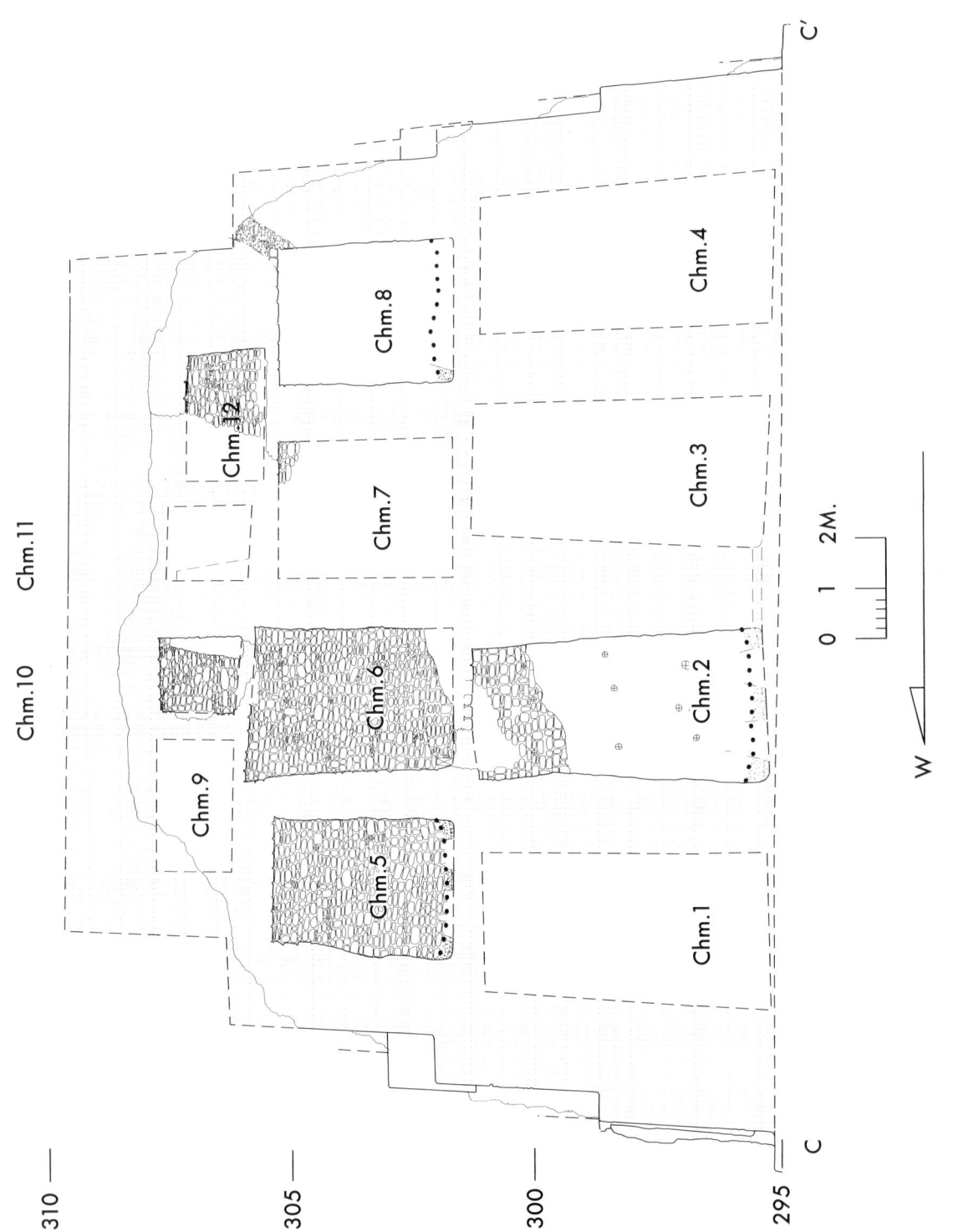

Str. 5D-5 Roofcomb Section/Profile C-C' (scale 1:125).

FIGURE 46

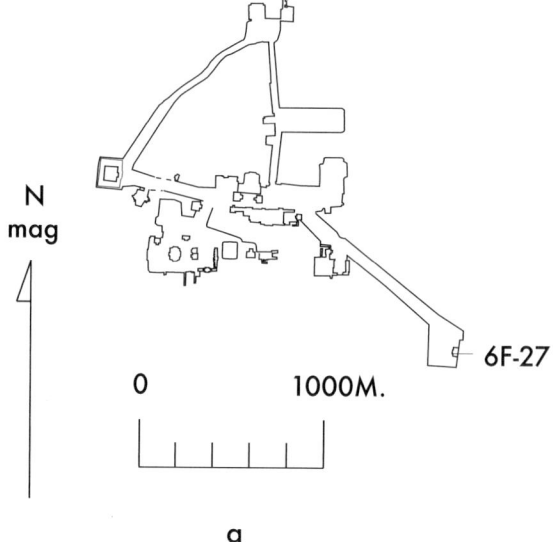

N
mag

0   1000M.

6F-27

a

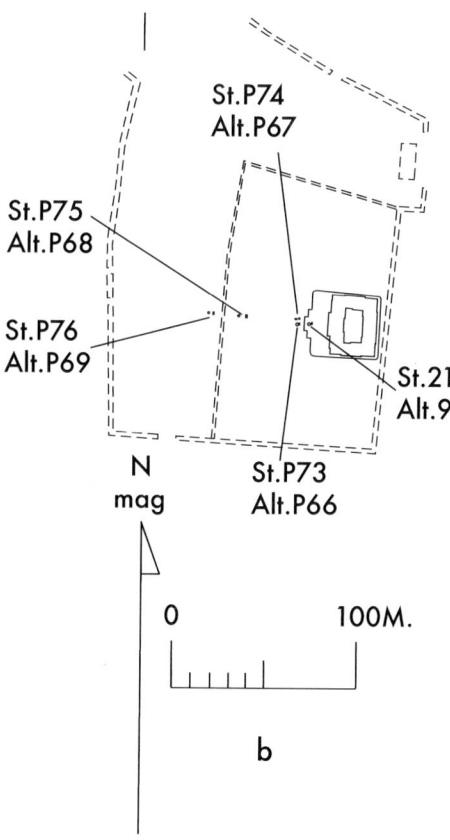

St.P74
Alt.P67

St.P75
Alt.P68

St.P76
Alt.P69

St.21
Alt.9

N
mag

St.P73
Alt.P66

0   100M.

b

Str. 6F-27-1st Location.
a. Location map after TR. 11 (scale 1:40,000). *b.* Precinct plan (scale 1:4,000).

FIGURE 47

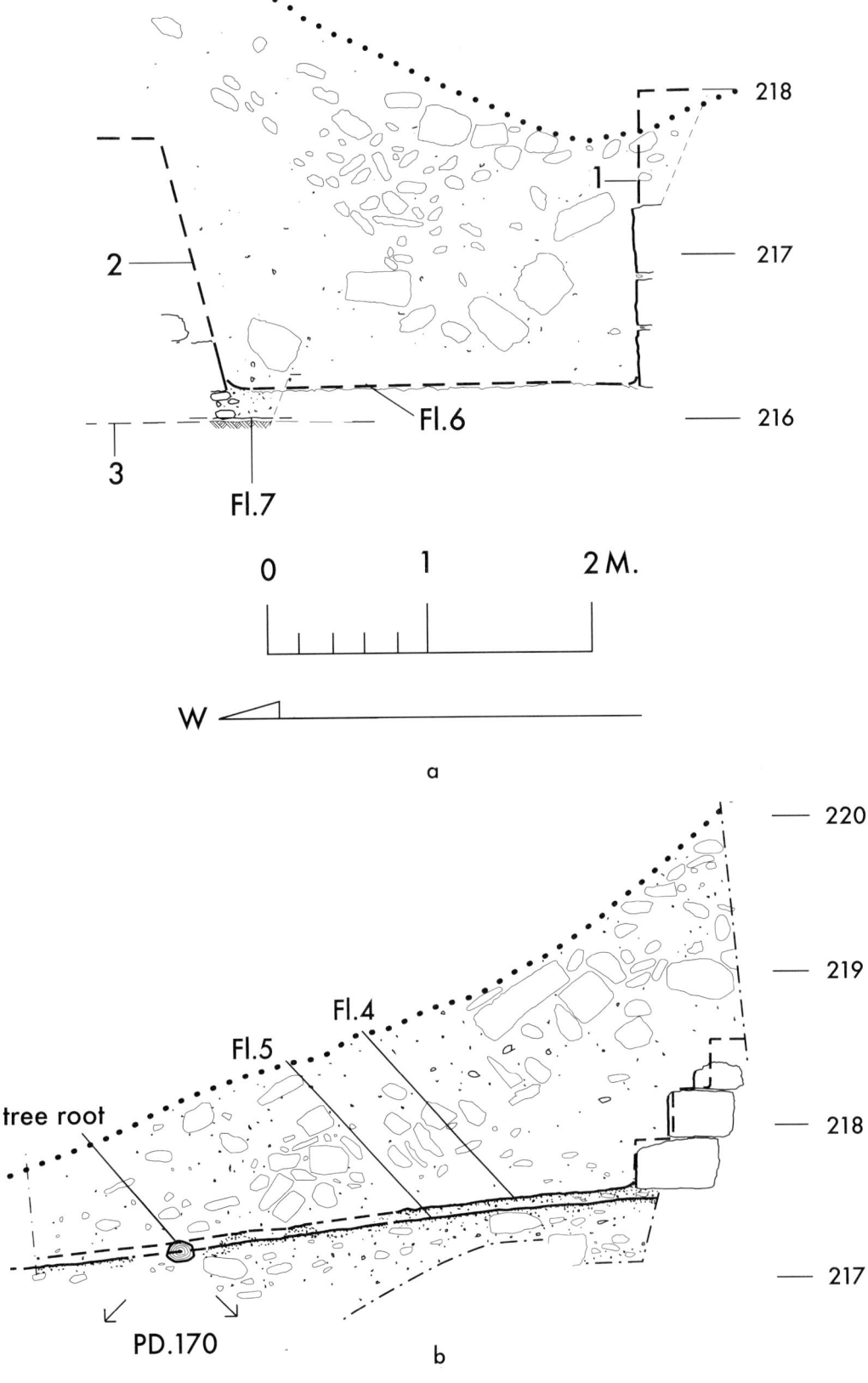

Str. 6F-27-1st Basal Platform Details (scale 1:50).
a. Cut at rear center. *1,* Precinct wall. *2,* Basal platform face. *3,* Leveled bedrock. *b.* Cut at base of stair.

FIGURE 48

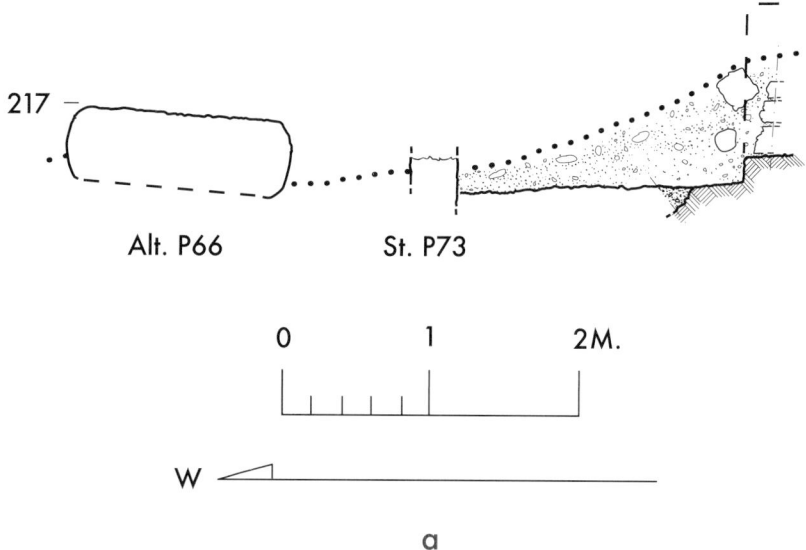

217

Alt. P66   St. P73

0   1   2M.

W

a

b

Str. 6F-27-1st Associated Stelae. a. St. P73 and Alt. P66 (scale 1:50). b. St. P74 photo. Courtesy of the Penn Museum; Tikal Project image 56-3-107.

FIGURE 49

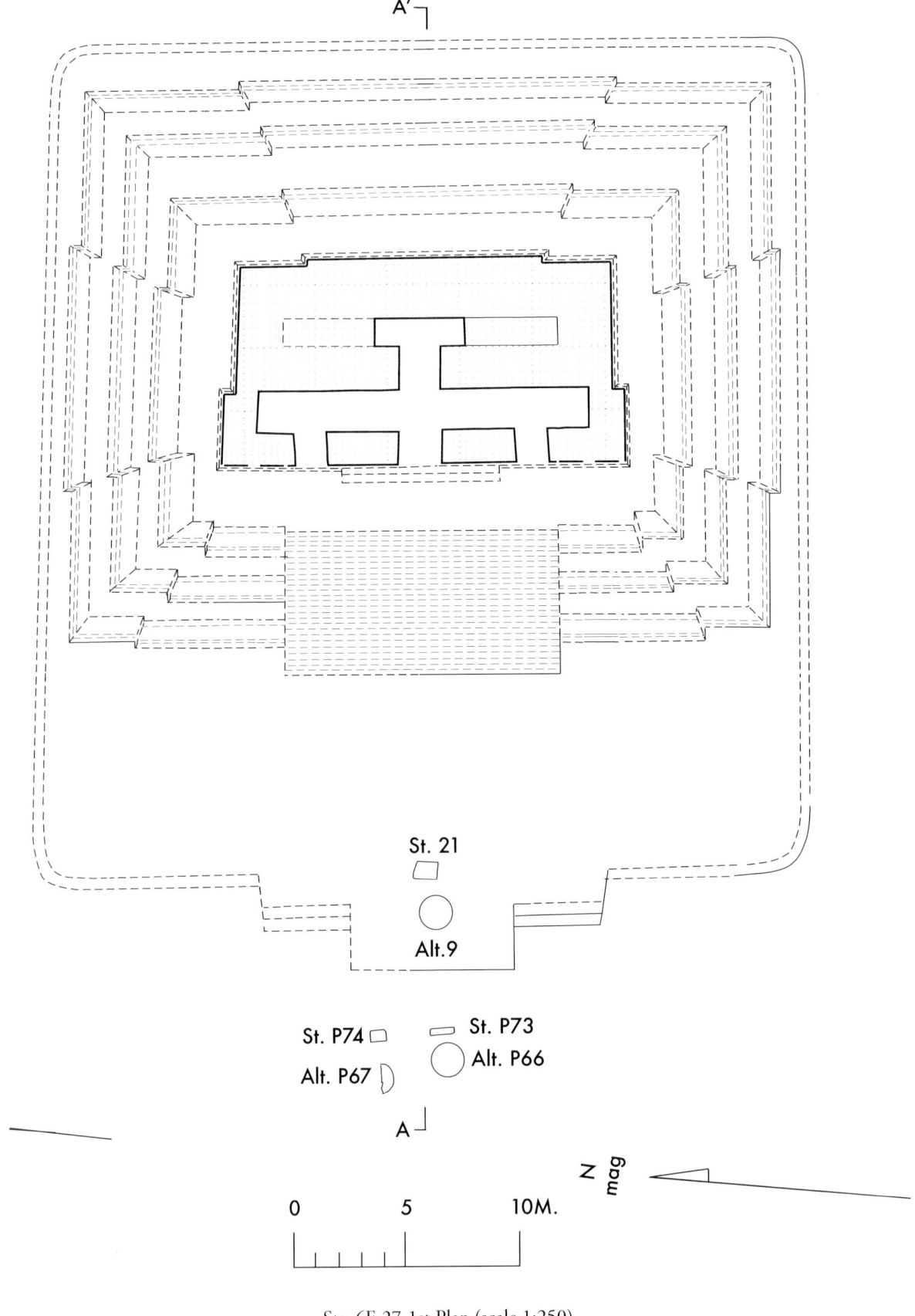

St. 21

Alt.9

St. P74   St. P73

Alt. P67   Alt. P66

A

N mag

0   5   10M.

Str. 6F-27-1st Plan (scale 1:250).

FIGURE 50

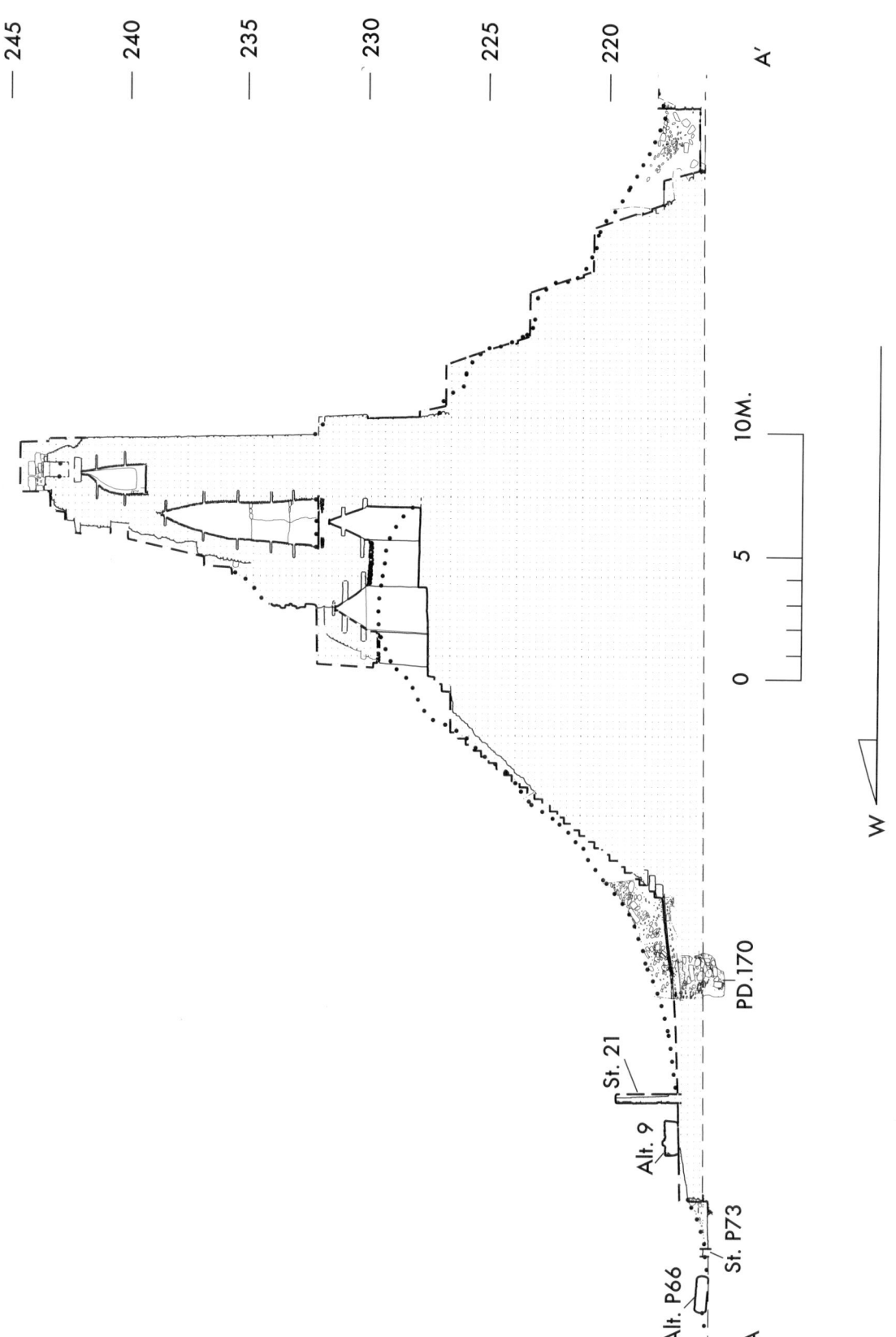

Str. 6F-27-1st Section/Profile A-A' (scale 1:250).

FIGURE 51

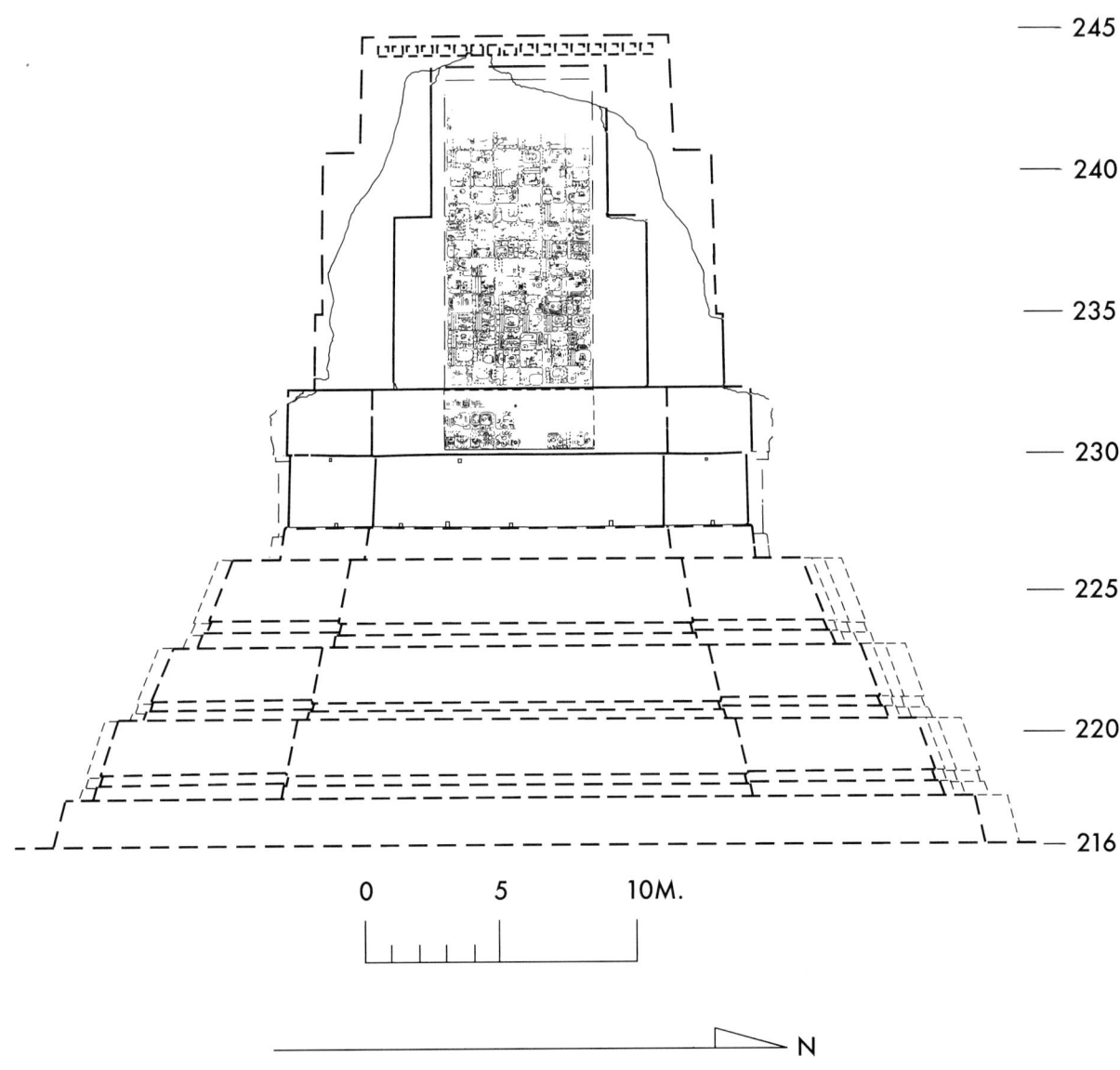

—— 245

—— 240

—— 235

—— 230

—— 225

—— 220

—— 216

0   5   10M.

N

Str. 6F-27-1st E (Rear) Elevation (scale 1:250).

FIGURE 52

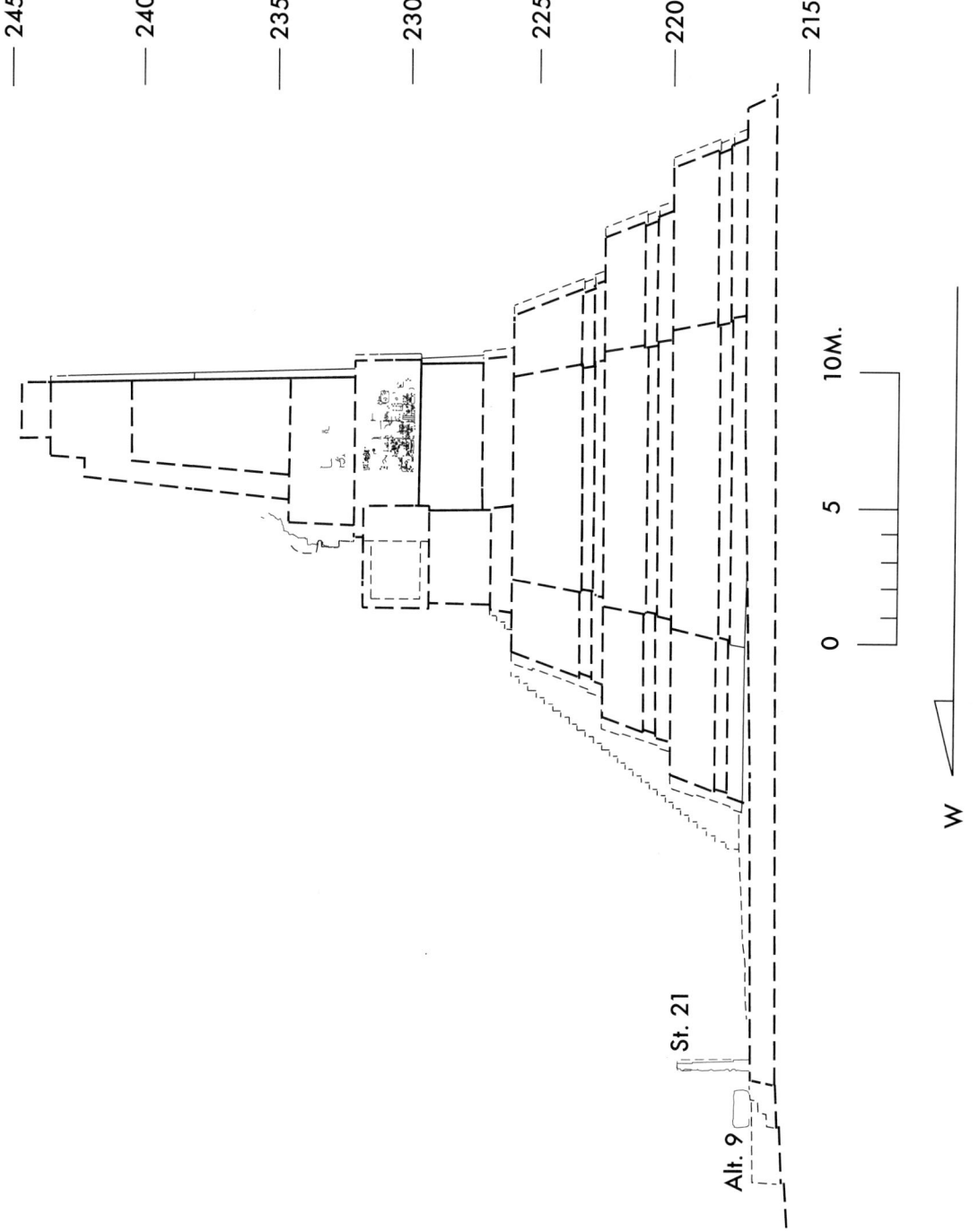

245

240

235

230

225

220

215

St. 21

Alt. 9

W

0 5 10M.

Str. 6F-27-1st S (Right Side) Elevation (scale 1:250).

FIGURE 53

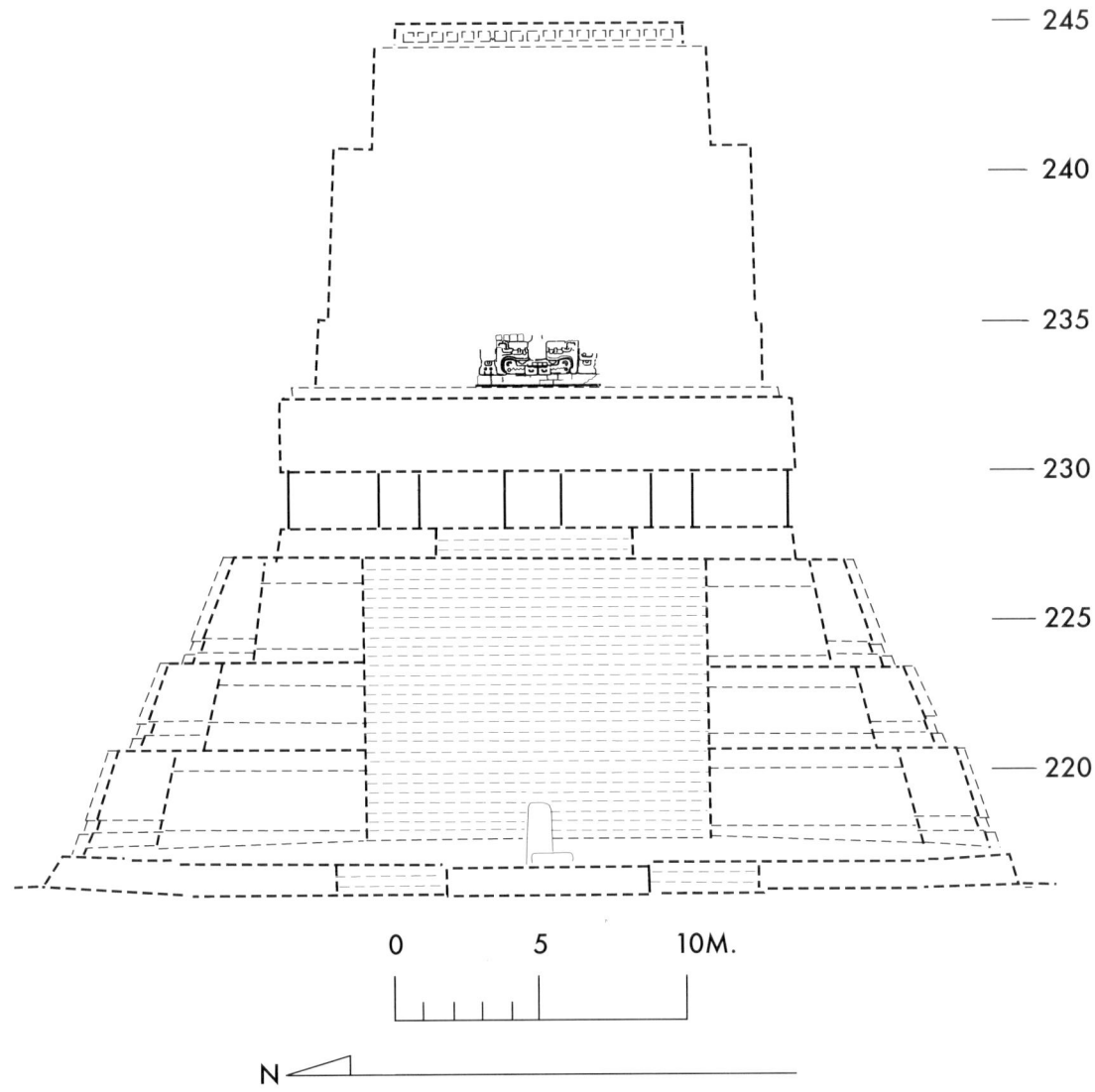

245

240

235

230

225

220

0   5   10M.

N

Str. 6F-27-1st W (Front) Elevation (scale 1:250).

FIGURE 54

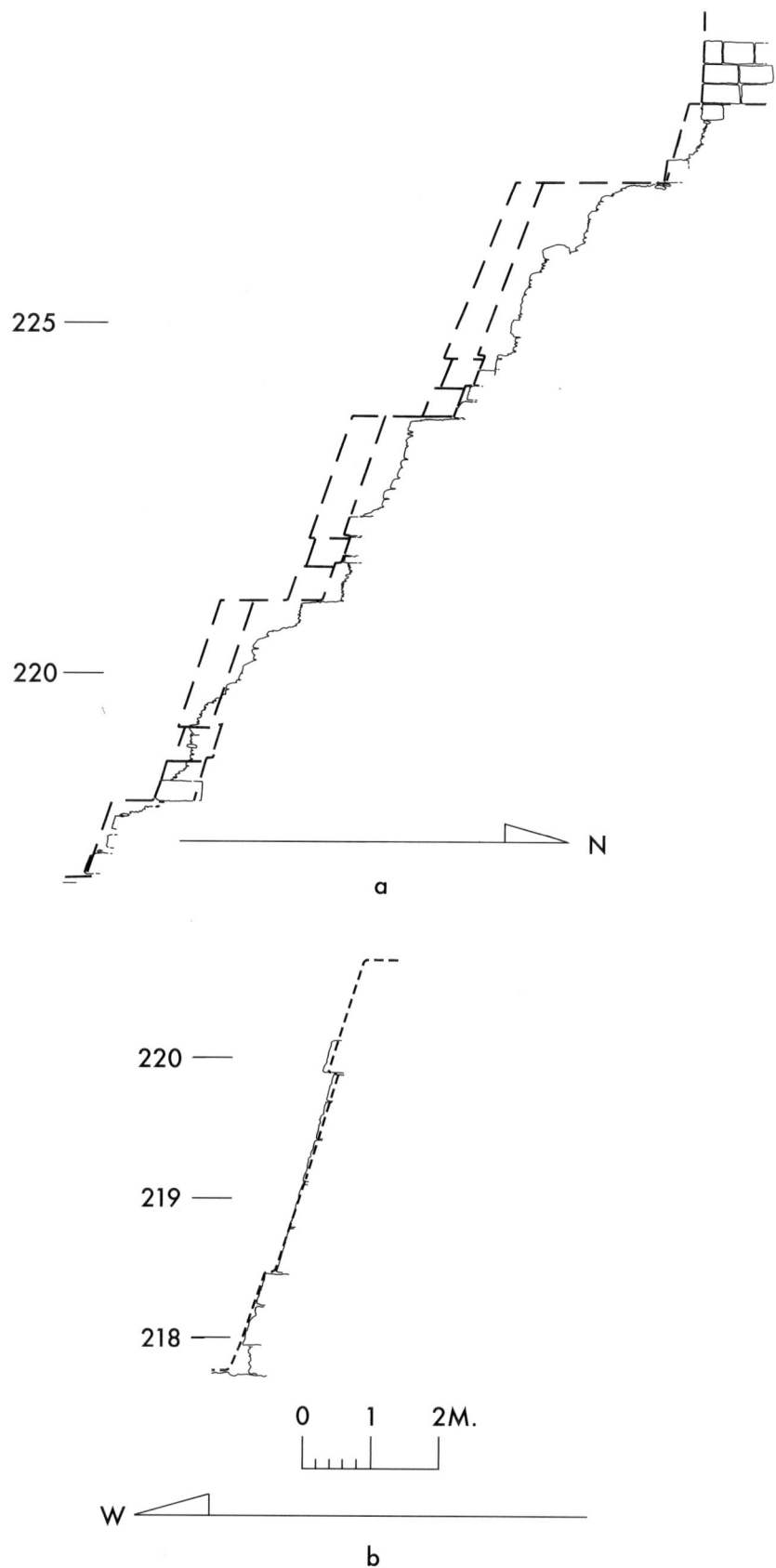

225 —

220 —

N

a

220 —

219 —

218 —

0   1   2M.

W

b

Str. 6F-27-1st Substructure Profiles (scale 1:100).
a. Terrace profiles. *b*. Stair-side profile.

FIGURE 55

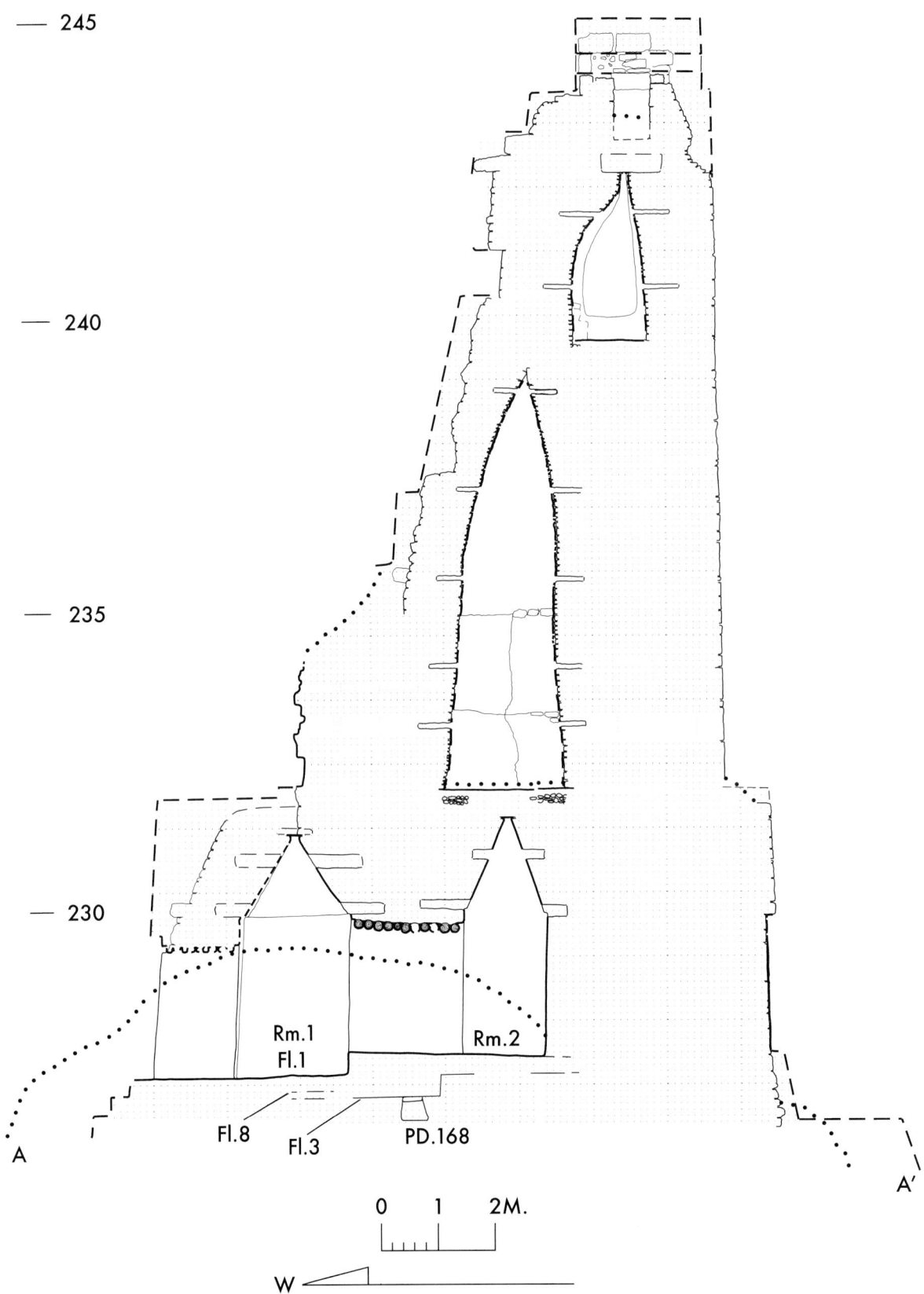

Str. 6F-27-1st Section/Profile A-A' Superstructure (scale 1:100).

FIGURE 56

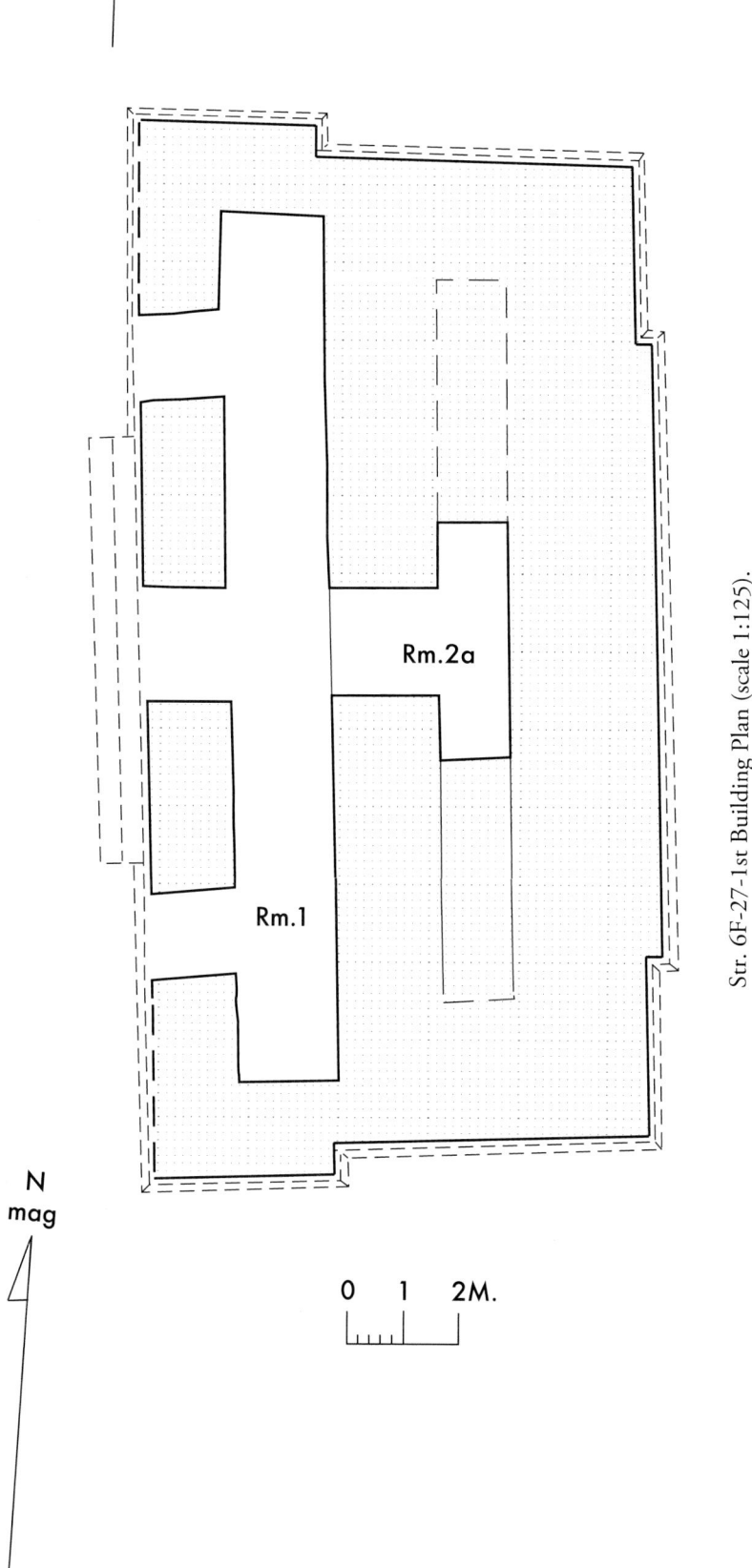

N
mag

Rm.2a

Rm.1

Str. 6F-27-1st Building Plan (scale 1:125).

0   1   2M.

FIGURE 57

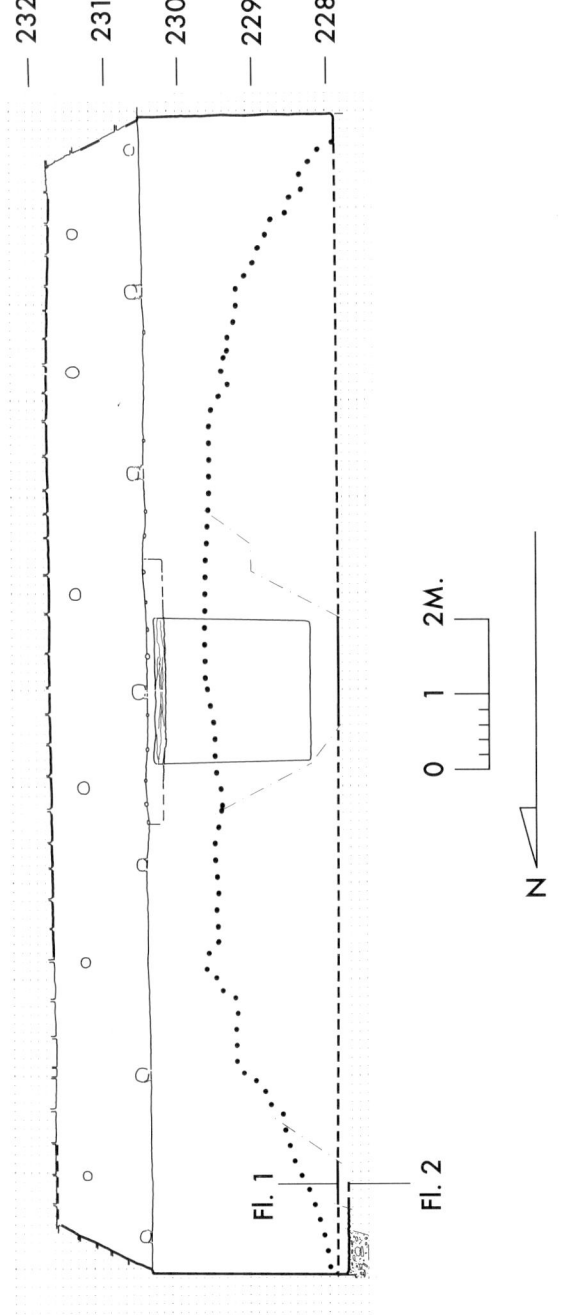

232
231
230
229
228

Fl. 1
Fl. 2

0 1 2M.

N

Str. 6F-27-1st Section/Profile Room 1 (scale 1:100).

FIGURE 58

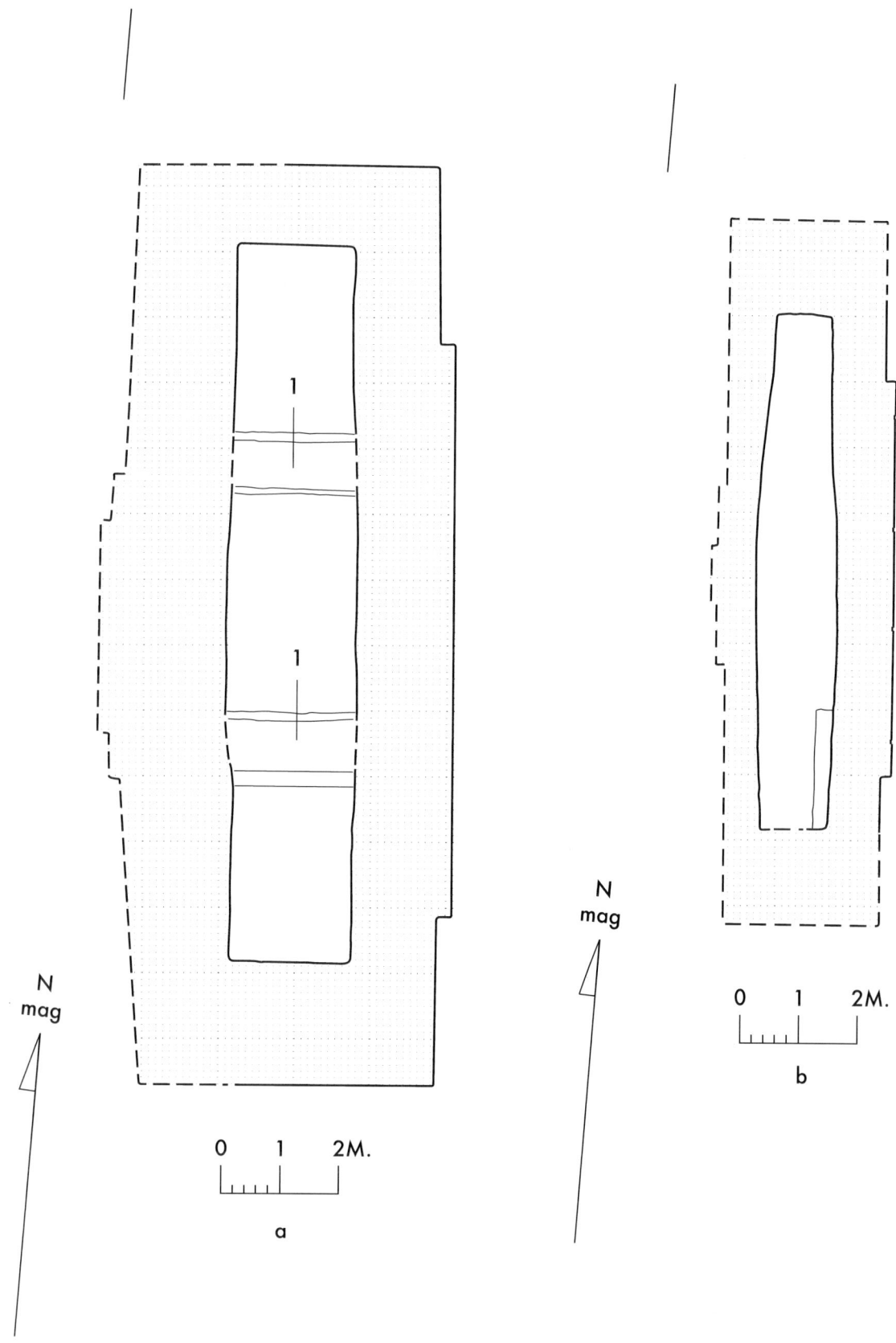

Str. 6F-27-1st Roofcomb Chambers (scale 1:100).
a. Plan at lower level. *1*, Dwarf wall. *b*. Plan at upper level.

FIGURE 59

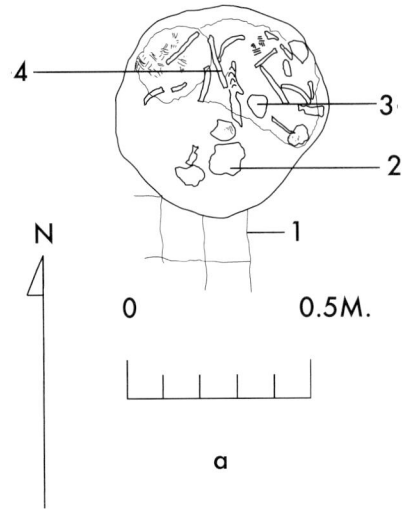

a

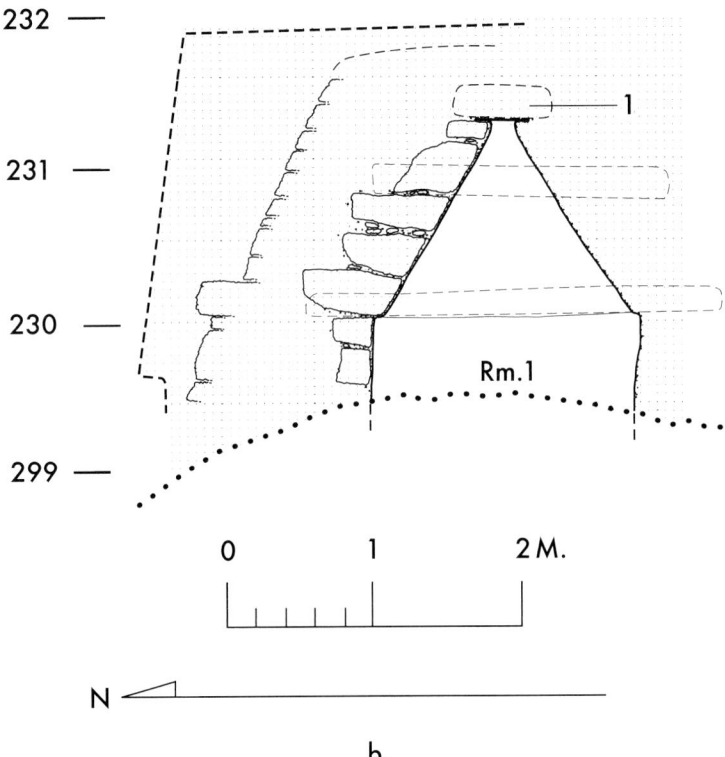

b

Str. 6F-27-1st Building Details.
a. PD. 168 plan (scale 1:20). *1*, Patolli game on Fl. 3. *2*, Human bone fragments. *3*, Patella. *4*, Long bone. *b*. Vault detail (scale 1:50). *1*, Pre-plastered capstone.

FIGURE 60

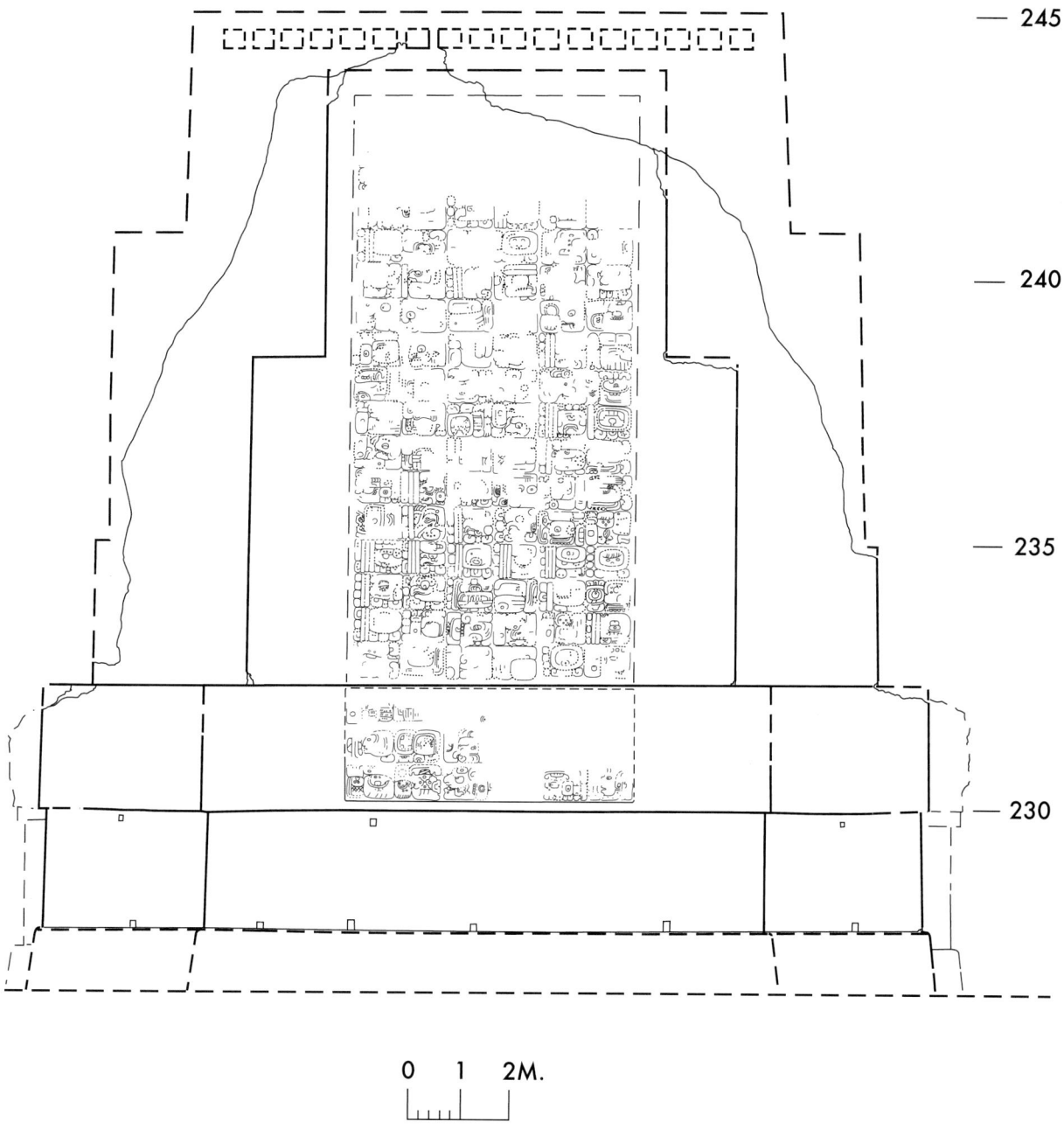

245

240

235

230

0 1 2M.

N

Str. 6F-27-1st E (Rear) Elevation Superstructure (scale 1:125).

FIGURE 61

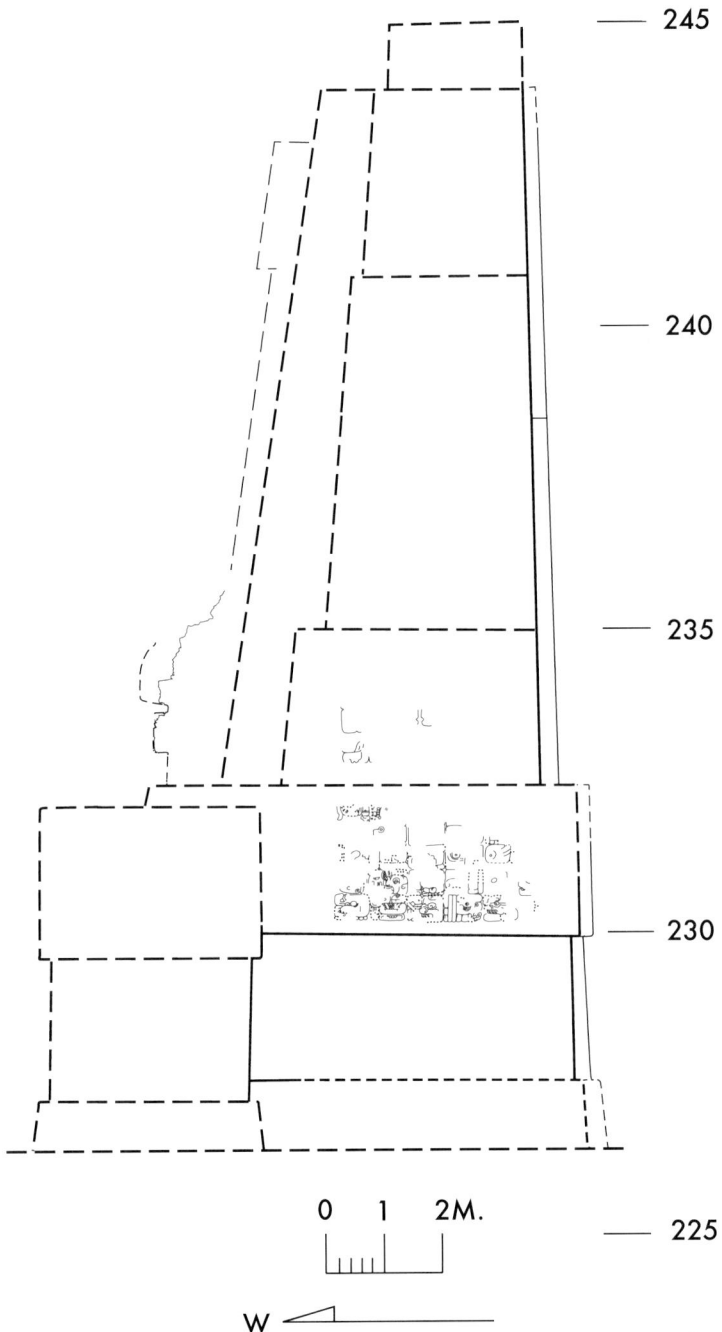

Str. 6F-27-1st S (Right Side) Elevation Superstructure (scale 1:125).

FIGURE 62

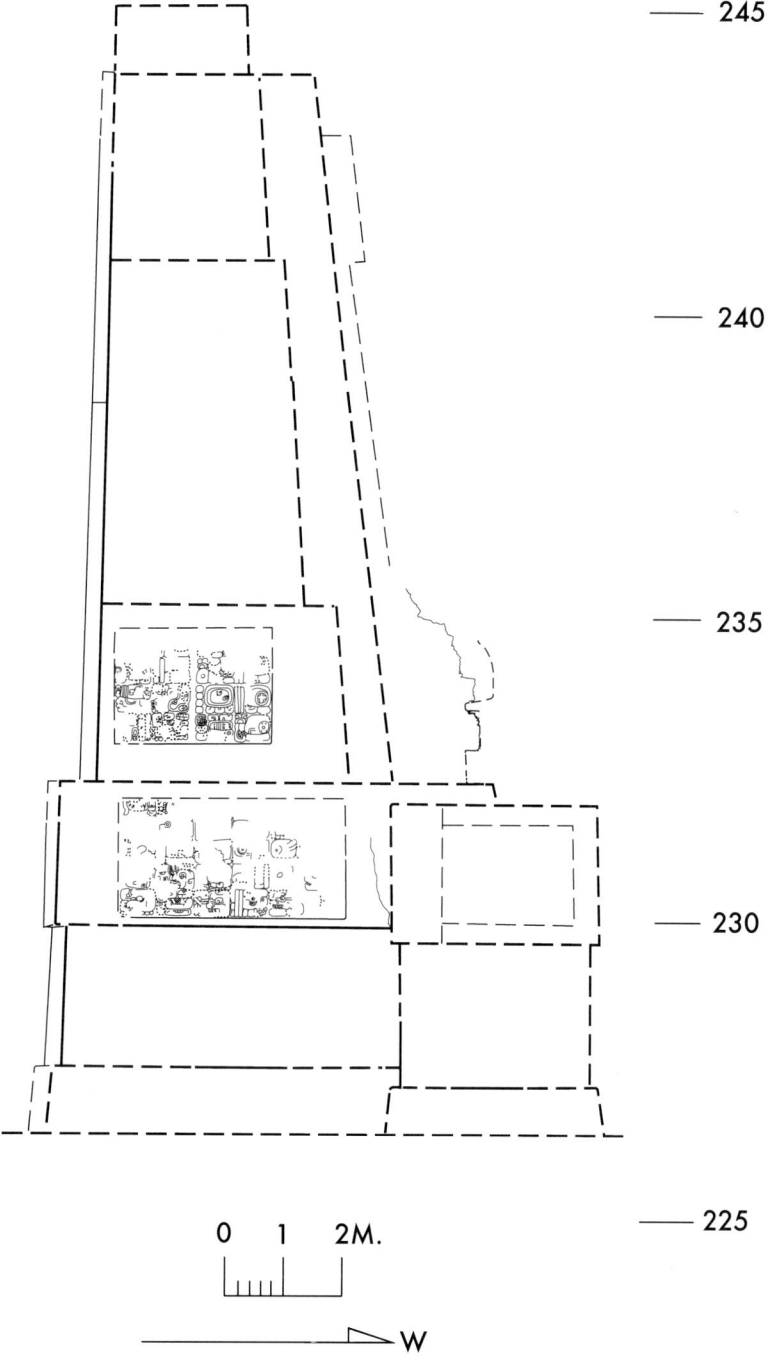

245

240

235

230

225

0   1   2M.

W

Str. 6F-27-1st N (Left Side) Elevation Superstructure (scale 1:125).

FIGURE 63

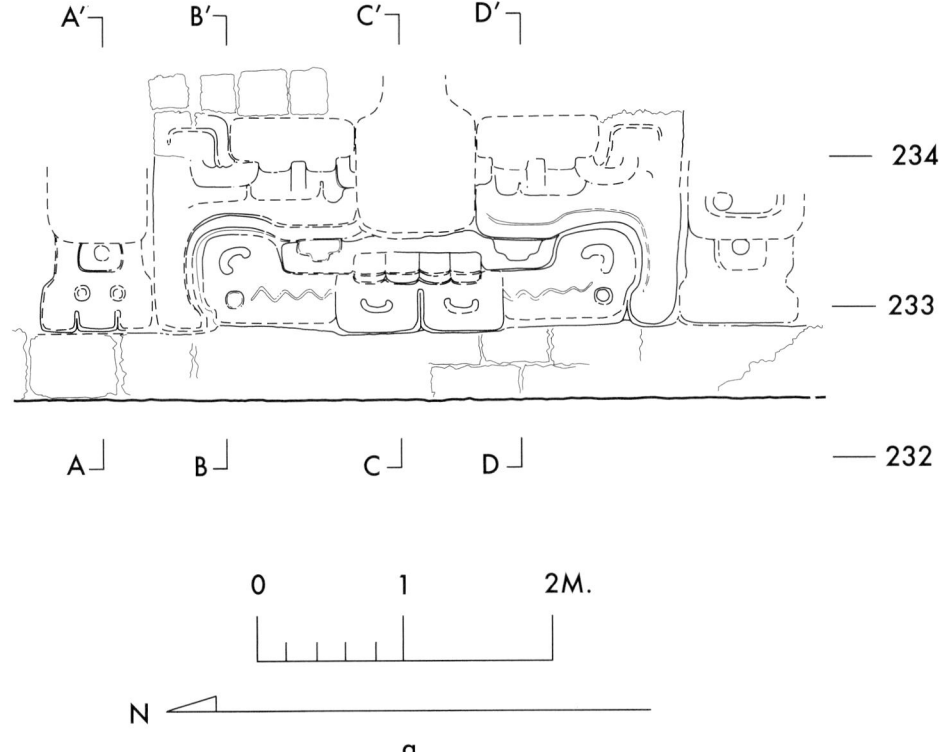

a

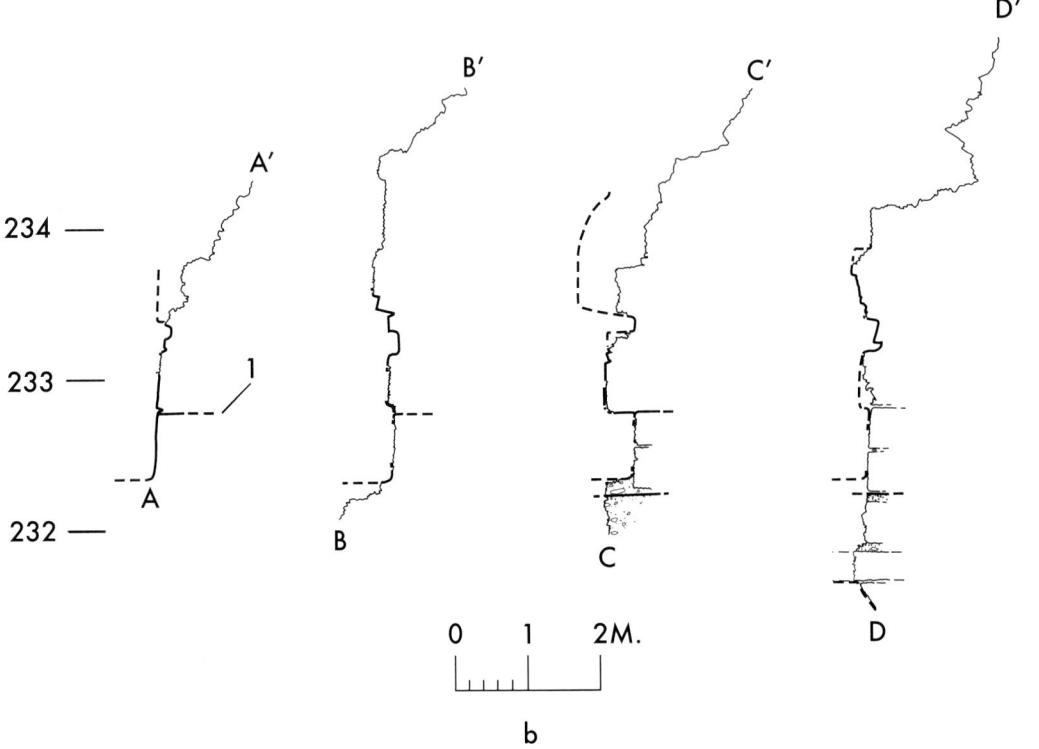

b

Str. 6F-27-1st Roofcomb Mask.
a. Elevation (scale 1:50). *b*. Profiles (scale 1:100).

FIGURE 64

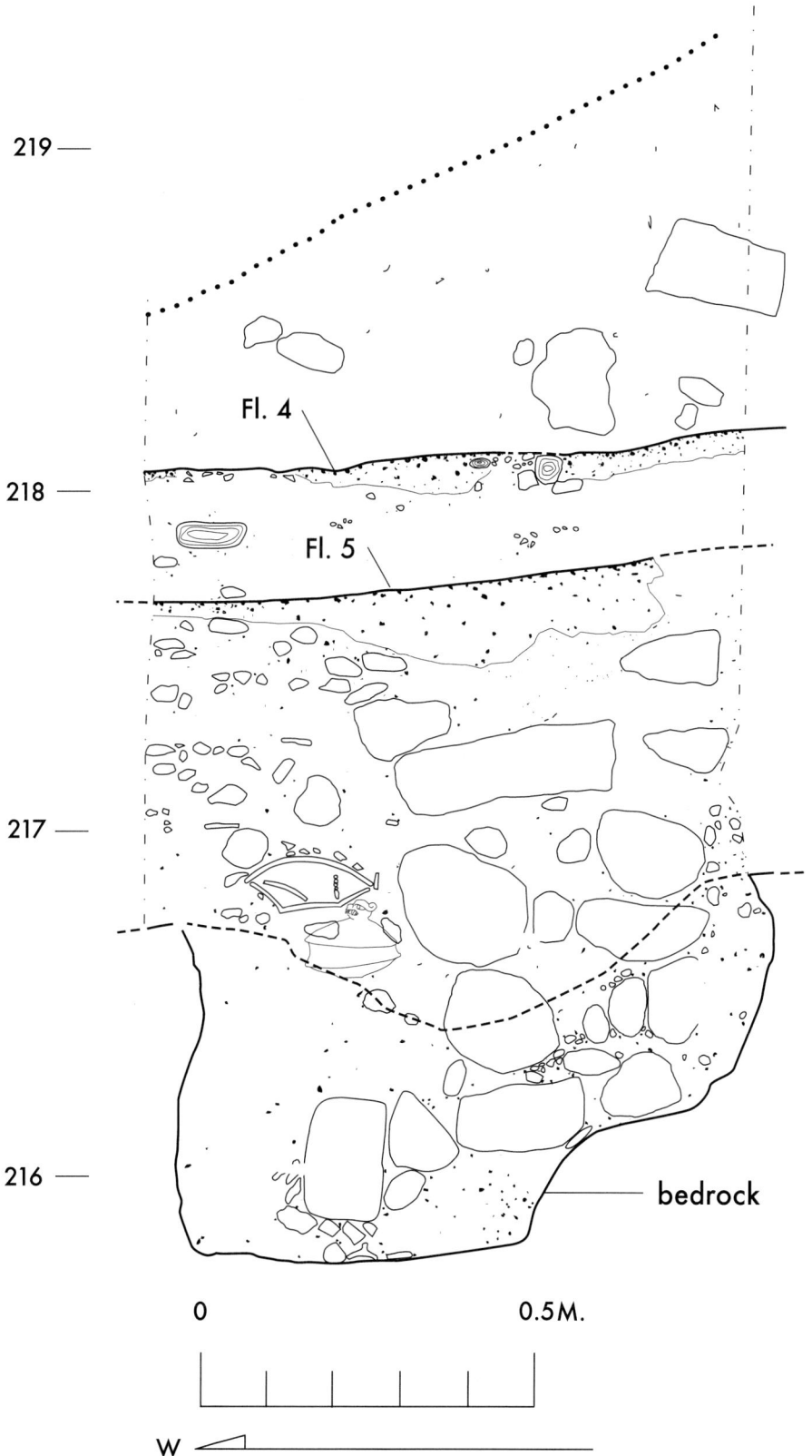

219 —

Fl. 4

218 —

Fl. 5

217 —

216 —

bedrock

0   0.5 M.

W

Str. 6F-27-1st PD. 170 Section/Profile (scale 1:20).

FIGURE 65

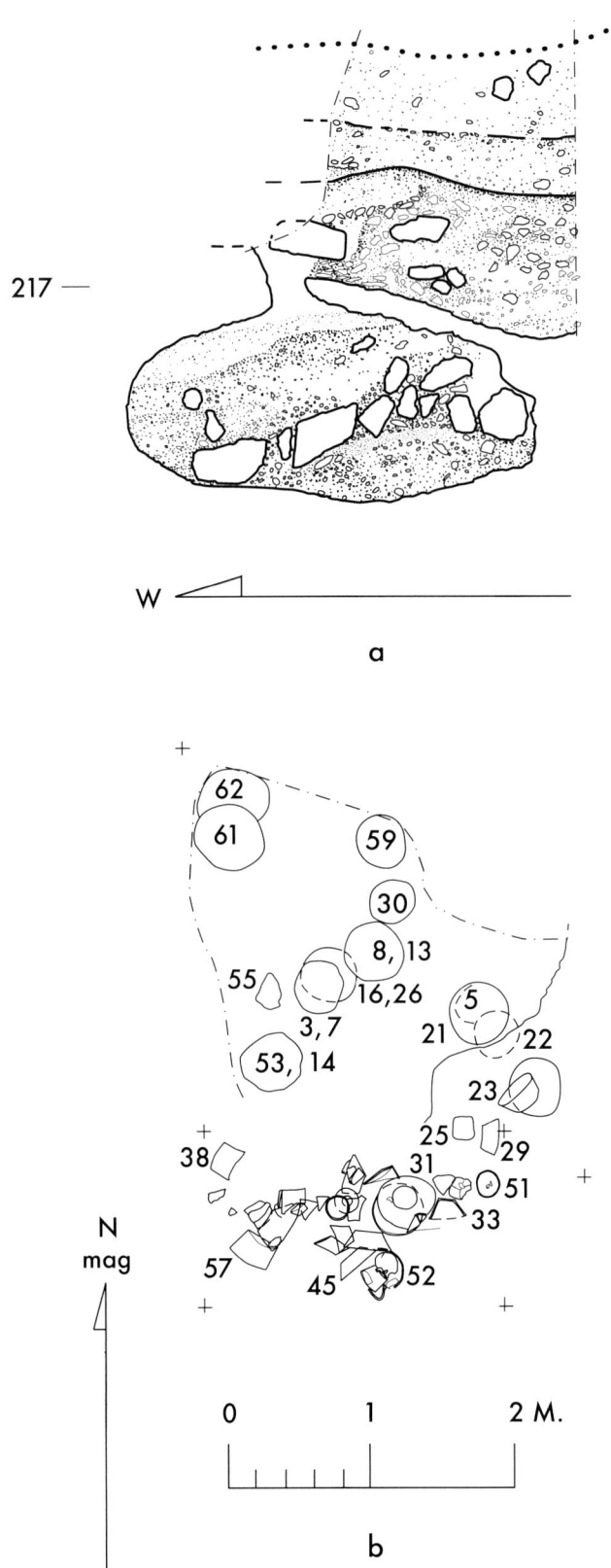

Str. 6F-27-1st PD. 170 Details (scale 1:50).
a. Section/profile through Ch. 6F-6. *b*. Plan.

FIGURE 66

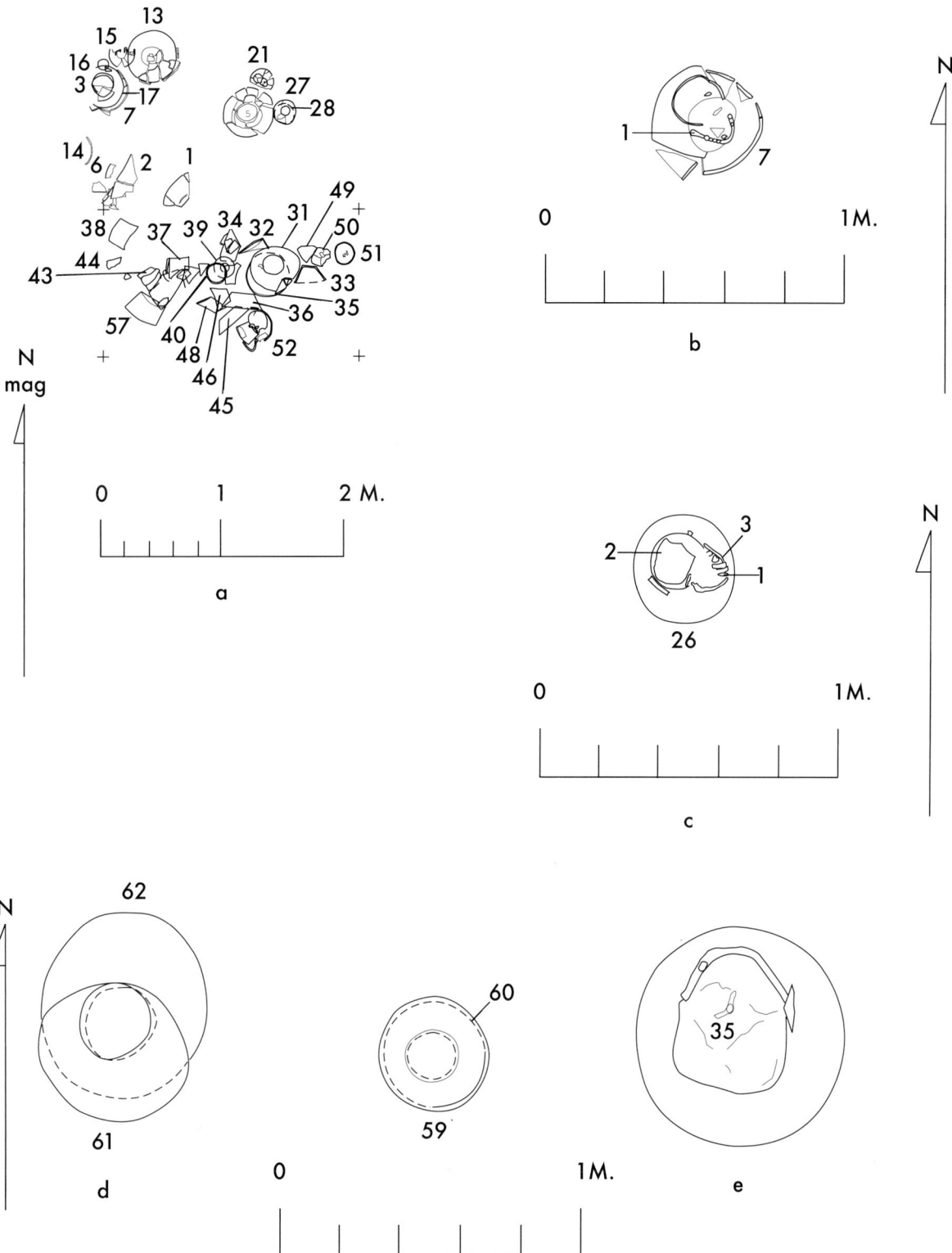

Str. 6F-27-1st PD. 170 Details.
a. Plan (scale 1:50). *b*. Vessel 7 (scale 1:20). *1*, Mandible. *c*. Vessel 26 (scale 1:20). *1*, Inlaid incisor. *2*, Fallen frontal bone. *3*, Mandible articulated. *d*. Vessels 59 and 61 (scale 1:20). *e*. Vessel 35 (scale 1:20).

FIGURE 67

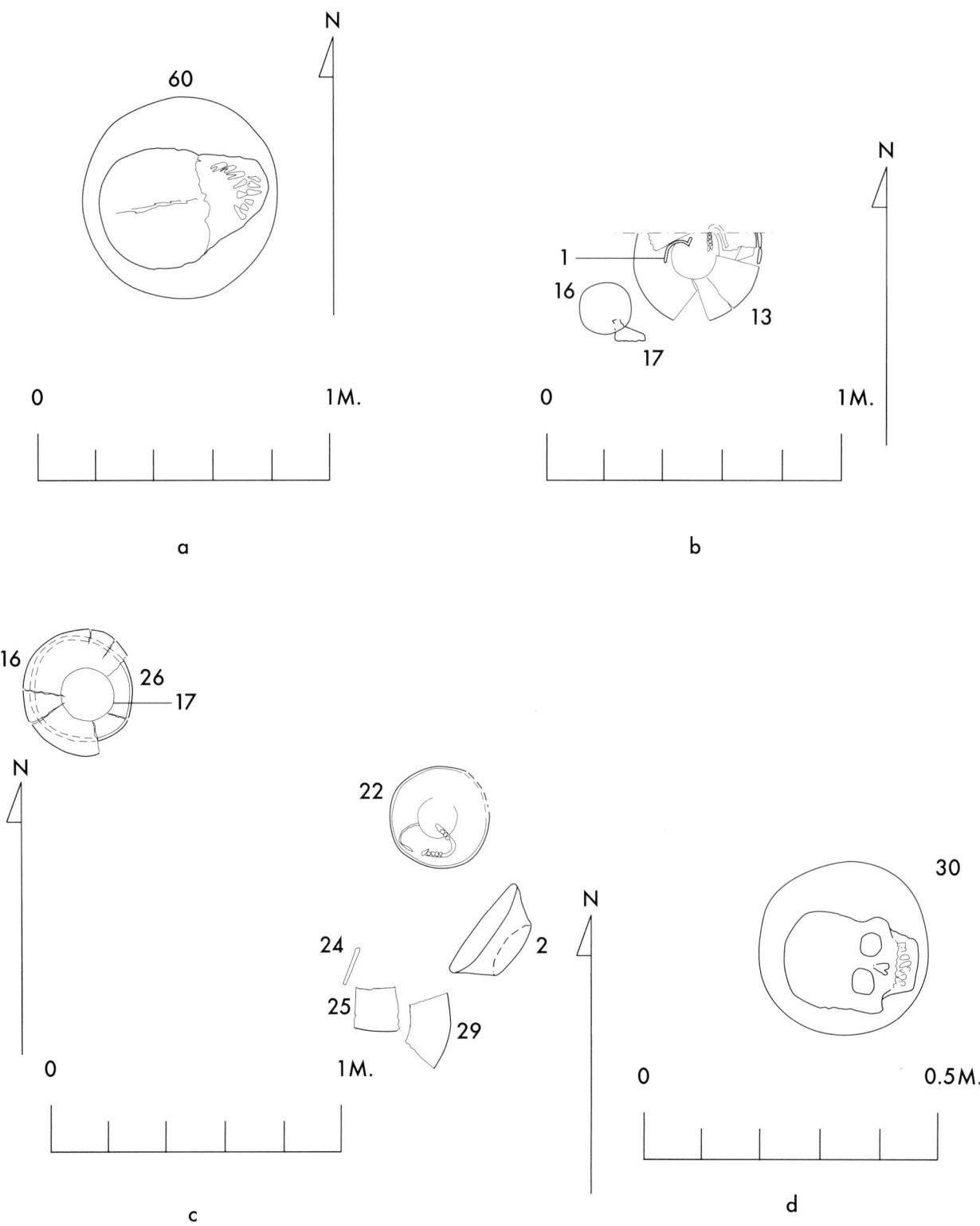

Str. 6F-27-1st PD. 170 Details (scale 1:20).
a. Vessel 60. *b.* Vessels 13, 16, and 17. *c.* Vessels 2, 16, 17, 22, 24–26, and 29. *d.* Vessel 30 (scale 1:10).

FIGURE 68

a

b

Str. 6F-27-1st Facade Texts.
a. E facade glyph panel. *b*. N facade glyph panel.

FIGURE 69

a

b

Str. 6F-27-1st Views.
a. S facade. *b*. E facade. Courtesy of the Penn Museum; Tikal Project image 56-3-101.

FIGURE 70

Great Temples Perspectives

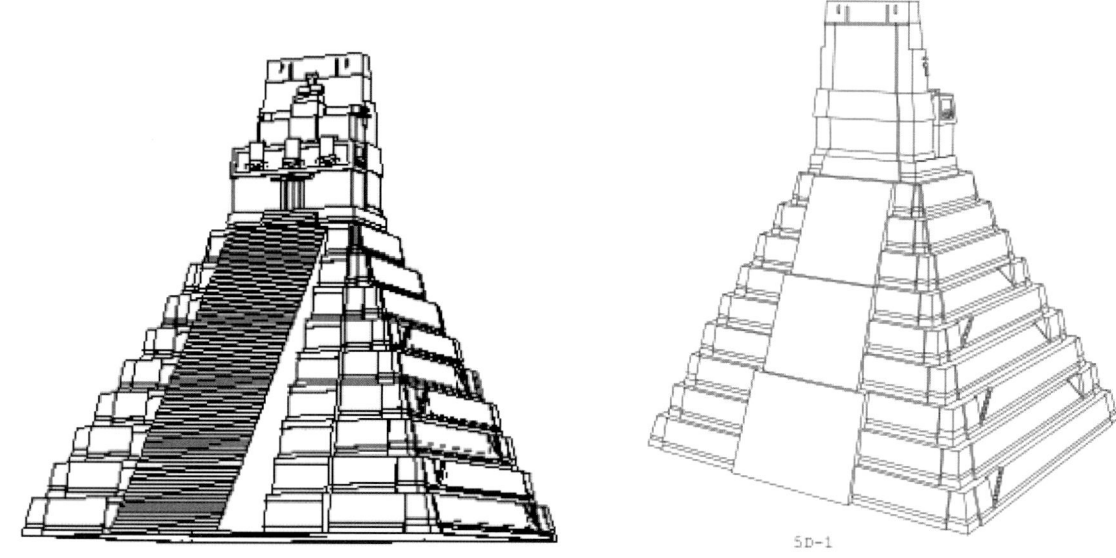

Great Temple I

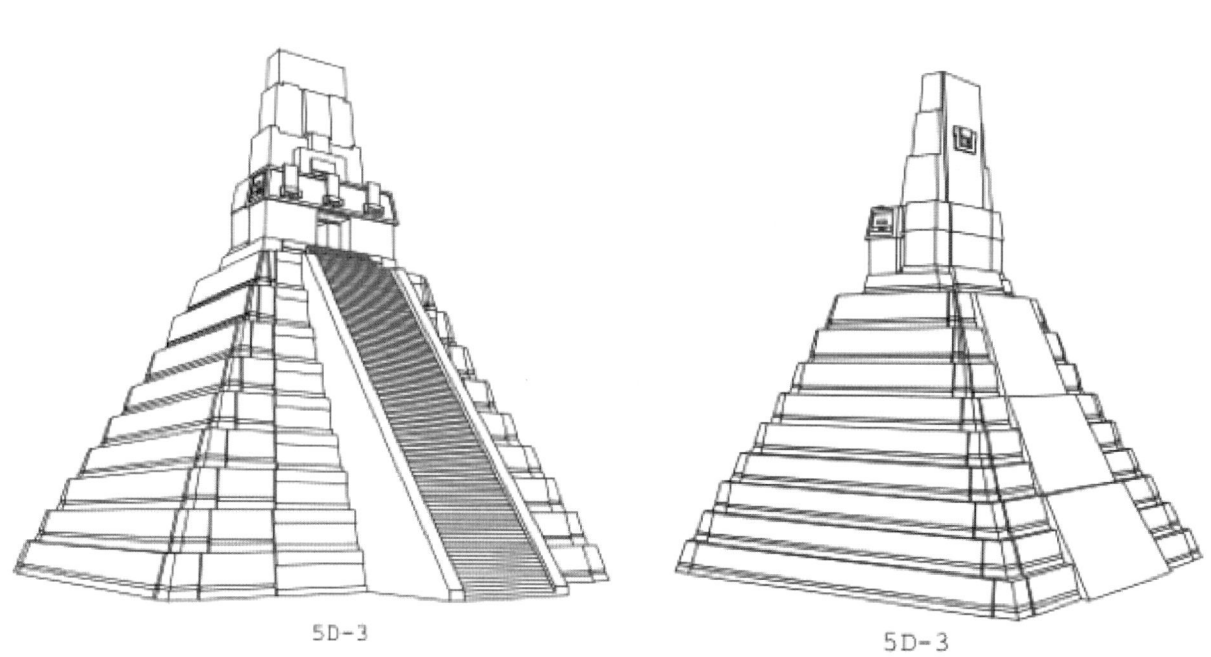

Great Temple III

Visual comparison of Great Temple I (5D-1) and Great Temple III (5D-3).

FIGURE 71

Great Temple V   Structure 5D-33-1st

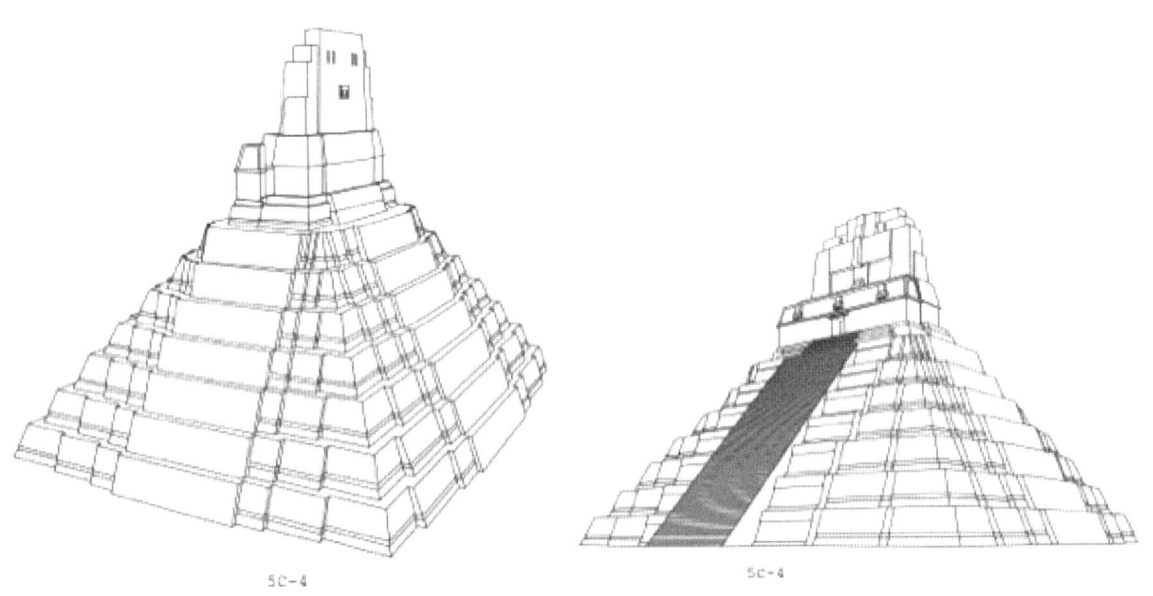

Great Temple IV

Visual comparison of Great Temple V (5D-33-1st) and Great Temple IV (5C-4).

FIGURE 72

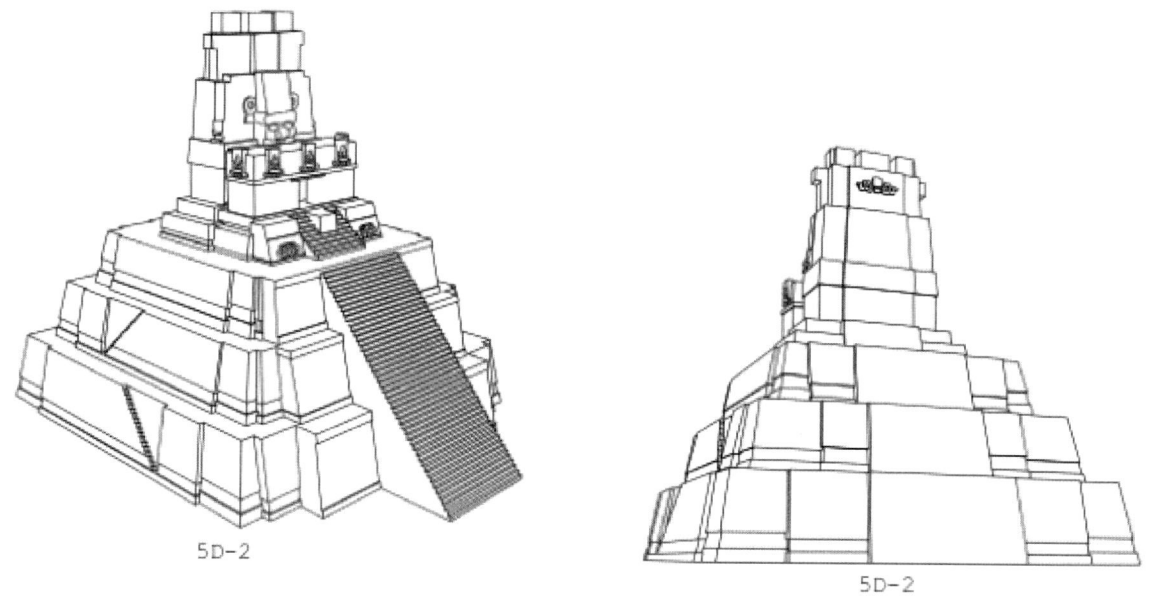

5D-2

5D-2

Great Temple II

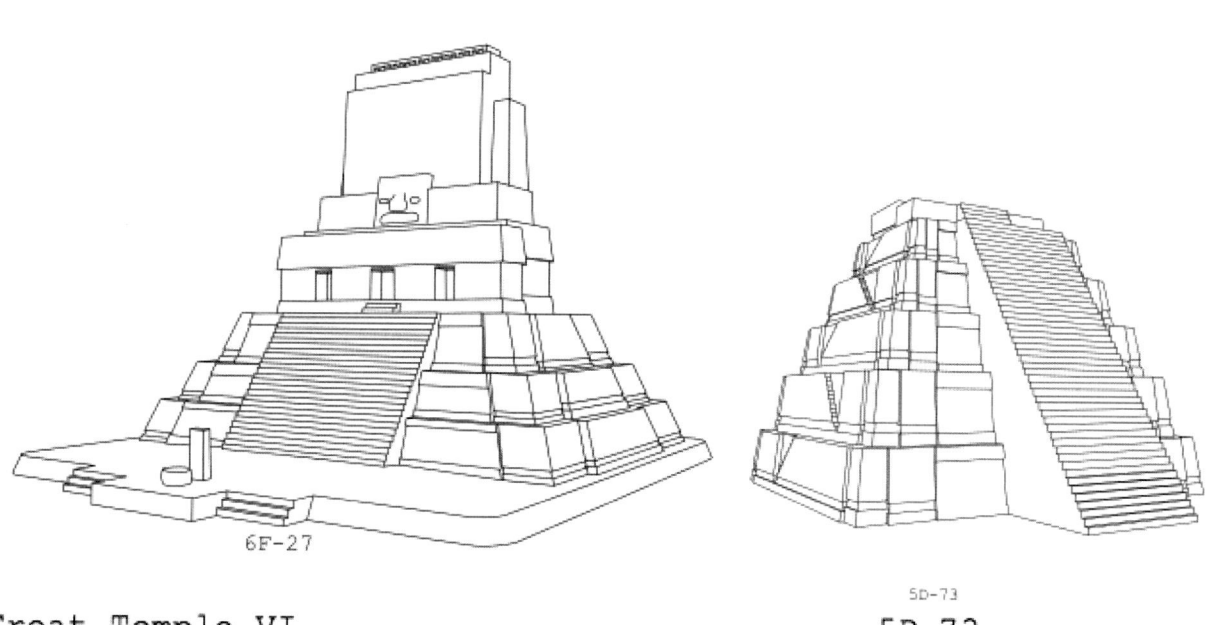

6F-27

5D-73

Great Temple VI

5D-73

Visual comparison of Great Temple II (5D-2) and Great Temple VI (5D-73).